Emerging Approaches to Educational Research

Emerging Approaches to Educational Research: tracing the sociomaterial recognizes that in the past fifteen years there has been significant innovation in the research of education and learning across the lifecourse, bringing with it both fresh insights and new dilemmas. Since the emergence of post-structuralism and postmodernism in the social sciences, a further range of conceptual and methodological orientations have attracted interest. These orientations focus more on the material aspects of relations, systems and practices than their earlier counterparts and offer approaches for tracing sociomaterial dynamics in education. They are described here as sociomaterial arenas.

This book explores four orientations that appear to be most widely used in research in fields of education and learning across the lifecourse. The discussion explores how these are being embraced and utilized, as well as their individual possibilities and limitations. These orientations are:

- complexity science
- cultural historical activity theory (CHAT)
- actor-network theory (ANT)
- spatiality theories.

Emerging Approaches to Educational Research is illustrated throughout with examples garnered from educational contexts across the lifecourse. These include schooling, post-compulsory education and training, educational policy, and workplace- and community-based education from North America, the UK and Australia. This guide to fresh ways of conducting and understanding research is a must for anyone undertaking educational research in the modern world.

Tara Fenwick is Professor of Professional Education at the School of Education, University of Stirling, UK.

Richard Edwards is Professor of Education and Head of the School of Education, University of Stirling, UK.

Peter Sawchuk is Associate Professor of Sociology and Equity Studies at the Ontario Institute for Studies in Education, University of Toronto, Canada.

Emerging Approaches to Educational Research

Tracing the sociomaterial

Tara Fenwick, Richard Edwards and Peter Sawchuk

Routledge
Taylor & Francis Group

LONDON AND NEW YORK

University Library of Columbus
4555 Central Avenue, LC 1600
Columbus, IN 47203-1892

First published 2011
by Routledge
2 Park Square, Milton Park, Abingdon, Oxon OX14 4RN

Simultaneously published in the USA and Canada
by Routledge
711 Third Avenue, New York, NY 10017

Routledge is an imprint of the Taylor & Francis Group, an informa business

© 2011 T. Fenwick, R. Edwards, P. Sawchuk

The right of T. Fenwick, R. Edwards, P. Sawchuk to be identified as
authors of this work has been asserted by them in accordance with
sections 77 and 78 of the Copyright, Designs and Patents Act 1988.

All rights reserved. No part of this book may be reprinted or reproduced
or utilized in any form or by any electronic, mechanical, or other means,
now known or hereafter invented, including photocopying and recording,
or in any information storage or retrieval system, without permission in
writing from the publishers.

Trademark notice: Product or corporate names may be trademarks or
registered trademarks, and are used only for identification and
explanation without intent to infringe.

British Library Cataloguing in Publication Data
A catalogue record for this book is available from the British Library

Library of Congress Cataloging in Publication Data
A catalog record for this book has been requested

ISBN: 978-0-415-57091-6 (hbk)
ISBN: 978-0-415-57092-3 (pbk)
ISBN: 978-0-203-81758-2 (ebk)

Typeset in Bembo
by Swales & Willis Ltd, Exeter, Devon

MIX
Paper from
responsible sources
FSC
www.fsc.org   FSC® C004839

Printed and bound in Great Britain by
TJ International Ltd, Padstow, Cornwall

Contents

Preface   vi

1 Why sociomateriality in education? An introduction   1

2 Emergence and perturbation: understanding complexity
theory   18

3 Complexity theory in educational research   35

4 Contradiction and expansion: understanding cultural historical
activity theory   56

5 Cultural historical activity theory in educational research   74

6 Translation and network effects: understanding actor-network
theory   94

7 Actor-network theory in educational research   110

8 Spatiality and temporality: understanding cultural geography   129

9 Spatial theory in educational research   148

10 Sociomaterial approaches: contributions and issues for
educational research   165

Bibliography   184
Index   209

Preface

A prominent shift is occurring in social sciences that are interested in knowledge, change, practice and politics, and the flows among them. We argue that this shift is also evident in educational studies, and that it deserves closer attention by researchers. This shift counters theoretical positions that assume the social/cultural and the personal to be the defining parameters of what it means to learn. It challenges the centring of human processes in learning (often conceived as consciousness, intention, meaning, intersubjectivity and social relations) derived from perspectives associated with phenomenology and social constructivism. This shift foregrounds materiality in learning.

The material includes tools, technologies, bodies, actions and objects, but not in ways that treat these as brute or inherently distinct from humans as users and designers. The material also includes texts and discourses, but not in ways that focus solely on linguistic, semiotic, intertextual and cultural matters. The material is entangled in meaning, not assumed to be separate from it. Overall, in education and other fields, this shift is away from a central preoccupation with human meaning, including meanings attributed to objects, as we might see in hermeneutic, narrative or symbolic interactionist approaches. The shift is also away from analysing such objects as simply traces of something assumed to be culture, as we might see in conventional anthropological accounts.

Instead, among perspectives that seem to be part of this pervasive shift, the material world is treated as continuous with, and in fact embedded in, immaterial energies, such as certain social relations and human intensities. Therefore, in this discussion, we have adopted the term 'sociomaterial' to refer to perspectives that are contributing to this shift. Of course, any transcendent term like sociomaterial must be used cautiously, particularly when diverse writers and positions are being called into presence under one umbrella that may fit uneasily with their particular projects. We are not arguing for a new grand ontology, nor for replacing other perspectives with those interested in the sociomaterial. Instead, we are calling attention to the importance of materiality in education and learning, and in foregrounding those interventions and studies in educational research that have specifically explored the influences of materiality in educational phenomena. But why this focus on the material? What can it bring to educational research?

A first response is perhaps an obvious one. Let us begin by acknowledging that, by education, we mean intentional activity to promote learning for particular purposes in any situation: classrooms, worksites, virtual spaces, mentoring meetings, community projects, social movements, and so forth. Education in all of these enactments is centrally material – its energies, processes, motives and outcomes are fully entangled with material practice, nature, time, space, technologies and objects of all kinds. These material entanglements are often not acknowledged in the conventional educational preoccupations with understanding human cognition, human activity and intentions, human meaning-making and human relationships.

A second response is that attention to the sociomaterial makes visible the mundanity of everyday life. Sociomaterial studies try to reveal the minute dynamics and connections that are continuously enacting the taken-for-granted in educational events: the clothing, timetables, passwords, pencils, windows, stories, plans, buzzers, bubblegum, desks, electricity and lights – not as separate objects, but as continually changing patterns of materiality. These patterns comprise human and non-human energies, each with historical trajectories, continually combining with (and dissolving away from) other assemblages. Humans, and what they take to be their learning and social processes, do not float, distinct, in container-like contexts of education, such as classrooms or community sites, that can be conceptualized and dismissed as simply a wash of material stuff and spaces. The things that assemble these contexts, and incidentally the actions and bodies including human ones that are part of these assemblages, are continuously acting upon each other to bring forth and distribute, as well as to obscure and deny, knowledge. These things might be taken by a casual observer as natural and given – objects comprising a context. But a more careful analysis notes that these objects, including objects of knowledge, are very messy, slippery and indeterminate things. Indeed, some sociomaterial analyses discussed in this book accept the simultaneous existence of multiple ontologies that can be detected in the play of things. This has enormous implications for understanding education and the purposes and processes of learning.

A third response to 'why sociomaterial?' is its fundamental questioning of the taken-for-granted categories that have become problematic conventions in educational analyses, despite long-standing critiques that by now are (or should be) well known. Sociomaterial analysis asks, how did these categories come to be materialized? What patterns of materiality support their continued enactment? Such categories include problematic binaries such as theory/practice, knower/known, subject/object, doing/reflecting, meaning/matter, informal and formal learning human/non-human and so forth. They also include all the categories – all the things – that are commonly used to conceive, think about and act upon education: policy, curriculum, learning, development, achievement, teacher, student and so forth. These categories suggest that such things exist as knowable and distinct, when research has struggled with the inseparability, uncertainties and fluidities of the phenomena that such categories are intended to describe. Sociomaterial approaches highlight the actual processes of boundary-making that create educational phenomena and produce knowledge and objects. They trace the actual dynamics through which powerful entities and linkages are assembled, reassembled and occasionally transformed, showing how they can be disassembled but also moved forward in the course of assemblage.

The purpose of this book is to open a dialogue among theoretical conceptions that reclaim and rethink material practice – how *matter* comes to matter in the social and personal mix – specifically in terms of educational processes and educational research. Four arenas have been selected for discussion: complexity theory, cultural historical activity theory or CHAT, actor-network theory or ANT, and theories of spatiality. Each appears to be attracting reasonable attention from educational researchers, judging from the numbers of available published studies working with such theories (for reviews, see Sawchuk *et al.* 2006; Gulson and Symes 2007; Edwards and Usher 2008; Mason 2008a; Daniels *et al.* 2009; Fenwick and Edwards 2010; Osberg and Biesta 2010). And further, some educational researchers are not simply applying these conceptions, but are raising educational questions that highlight oversights and that can push these theories forward. The four arenas bear some similarities in their conceptualization of knowledge and capabilities as emerging – simultaneously with material elements, identities, policies, practices and environment – in webs of interconnections between heterogeneous entities, human and non-human. Each illuminates very different facets of the sociomaterial that can afford important understandings related to conceptions of learning and knowledge in education: about how subjectivities are produced, how knowledge circulates and sediments into formations of practice and power, how agency might be understood as material as well as relational, and how practices are configured, reconfigured and transformed. Yet each perspective is itself a heterogeneous and contested site of inquiry. Learning itself is a slippery term that has come to be applied to a vast range of processes, from information processing, transmission, acquisition, transfer and individual development to emancipatory sociomaterial expansions and transformations. There is no unitary definition that can adequately represent the multiple and contested positions. In this book, learning is treated differently in each arena, and no attempt is made to synthesize the different positions into one transcendent pronouncement.

Important critiques and responses have been generated as these theoretical conceptions have proliferated across a range of social sciences, not just in education, but also in organization studies, environmental research, sociologies of technology, science and work, cultural studies, and human geography. Problematic issues of subjectivity, ethics, power relations, dangers of totalization and formulaic models, researchers' presence, representation of absence and multiplicity, etc. have been widely debated within each area, and are outlined in the respective chapters of this book. Beyond these critiques, each of these four arenas, like any approach to research, has particular limitations and pre-occupations that render it more useful for some questions and less so for others. Each, too, has a very different trajectory and set of origins in terms of its uses in education, although most have begun to appear only relatively recently in educational studies. In this respect, for example, those perusing this text for analyses of gender, race and multiculturalism, indigeneity, sexual difference, dis/ability, class issues, transnationalism and other complexities of inequity and identity politics may be partially disappointed. This may point to the inherent limitations of certain sociomaterial approaches, or to their relatively recent introduction in educational research, or their concentration so far on broader issues of curriculum, change and learning and their underdevelopment in other areas. We tend to believe that the potential analytical power offered by these sociomaterial approaches for questions of diversity and social justice in education is rich. In different ways, they provide a language as well as method-ological and analytical strategies to understand complex politics, hybridities, non-coherences, absences, problematic representations of presence, and materializing processes that are becoming important in educational accounts.

It is important to note that complexity, CHAT, ANT and spatiality are by no means the only sociomaterial orientations that are being explored in social science research. We have chosen them primarily because they each have become reasonably established in educational research through studies of diverse phenomena, ranging from teaching–learning processes and knowledge practices to curriculum, policy and educational change. If somewhat modest in number, these studies are demonstrating the explanatory power of these approaches, as well as their particular utility for educational questions. Other perspectives that bear mentioning, that could be described as sociomaterial and potentially very helpful in educational research, are enjoying uptake in fields such as organizational studies. For example, Schatzki's (2001, 2002) theory of practice – embodied, materially mediated networks of activity informed by meaning – has influenced much social theory. Schatzki is interested in collective agency, showing how activities, humans and objects develop, and at the same time become organized by, particular normative objectives. A similar practice-based approach that could be described as sociomaterial is Knorr Cetina's (1997, 2001) conception of the social as embodied practices of object relations. She highlights the intimate, emotional engrossment of humans with things, showing how objects, such as knowledge objects, inspire humans' desires for deeper understanding and engagements with them, and unfold indefinitely in close relation with humans' engagement. Again, there is not yet an established body of work using these ideas in education, although a few excellent educational studies employing Knorr Cetina's idea of epistemic objects are available in studies of professionals' knowledge practices and learning (see Jensen 2007, Nerland 2010). The 'practice turn' has been widely explored in organization and management studies, evidence by prominent special journal issues debating diverse perspectives and methodologies for tracing the sociomaterial in work life (e.g., see *Management Learning* 2009, 40 (2); *Organization Studies* 2009, 30 (12)). On a different tack, critical realism, developed in different ways by its key commentators Archer (1995) and Bhaskar (1998), has been proliferating in management and organization studies, particularly in qualitative empirical studies, where it offers well developed methods for empirical research in social sciences. Critical realism distinguishes between different modes of what is real according to the extent of human access to them. What is real is anything that has causal efficacy, affects behaviour and makes a difference. Material entities (oceans, trees, bricks, pencils) and non-material entities (God, love, racism) are all real: they can exist as real independently of particular humans' knowledge of them. They also can exist in different modes of real, according to the ways that humans conceptualize them, or participate in them, or even intervene to change them. While critical realism appears to offer interesting potential for educational analyses, particularly at organizational levels, there is yet little published educational research exploring this potential (exceptions include Clegg 2005, Scott 2010, Wheelahan 2010).

There is a long tradition of exploring embodiment and embodied knowledge in feminist writing (e.g. Grosz 1994) and various materialist feminisms (e.g. Hennessey 1993) that explicitly foreground materiality and the (gendered) interpenetration of cultural artefacts with modes of production and social relations. This has rather more focus on human materiality and the material effects of discourse than flows among natural, technical and human intensities. However, feminist analyses such as Haraway's cyborg (1991: 32) have been enormously influential in interrupting nature/technology binaries to develop hybrid, sociomaterial accounts of bodies and subjectivities. Educational writers also have drawn upon the material conceptions of Deleuze and Guattari (1987), applying notions of rhizomes, machines and bodies-without-organs to understand the flows not only of materiality, but also of desire in educational phenomena. New anthropologies (e.g. Henare *et al.* 2007) attempt what they characterize as a radical shift to erase the separation of humans and objects and appreciate their interpenetrations, and to understand the different simultaneous ontologies being performed in diverse cultural communities. Material cultural studies and sociologies of technology have a long tradition of exploring the human/non-human hybrids of social life, highlighting issues such as the politics of making infrastructure visible (Pinch 2010). Recent studies affiliating themselves with a mobility paradigm (Sheller and Urry 2006: 210) seek to redirect research 'away from static structures of the modern world to see how social entities comprise people, machines, and information/images in systems of movement', where all mobilities entail systems of (often immobile) materialities: transmitters, roads, docks, airports, fibre-optic cables, mobile phones. The list goes on, although educational voices, examples and questions are not always present in their debates.

This book does not pretend to be comprehensive. Nor are we presuming to offer a full comparison of four theories, which would be a problematic project at best. We decided that within each theoretical arena there is already so much debate and complexity that it might cause unnecessary confusion to link together debates framed separately within distinctly different analytical universes. Yet certain questions echo across these orientations, and certain terms arise in each, trailing similar conceptual associations. We have highlighted some of these echoes in the final chapter, trying to avoid reducing them to similarities that can be cited as a sort of primer of shared themes of sociomateriality. For that is our chief worry in presenting this book. While we have gathered these four arenas as each, in some way, contributing to a shared project of focusing analysis upon activity and materiality in education, they are each very distinct.

Overall, we are seeking here to do three things. First, we present an introduction: we aim to introduce new educational researchers (or researchers new to these arenas) to the possibilities of sociomaterial approaches as offered in complexity theory, CHAT, ANT and spatiality. Second, we highlight a distinctive sociomaterial orientation that seems to be emerging in educational research, through which studies such as those featured in this book can be positioned as opening some exciting directions and possibilities. Third, we offer an invitation: we hope to invite further dialogue among sociomaterial conceptions such as these four, in terms of their diverse principles, approaches and potentials for educational research. In sum, this book outlines our case for what might be called a 'sociomaterial turn' in research, approaches that illuminate important material dynamics that are too often neglected or underestimated in educational research. We hope to persuade readers how and why *matter* matters in the practices of becoming and knowing that constitute the spheres of education and learning.

Chapter 1

Why sociomateriality in education?

An introduction

There is a long-established tradition of researching the material aspects of education, from the design of school desks to the built environment of schools (Lawn and Grosvenor 2005). Indeed, Dewey's (1938) influential conception of learning emerging through transactions between an inquiring learner and objects of the environment could be argued to have inaugurated a sociomaterial view of education. And as we note in later chapters, Piaget, Dewey and Vygotsky each could be said to have theorized humans learning as active agents in the world. Practice – that is, *doing* – is not ontologically separable from learning and human development, but is the very substance of it. However, what is material is often taken to be the background context against which educational practice takes place or within which it sits, and material artefacts are often taken to be simply tools that humans use or objects they investigate. While giving a focus to the materiality of education, therefore, these approaches still tend to privilege the intentional human subject, which is assumed to be different or separate from the material; the material is the non-human. In educational research, therefore, Sørensen (2009: 2) argues that there is a 'blindness toward the question of how educational practice is affected by materials', and suggests that its consequence is to treat materials as mere instruments to advance educational performance. In her study of the materiality of learning, she shows how everyday educational activity and knowing are critically shaped through the material. She argues that the materiality is not consolidated within artefacts, but is distributed, such that social as well as physical processes can be understood as material. For her, things matter not as discrete and reified objects with properties, but as effects of dynamic materializing processes that cause them to emerge through gatherings and to act in indeterminate entanglements of local everyday practice. It is this relational materiality that is often overlooked in educational research.

To address this issue, in recent years a number of educational researchers have engaged with sociomaterial approaches to reclaim and rethink the material practices of education in different ways. In this book, we have chosen four different arenas within which such studies are situated: complexity theory, actor-network theory (ANT), cultural historical activity theory (CHAT), and spatiality theories. We prefer to discuss them as 'arenas' because these can be considered sites of contestation and performance of ideas. Each one represents a heterogeneous multiplicity of theories, or at least widely divergent uptakes of similar theoretical resources, so referring to each as a singular theory is problematic. Although each is called a 'theory' by its own users, most have featured debates criticizing this representation. Also problematic is the ocularcentric term of 'perspective', or 'view', to represent these explorations. Researchers in these arenas tend to emphasize knowing as enactment rather than as 'seeing' or as representation. In fact, they work to reveal the practices through which things become visible, conceptualizing knowledge, capabilities and subjectivities as emerging simultaneously in webs of interconnections among heterogeneous entities: human and non-human, social discourses, activities and meanings, as well as material forces, assemblages and transformations. In the hands of educational analysts, a rich body of literature has arisen that suggests useful interventions related to education, such as how sociomaterializing processes configure educational actors, subjectivities, knowledge and activities. Working within these arenas, educationists have shown possibilities for alternative imaginings of curriculum, learning and knowledge, and different ways to approach pedagogical interventions.

This chapter begins to examine the educational understandings offered by sociomaterial approaches such as those featured in this book. In the first section, we discuss in more detail what we believe to be the important contributions of these approaches, including how and why *matter* matters in constituting the actors, knowledge and activities of education. The second section offers a brief introduction to the four arenas, which are developed in detail in subsequent chapters in terms of their central principles and approaches. The third section introduces general themes that are taken up throughout the book. Here we outline educational issues and how they become approached through sociomaterial sensibilities, as well as issues of research and knowledge that emerge in sociomaterial studies. Overall, this chapter attempts to set the stage for the remaining text, which examines the different entanglings and possibilities for educational research offered by these intriguing arenas.

Sociomateriality as an approach to educational research

What sociomaterial approaches offer to educational research are resources to consider systematically both the patterns and the unpredictability that make educational activity possible. They promote methods by which to recognize and trace the multifarious struggles, negotiations and accommodations whose effects constitute the 'things' in education: students, teachers, learning activities and spaces, knowledge representations such as texts, pedagogy, curriculum content, and so forth. Rather than take such concepts as foundational categories, or objects with properties, they become explored as themselves effects of heterogeneous relations. In all four arenas discussed in this book, researchers focus on the relations and forms of connections/disconnections among things, where things are taken to be gatherings rather than existing as foundational objects with properties. They challenge assumptions that a subject is separable from an object, or a knower from the thing that is known, and in some instances that a learner is necessarily human. They interrupt understandings of knowledge, learning and education as solely social or personal processes, and insist upon attending to the material that is enmeshed with the social, technical and human. In the most radical expression of this view, which is not shared to the same extent across all the arenas discussed in this volume, things are performed into existence in webs of relations. All things – human and non-human, hybrids and parts, knowledge and systems – emerge as *effects* of connections and activity. There are no received categories. The shift here is what Jensen (2010: 7) characterizes as 'from epistemology and representation to practical ontology and performativity'. The question of producing knowledge and learning shifts from a representational idiom, mapping and understanding a world that is out there, to a view that the world is doing things, full of agency. Not only humans act, because non-humans act on and with humans.

Bennett (2010: 1) describes this as the 'force of things', 'the agency of assem-blages' and 'the vitality of materiality', drawing from Deleuze and Guattari's (1987) vital materialism of energies coursing through matter. In her treatise on why materiality is critical to reformulating a politics of ecology that moves beyond oppositions, blame and self-interest, Bennett shows how public life is dramatically acted upon by matter such as food and fat, stem cells, metal and electricity. The North American electricity blackout of 2003 that affected 50 million people, for example, was enacted through a heterogeneous assemblage including electricity, power plants (with overprotective mechanisms and under-staffing), transmission wires (with limits on their heat capacity), a regulatory commission and policy act (that privatized electricity and separated transmission of electricity from distribution), energy-trading corporations (profiting from the grid at the expense of maintaining infrastructure), consumers (with growing demand for electricity), and a brush fire in Ohio. The point is not that individual objects have agency, but that force is exercised through these sociomaterial assemblages. Non-human materiality, Bennett argues, is interpenetrated with human intensities in these assemblages in ways that must be treated sym-metrically. Human agency is simply the effect of particular distributions and accumulations enacted through such assemblages. This view

> multiplies the potentially relevant actors and forces attention on their dif-ferences and relations. The aspiration is to thereby facilitate more nuanced analyses of how humans and things (broadly construed) together create, stabilize and change worlds. Analyses, in other words, that are sensitive to human and nonhuman activities as *practical ontology*: efforts to concretely shape and interrelate the components that make up the worlds they inhabit.
> (Jensen 2010: 5)

In education, voices like Sørensen (2009) are increasingly arguing not just for greater attention to materiality, but for this more symmetrical approach. Waltz (2006) claims that in educational analyses, material things too often are denied their vitality. Materiality is subsumed by human intention, design and drive, and treated merely as things representative of human ends. This hides the qualities and contributions of material entities themselves, particularly the ways they act within educational processes. Textbooks, for example, exert force. Depending on their form, they can enact certain pedagogical activities and sequences, align curricula across space and time, limit the teacher's academic freedom, and affect student funds. They generally function as 'co-conspirators, law-enforcement officers, administrators, racists, quality control agents, seducers, and investment advisors' (Waltz 2006: 57).

The point is that material things are performative and not inert; they are matter and they matter. They act together with other types of things and forces to exclude, invite and regulate particular forms of participation in enactments, some of which we term education. What then is produced can appear to be policy, or gender identity, or expertise, or a social structure such as racism. A focus on the sociomaterial therefore helps us to untangle the heterogeneous relationships holding together these larger categories, tracing their durability as well as their weaknesses. From this approach, no anterior distinctions, such as human beings or social structures, are presupposed. Everything is performed into existence: 'the agents, their dimensions and what they are and do, all depend on the morphology of the relations in which they are involved' (Callon 1998: 8).

These relations are conceptualized very differently in different arenas. In some complexity accounts, these connections are co-specifications between elements that are immediately adjacent to one another, that interact and begin actually to affect each other's movements. They even participate in each other's emerging movements – in ways that reconfigure the whole, sometimes dramatically, as a multifarious system self-organizes into a new pattern. For instance, a flock of geese resting on the water will suddenly rise and sweep upwards in a single curve, if a bystander perturbs those closest to the path. Or a new pedagogical idea such as 'cooperative learning' appears to sweep an entire region with neither a policy mandate nor evidence for success.

Actor-network theory calls the micro-connections that create such assemblages 'translation', and understands them to be negotiations between elements. A thing, a text or a person may try to reconfigure something else, but that something can resist despite persuasion or incentives, or compromise. At the moment when one thing encounters another, they can perform something new, or something familiar. Cultural historical activity theory shows how people and processes become transformed through particular ways of participating in complex and interpenetrating artefact-mediated spheres or systems of activity. These systems are understood to contain contradictions and to be organized around particular objects/motives shaping unselfconscious operations and goal-directed actions. Spatiality orientations are concerned with how space is shaped, altered, coloured, refracted by the human activity within it, and how space arrangements alter human movement, identifications and meanings: what Massey (2005: 24) calls the 'dimension of multiple trajectories, the simultaneity of stories-so-far'. Most important, all these links are precarious. Links can be co-configured, dissolved, translations refused, and mediation attempts transformed into unanticipated directions. Importantly, there is no all-powerful system pre-existing these many negotiations between the different entities. For example, what may appear to be an immutable system of performance measurement is in fact held together very provisionally by myriad connections that can be identified and reopened. Here, and across the arenas we examine, we thus find a shared appreciation for the fundamental importance of the local understood as the actual instances of 'translation', or 'mediation', and so on.

Sociomaterial analysis also steps outside conceptions of local–global scalar distinctions in considering educational activity. To view educational instruction, curricula, texts, standards, etc. as developed in hierarchical levels and implemented locally, or to conceptualize 'globalized' knowledge as distinct from local knowledge and practices, is to accept an ontological distinction between the scalar levels of the local, regional, national and global. Neither complexity, CHAT, ANT nor spatiality approaches conceptualize distinctions in this way. In complexity, for example, layers of activity are understood to be nested within each other. Micro-interactions comprising the system of classroom practice are nested within the institutional system, which is nested within community systems, curriculum systems, biosphere, and so forth. In ANT, what appear to be macro entities, or social structures, or even global spheres of activity, are simply far-flung, numerous networks or assemblages consisting of a plethora of mundane materials all held together by a series of connections, which are often mighty precarious. The question is not what occurs at local and global levels and how they influence one another, as it is so often framed in the explanation of education practices. It is rather how systems and practices and knowledge become more or less connected, performing comparable (if often distinctly different) activities across space–time. What appears to be difference in size and scale is simply the end product of network extension actions. There are not hierarchal levels, but different spacings and timings through the connections. There is no all-powerful system pre-existing these many negotiations between the different materials. Whatever may be manifested as powerful educational activity, whether in explicit systems such as state-mandated curricula, teaching standards and high-stakes testing, or as social structures of institutionalized racism and class exclusion, is in fact held together very provisionally by myriad connections – as well as spaces between them – that can be identified and reopened.

Consider the concept of learning, central in educational discussions and extremely slippery in meaning. It is by now a commonplace in educational theory to understand learning as more than the purely individual, cognitive and acquisitive process that has driven some educational approaches. Conceptions of learning have long acknowledged the importance of transactions among concepts, language, cultural mediation and experimentation with environmental objects. Notions of learning as socio-cultural participation, embedded in particular joint activity, tools and routines, have become ubiquitous in educational writings that suggest less instruction and more scaffolding of active processes as a pedagogical approach. However, such conceptions still tend to focus on individual learning subjects, and on their particular development through the processes of mediation and participation. What is placed in the background is how the entities, knowledge, other actors, and relations of mediation and activity – all the forces directly engaged in learning activities – are also being brought forth in practices *as* learning. As the material is not secondary, but integral to the human, it is through the being-together of things that actions, including those identified *as* learning, become possible. Learning is an effect of the networks of the material, humans and non-humans, that identify certain practices *as* learning, which also entails a value judgement about learning something worthwhile. Thus teaching is not simply about the relationships between humans, but is about the networks of humans and things through which teaching and learning are translated and enacted. Teaching and learning do not exist, and cannot be identified, separately from the networks through which they are themselves enacted. They are not independent transcendental entities or processes, but immanent assemblages.

Four research arenas that we call 'sociomaterial'

All four arenas – complexity theory, cultural historical activity theory, actor-network theory and spatiality theories – while deriving from very different theoretical roots and premises, bear some important resemblances. First, all four take *whole systems* into account, regardless of what small slice of material or activity has been chosen as a primary focus for study. All four explore the webs of entangled human/non-human action and knowledge that give rise to systems, and acknowledge the processes of boundary-making and exclusion that establish what we take to be systems and their internal elements. Second, they all focus on closely tracing the formations and stabilization of elements – all bodies, including bodies of knowledge – that are produced, reinforced or transformed by subjects that emerge with/in a particular activity. That is, they all trace *interactions among non-human as well as human* parts of the system, emphasizing both the heterogeneity of system elements and the need to focus on relations and mediations, not separate things or separate individuals. Third, they all understand human knowledge and learning in the system to be embedded in *material action and inter-action (or intra-action)*, rather than focusing strictly on internalized concepts, meanings and feelings of any one participant. In other words, they do not privilege human consciousness or intention in any conventional sense, but trace how knowledge, knowers and known (representations, subjects and objects) emerge together with/in activity.

Complexity theory: learning as emergence of collective cognition and environment

Complexity theory is actually a heterogeneous body of theories originating in evolutionary biology, mathematical fractals, general systems theory, cybernetics and so on. The present discussion draws from analysts who have theorized complexity theory in terms of human and organizational learning (e.g. Stacey 2005; Davis and Sumara 2006; Osberg and Biesta 2007). Complexity theory provides one approach to understanding learning processes in a system such as a work organization. The first premise is that the systems represented by person and context are inseparable, and the second that change occurs from emerging systems affected by the intentional tinkering of one with the other. The key theme is emergence, the understanding that in complex adaptive systems, phenomena, events and actors are mutually dependent, mutually constitutive, and actually emerge together in dynamic structures.

Davis and Sumara (2006), among others, have applied these concepts to human learning, showing how environment and learners emerge together in the process of cognition. Elements that come to comprise a system interact according to simple rules that are recursively re-enacted. Elements often couple, in a process of co-specification (Varela et al. 1991). As each element interacts and responds within the activity, the overall shape and direction of the system shifts, as does the emerging object of focus. Other elements are changed, the relational space among them all changes, and the looping-back changes each element's form and actions. The resultant coupling changes or co-specifies each participant, creating a new transcendent unity of action and identities that could not have been achieved independently. These interactions are recursive, continuing to elaborate what is present and what is possible in the system. They also form patterns all by themselves. They do not organize according to some sort of externally imposed blueprint, so complexity theorists describe such systems as *self-organizing*. Through the ongoing processes of recursively elaborative adaptation, the system can maintain its form without some externally imposed discipline or organizing device, such as hierarchical management.

In education, people constantly influence and adjust to each other's emerging behaviours, ideas and intentions, as well as with objects, furniture, technologies, etc., through myriad complex interactions and fluctuations. A whole series of consequences emerge from these micro-actions. Most of this complex joint action leaks out of individuals' attempts to control what they are doing. No clear lines of causation can be traced from these interactions to their outcomes, because at any given time among all these interconnections, possibilities are contained in the system that are not visible or realized. This means, among other things, that humans are fully nested within and interconnected with many elements of the systems comprising them and in which they participate. They are not considered to be autonomous, sovereign agents for whom knowledge can be acquired or extracted.

And yet, in our observation and recall of such occurrences, the tendency is to focus on the (human) learning *figure* and dismiss all these sociomaterial complex interactions within which the figure becomes visible as background. Complexity science urges a refocusing on the relations that produce things, not the things themselves. Out of these continuous and non-linear interactions emerge dynamic wholes that exceed their parts. Osberg and Biesta (2007) call this strong emergence: conditions where the knowledge and capability that emerges is more than the sum of its parts, and therefore not predictable from the ground from which it emerges. Johnson (2001) shows that this emergence is enabled in systems characterized by diversity, decentralization, redundancy, open constraints and feedback.

Overall, in complexity theory, knowledge and action are understood as continuous invention and exploration, produced through relations among consciousness, identity, action and interaction, objects and structural dynamics. New possibilities for action are constantly emerging among these interactions of complex systems, and cognition occurs in the possibility for unpredictable shared action. Knowledge or skill cannot be contained in any one element or dimension of a system, for knowledge is constantly emerging and spilling into other systems. No actor has an essential self or knowledge outside these relationships: nothing is given in the order of things, but performs itself into existence. In human resource development applications of complexity theory, attention would be drawn to the relationships among learners and the environment. For example, an organizational change initiative would focus on enabling connections instead of training individuals to acquire understanding of the new policy. These are connections between this initiative and the many other initiatives likely to be lurking in the system; between parts of the system; between the initiative and the system's cultures; and between people, language and technologies involved in the change. It would encourage experimentation among people and things involved in the change, and would focus on amplifying the advantageous possibilities that emerge among these connections as people tinker with the things and language involved. Learning is defined as expanded possibilities for action, or becoming 'capable of more sophisticated, more flexible, more creative action' (Davis and Sumara 2006).

Cultural historical activity theory: contradiction and expansion

Cultural historical activity theory (CHAT) analyses the ongoing dynamic interactions of people and artefacts with an expansive view of learning (Engeström 1987, 2001). Derived from an almost century-long dialogue across psychology and a host of other disciplines and perspectives, notably dialectical philosophy and Marxism, CHAT began with elementary explorations of thought, speech and social practice, culminating in the idea of activity as the minimal meaningful unit of analysis for learning and human development. It highlights the sociomaterial interactions, particularly among artefacts, system objects and patterns, individual/group perspectives, and the histories through which these dynamics emerged. Configurations of material as well as symbolic artefacts (tools, technologies, signs, internalized schema) are considered a primary means of transmitting knowledge historically, as they are understood to consolidate and mediate social interaction and the negotiation of knowledge, and suggest alternative modes of operation (Miettinen *et al.* 2008). CHAT studies examine a system's historical emergences and relations among these material artefacts, as well as divisions of labour, cultural norms, rules and perspectives enmeshed in the system: 'how things came to be as they are, how they came to be viewed in ways that they are, and how they are appropriated in the course of developmental trajectories' (Sawchuk 2003). Close attention is given to the system's object/motives – the realization of need in the object-relatedness of activity. Emphasis is placed on the contradictions inherent to activity, as expressed in the common tension between forms of control and the myriad of human purposes that bump up against it whether in a classroom, a school system, an organization or across organizations. When these contradictions become sufficiently exacerbated, alternative practices seep through activity; questions emerge; actors struggle, negotiate, accommodate; learning occurs; people are transformed. And, in the instances in which activities themselves are collectively transformed, new expansive object/motives and the multitude of practices, internalizations as well as externalizations, which sustain it can take hold.

In the arenas of CHAT research, then, learning is explained as the 'construction and resolution of successively evolving tensions or contradictions in a complex system that includes the object or objects, the mediating artifacts, and the perspectives of the participants' (Engeström 1999a: 384). What becomes distinguished as novel or useful depends on what problems become uppermost in a particular activity system, what knowledge is most valued there, and what knowledge is recognized and responded to by the system elements.

Sawchuk's (2003: 21) study of technology learning among workers showed how people's participation in computer learning practices was inseparable from sociomaterial dynamics: 'integrated with everyday life and mediated by artifacts including computer hardware and software, organizational settings, oral devices, class habitus, trade unions, and working-class culture'. He analysed encounters among participants to reveal how their patchwork of learning opportunities unfolded in informal networks across overlapping systems of activity – on the job as well as at home with the kids, fixing a car with buddies, struggling in computer labs. The material dynamics of these systems, their artefacts and the histories and cultures embedding them in practices are as important as the social dimensions of community, language, routines and perspectives in tracing the knowledge that is produced and the changes in people and practices that emerge through contradictions.

Actor-network theory: learning as translation and mobilization

Actor-network theory (ANT), claim its continuing proponents, is not a theory but a sensibility – indeed, many diffused sensibilities, evolving in ways that eschew its original tenets. Their shared commitment is to trace the process by which elements come together and manage to *hold* together, to assemble collectives or networks. These networks produce force and other effects: knowledge, identities, rules, routines, behaviours, new technologies and instruments, regulatory regimes, reforms, illnesses and so forth. No anterior distinctions such as human being or social structure are recognized. Selected concepts of this field that have been most frequently applied to questions of learning, knowledge generation and practice include central notions of:

> *symmetry* – that objects, nature, technology and humans all exercise influence in assembling and mobilizing the networks that comprise tools, knowledge, institutions, policies and identities;
> *translation* and *stabilization* – the micro-negotiations that work to perform networks into existence and maintain them while concealing these dynamic translations;
> the processes of *enrolment* and *mobilization* that work to include and exclude; and
> the *fluid objects* and quasi-objects produced by networks that perform themselves as stable, even 'black-boxed', knowledge and bodies.
>
> (Fenwick and Edwards 2010)

ANT takes knowledge generation to be a joint exercise of relational strategies within networks that are spread across space and time, and performed through inanimate (e.g. books, mobile phones, measuring instruments, projection screens, boxes, locks) as well as animate beings in precarious arrangements. Learning and knowing are performed in the processes of assembling and maintaining these networks, as well as in the negotiations that occur at various nodes comprising a network. ANT studies are particularly useful for tracing the ways that things come together. They can show how things are invited or excluded, how some linkages work and others do not, and how connections are bolstered to make themselves stable and durable by linking to other networks and things. Further, and perhaps most interesting, ANT focuses on the minute negotiations that go on at the points of connection. Things – not just humans, but the parts that make up humans and non-humans – persuade, coerce, seduce, resist and compromise each other as they come together. They may connect with other things in ways that lock them into a particular collective, or they may pretend to connect, partially connect, or feel disconnected and excluded even when they are connected.

Spatiality: learning as (im)mobilities

Spatial theory is used by both educationalists and geographers to research education following what is sometimes referred to as the spatial turn in social sciences in the 1990s. In such approaches, space is not considered a static container into which teachers and students are poured, or a backcloth against which action takes place, but a dynamic multiplicity that is constantly being enacted by simultaneous practices-so-far. Space is not to be considered simply an object of study, as, for instance, in examining how classroom spaces are designed and used. It is also, more critically, a theoretical tool for analysis. Issues for education that are often identified include how spaces become learning spaces, how they are constituted in ways that enable or inhibit learning, create inequities or exclusions, or open and limit possibilities for new practices and knowledge. Particularly in new educational arrangements incorporating rapidly developing media and communications technologies, the ordering of space–time has become a critical influence on, and way of analysing, curriculum and pedagogy. Spatial theories raise questions about what knowledge counts, where, how it emerges in different time–spaces, how subjectivities are negotiated through movements and locations, and how learning is enmeshed as, and in, the making of spaces.

In recent decades, there has been a shift from considering space as universal and abstract in favour of conceptions that bring to the fore the hybrid, entangled and turbulent nature of space. This is reflected most notably in what is referred to as a materialist turn in framings of space (Anderson and Wylie 2009). The materialist turn takes many forms, but for our purposes, the significant work in this thread is associated with what might be called a (im)mobilities paradigm (Urry 2007). Influenced in part by post-humanist and non-representationalist theories, this work has focused on space as material orderings and disorderings, as enactments and performative. Here there is a movement away from assuming the primacy of human intention and action, for 'human life . . . is never just human' (Urry 2007: 45). Spatial orderings are not about human subjects *per se*, but are material assemblages of subjects–objects that interrupt and affect, question and promise.

The mobilities theoretical framing can be seen as contributing to the materialist turn in geography, as 'there are hybrid systems, "materialities and mobilities" that combine objects, technologies, socialities and affects out of which distinct places are produced and reproduced' (Hannam *et al.* 2006: 14). Here place is not bounded or separated from flux and networks, but arises from them, and *vice versa*. This approach provides a sophisticated set of resources through which to rework spatial framings generally, and the analysis of education more specifically.

A focus on mobilities points us towards a tracing of the movements, relations and networks of objects, people, information and images, and the ways in which flux is regulated, made possible and constrained. Rather than starting analysis from a space out of which objects move, this approach aims to map mobilities, the ways in which spaces are moored, bounded and stabilized for the moment, and the specific (im)mobilities associated with such moorings. We might take such spaces for granted, as for instance, universities, but a mobilities analysis would examine how such spaces are enacted and become sedimented across time. This has implications for how we might research education, and the extent to which curriculum and pedagogy are moored and bounded through particular enactments of relations. It entails examining education as a spatio-temporal ordering of mobilizing, mooring and bounding in the valuing and enacting of certain forms of subjectivities and practices.

Contrasting arenas of sociomateriality

More, perhaps, than the other arenas, complexity theory provides a rich analysis of the *biological* (as well as social, personal, cultural) flows inherent in material-ization processes. It highlights the elaborate intertwining of human/non-human elements, and the non-linear simultaneous dynamics and conditions which produce *emergence*. The system in complexity theory is an effect produced through self-organization via these dynamics and is continuously adaptive. Studies are able to model system patterns in various scalar spaces as they interact, shift and change. Knowledge (e.g. new possibilities, innovations, practices) emerges along with identities and environments when the system affords sufficient diversity, redundancy and multiple feedback loops. Diversity is not to be managed towards producing greater homogeneity, as some approaches to workplace learning might advocate, but to be interconnected. In elaborating this point, Davis and Sumara (2006) explain that difference in an identified system needs ways to become visible – the conditions must enable the enactment of difference – which it often is not. As diverse elements become enacted, they must also be able to interconnect through overlap. In classrooms or organi-zations, emergence can be enabled where there are diversity and constraints (purposes and rules of engagement) by amplifying difference and perturbations, decentralizing organizing processes, encouraging continuous interaction and ensuring ongoing feedback among various elements/sites (Stacey 2005; Davis and Sumara 2006).

By contrast, in cultural historical activity theory, activity and the overlapping systems of activity are viewed as sites of domination, accommodation and resistance as well as struggle, shaped in myriad ways by the contradictory mutuality of those who control the means of production and those whose labour and knowledge are exploited. These are the Marxist roots of this theory, although it moves well beyond binary conceptions of activity as unidimensional sites of class struggle alone. The Marxist notion of dialectical contradictions is central to CHAT, and individual perspectives and interests are constantly at play in negotiating these contradictions. In these features, CHAT retains a more humanist orientation than either complexity or ANT. This human-centric analysis is also evident in the clear delineation of non-human artefacts as bounded, distinct from humans and, while embedding cultural histories, relegated to the role of mediating human activity. CHAT also foregrounds a sociopolitical analysis of human activity, including constructs such as division of labour and community, which are historical and in this sense anterior to the emergence of elements that may or may not comprise a system. However, CHAT affords a rich approach to analysing precisely these political dynamics that are so important to all forms of learning and human development, while insisting that these dynamics intermingle the material, the symbolic, the social relational and the transformational. Complexity theory can address the political only through severe, and some would argue inappropriate, stretching of its constructs. CHAT also theorizes the historical emergence of the sociocultural/material in activity systems in ways that complexity theory cannot.

ANT approaches have been compared with CHAT, although they share little in their ontological assumptions (for comparisons of ANT and CHAT, see Engeström 1996b; Latour 1996; Miettinen 1999). ANT, including the many *after* ANT commentaries, perhaps offers the more radical material challenge to understandings of learning, education and organizations. When anyone speaks of a system or structure, ANT asks, how has it been compiled? Where is it? What is holding it together? All things are assemblies, connected in precarious networks that require much ongoing work to sustain their linkages. ANT traces how these assemblages are made and sustained, how they order behaviours as well as space and objects, but also how they can be unmade and how counternetworks or alternative forms and spaces can take shape and develop strength. ANT has also challenged the tendency to seek relations, showing that the relative stability of certain networks occurs not through their coherences, but through their incoherences and ambivalences. ANT commentators play with scale, and reject dualisms of local/global or micro/macro. There are no suprastructural entities, explains Latour (1999: 18), because 'big does not mean "really" big or "overall" or "overarching", but connected, blind, local, mediated, related'. ANT also shows how knowledge is generated through the process and effects of these assemblages coming together. ANT offers us, finally, a way to challenge notions of learning as a process occurring in individuals' conscious minds. In ANT, all things are network effects: a concept, a text, an organizational routine or breakdown, an oppressive regime, a teacher, worker or manager. In fact, any thing or human being, human intention, consciousness, desire, etc. emerges and oscillates through various translations at play in material network effects, sometimes appearing simultaneously as multiple ontologies. ANT focuses on the circulating forces and minute interactions that get things done through the networks/*assemblages* of elements acting upon one another. As Latour (2005: 44) wrote:

> Action is not done under the full control of consciousness; action should rather be felt as a node, a knot, and a conglomerate of many surprising sets

of agencies that have to be slowly disentangled. It is this venerable source of uncertainty that we wish to render vivid again in the odd expression of actor-network.

Issues in sociomaterial approaches to educational research

There is a danger in becoming overly fascinated with conceptions that trace complexity, without asking why such analysis is any more productive in understanding and responding to educational concerns. Educational researchers, such as those we have gathered in this book, in fact bring important educational questions to sociomaterial arenas around core educational dimensions of knowledge, pedagogy and purpose. What forms of knowledge are produced in current educational arrangements, what productive forms of knowledge are possible, and what engagements can develop these? What is competency, and what is expertise, in sociomaterial flows? How is pedagogy achieved socio-materially, and what effects are produced by different pedagogies? How are educational purposes produced (or resisted, defused, undermined) through different heterogeneous assemblages, and how can these be influenced? How can we conceptualize 'good education' in a sociomaterial orientation? How can we understand and promote productive enactments of educational respon-sibility? What does education for equity and justice look like if we approach it as vital materiality, and how can it be promoted?

Educators also have for some time worked with notions of situated learning, accepting metaphors of learning as more about participation than acquisition. But who participates, and how, with what effects? Sociomaterial orientations offer more fine-grained analyses of participation than are commonly under-taken in conceptions of communities of practice. Similarly, the concept of practice in education, while recently reclaimed in the 'practice-based turn' of learning (Hager *et al.* 2011), is a vast domain that needs more nuanced con-sideration: visible activity and invisible infrastructure, forms and purposes of knowing activity, and various practising combinations of materials, meanings and energies that sociomaterial analyses can help us to appreciate.

Educators working in sociomaterial arenas, too, continue to raise the ques-tion of human subjectivity and human meaning. As we will see in subsequent chapters focusing in detail on the different arenas, educational researchers wonder, when we move away from the individual, are we then in a world of techno-determinism? Or, from a different set of concerns, do these approaches simply remain at a systemic level that abstracts, or omits, the person and the personal that are crucial in education? For some, sociomateriality represents a post-human orientation. However, this is not an anti-human post-humanism, where technological enhancements and digitized bodies are the nightmare of lost human dignity and subjectivity (Hayles 1999; Fukuyama 2002). Rather, this is a post-humanism that refutes anthropomorphic centrality of human beings and human knowledge in defining the world and its relations. It accepts the value of transgressing boundaries and disrupting uniform ideas about what it means to be human. It even may suggest expansion of human being-ness beyond current naturalized limitations of physical body and brain-based intelligence.

Questions of power and the normative inspire continuing debate among educators and other commentators within all four arenas discussed here. Some approaches, such as ANT, have been critiqued for offering a flat ontology where nothing can be challenged and no standpoint for intervention formulated. As we shall see, other researchers have shown clearly that ANT traces very well how powerful assemblages – whether ideas, institutions, machines or dictators – emerge and extend themselves. Sociomaterial approaches can reveal materialist dynamics of oppression, exclusion and agonism that are at play, but often overlooked, in educational processes. They also can illuminate openings and ambivalences for entry, opportunities for interruption, and strategies for productive materialist coalitions. More importantly, as Bennett's (2010: 107) work shows, a materialist theory of democracy is enabled when we encounter the world 'as a swarm of vibrant materials entering and leaving agentic assemblages'. She follows the French philosopher Rancière in accepting that a political act not only disrupts, but also disrupts so as to radically change how people perceive the dominant 'partition of the sensible': the boundaries that distribute bodies so that some are visible as political actors and others ignored. But, Bennett asks, why is the power to disrupt limited to human speakers, and the power to provoke dramatic public perceptual shifts assumed to exclude non-humans?

> We might then entertain a set of crazy and not-so-crazy questions: Did the typical American diet play any role in engendering the widespread susceptibility to the propaganda leading up to the invasion of Iraq? Do sand storms make a difference to the spread of so-called sectarian violence? Does mercury help autism? In what ways does the effect on sensibility of a video game exceed the intentions of its designers and users? Can a hurricane bring down a president? Can HIV mobilize homophobia or an evangelical revival?
>
> (Bennett 2010: 107)

As Bennett concludes, when the sensible is repartitioned, and the regime of the perceptible overthrown, new tactics emerge for enhancing, or weakening, particular arrangements of the public.

A final contribution of sociomaterial approaches is to debates around the difficulties of conducting research amongst a 'swarm of vibrant materials entering and leaving assemblages'. Suchman (2007) explains that sociomaterial orientations call us to constant reminder that we are an integral part of the apparatus through which our research objects are made. Once we step outside a representational idiom of (re)searching phenomena, we must confront the ways in which our practices of knowing are specific material entanglements that participate in (re)configuring the world. Sociomaterial approaches offer two starting points for this, elaborated in the ensuing chapters here. The first is a sensibility for, and a language for speaking about, both the order and the mess that are mutually constituted in the material swarms of educational worlds. The mess is the lumpy stuff that continually spills out of categorizations and models: a necessary hinterland of details, contingency and banality, that so often disappears in a focus on what appears to be self-evidently important. As Suchman (2007) has been reminding us for over two decades, we keep trying to order the mess with prescriptive devices – plans, maps, procedures and instructions – but these are in themselves practices that are mutually constituted of ordering impulses and messy hinterlands. Sociomaterial approaches such as the four we trace here all emphasize responsible knowing, research that explicates the boundary-making and the exclusions crafted through its own processes, and that traces the entanglement of the researcher in the vital swarms of the researched. This is a fraught endeavour, of course, particularly when a human researcher is, in the final representation, speaking for the swarms. This book does not promise any clear solution to this and the other research dilemmas raised through sociomaterial approaches. In fact, it might be most accurate to characterize these arenas in terms of *what* they attend to, rather than how – perhaps their most valuable contribution is the questions they raise about the purposes and activities of research.

We have been arguing that sociomaterial approaches offer useful sensibilities and questions for educational researchers. While we limit our examination in this book to the four arenas of complexity, CHAT, ANT and spatiality, and some of their diverse uptakes, there are many other sociomaterial approaches that do similar kinds of work, as noted in the Preface. Our interest is primarily in the emphasis on materiality offered by these approaches, which show how it is relational and distributed within webs of thought and activity, social and physical phenomena in education. Further, they offer methods for analysing how materializing processes are bound up with assembling and reassembling policies and practices, identities and knowledge. While very different in their points of departure and foci for analysis, these approaches analyse processes termed learning as phenomena of emergence and orderings within and across space–time. They show the interdependence of entities, which not only decentres the knowing subject, but also unseats idealizations of enterprising, autonomous knowers. Most important, perhaps, in the work of educational analysts, these approaches have offered resources to understand and engage, both pedagogically and critically, with the unpredictability of educational processes. They have been used to unpick the fragile stabilities of devices that appear to be immutable and to show the productive openings created in contradictions.

For all four arenas, questions of interest are around how disparate elements and their linkages are performed and reconfigured through local practices of materialization. All four examine how practices become fixed and durable in time and space, and seek out the ambivalences, uncertainties and contra-dictions – the openings. A key contribution of them all is to decouple learning and knowledge production from a strictly human-centred socio-cultural ontology, and to liberate agency from its conceptual confines as a human-generated force. Instead, agency as well as knowledge is understood as *enacted* in the emergence and interactions – as well as the exclusionings – occurring in the smallest encounters. In these material enactments bursting with life, this 'vital materiality', or 'material-discursive agency', boundaries and properties of elements come into being, subjects and objects are delineated, and relations are constituted that produce force. Nothing is determined. Therefore (unknown) radical future possibilities are available at every encounter. Perhaps this is most apparent in the arena of complexity, which we explore in the next two chapters.

Chapter 2

Emergence and perturbation
Understanding complexity theory

Complexity theory is growing in usage among educational researchers. We can point to several recent books (Davis and Sumara 2006; Mason 2008a; Osberg and Biesta 2010), a journal (*Complicity*, inaugurated in 2004), an annual international conference dedicated to complexity studies in education, an annual meeting of a special interest group in complexity at the American Educational Research Association, and various special issues of educational journals featuring complexity studies (e.g. Mason 2008b,c; Osberg 2008). While its uptake is most evident in curriculum studies and school pedagogical writing, complexity theory also is beginning to appear in adult education and higher education (Karpiak 2000; Cutright 2001; Haggis 2007) and has become popular in workplace and vocational education, particularly organizational development and training (Kauffman 1995; Stacey 2005) and professional education (McMurtry 2010). This popularity is evident across the social sciences. In explaining the 'turn' to complexity, Urry (2005) noted that it is not surprising, given that complexity characterizes the global conditions of trade, migration, communications (and, we might argue, education) with the ever-evolving interconnectedness of ideas, processes and organizations and the tangled proliferation of technology-mediated networks.

To refer to 'complexity science' or complexity theory as though it is a singular, monolithic body of knowledge is a misrepresentation. The complexity field embraces diverse developments that have informed one another. These include theories of general systems, cybernetics, chaos, deep ecology and autopoesis. The historical distinctions among these developments are outlined briefly later in this chapter. However, in the main, the discussion here focuses upon the shared understandings of complexity that appear most frequently in educational writings, using a single term 'complexity theory'.

What is complexity theory? One definition is offered by David Byrne, who authored *Complexity Theory and the Social Sciences* back in 1998, and more recently described complexity as

> the interdisciplinary understanding of reality as composed of complex open systems with emergent properties and transformational potential. A crucial

corollary of complexity theory is that knowledge is inherently local rather than universal. Complexity science is inherently dynamic. It is concerned with the description and explanation of change.

(Byrne 2005: 97)

Complexity's definition in educational research, claim Davis and Sumara (2008), varies according to who is defining it and their obsessions. Some focus more on complexity as a way to understand knowledge as emergent and enacted rather than represented and acquired. They may do so to consider alternative approaches to curriculum, or to advise teachers about pedagogies that might generate more open, improvisational and collaborative learning activities. Other educators work with concepts of emergence and self-organization to understand how systems take shape in unexpected ways. They may do so to show how change actually occurs in these systems, to trace the unpredicted consequences of particular changes and actions, or even to advise practitioners about effective ways to intervene in a system to cause change. A system can be any assortment of entities – material and virtual, human and technical, seen or unseen – held together by some kind of interrelations with one another to form a collectivity: a classroom of children, a team of professionals, a *Facebook* site, an individual mind or digestive system, an infectious disease, a hurricane.

Complexity theory posits that these complex open systems emerge in unpredictable patterns that often defy attempts to control and direct. Some claim that a complex system is inherently a learning collective. Most agree that a complex system is disordered while balancing particular orders. It is ceaselessly dynamic, and does not exist in stasis or it would die. It constantly adapts to what surrounds it and what is nested within it, which is constantly changing. In this way, as Prigogine (1997: 189) explained, complexity science overcomes the popular but inaccurate dichotomy of 'a deterministic world and an arbitrary world of chaos'. Complexity views all things as formed through a dynamic conversation among order and disorder: recursive iterations of particular ordering rules and orders, and improvisational expansion through disordering perturbations and novel encounters.

This chapter offers various explanations of complexity theory. At best, this is a presumptuous and problematic project. It implies the existence of certain laws in a field that challenges analysis of parts according to laws. It also suggests a singularity of understandings where there is heterogeneity. It potentially contributes to the simplistic and romantic descriptions of complexity theory that have proliferated in popular literature. Nonetheless, certain concepts appear frequently in the work of educationists using complexity, and it is difficult to understand their questions without some background. Following a brief history of this background, some of these key concepts are outlined below: emergence, non-linear dynamics and uncertainty, positive feedback, self-organization and the balance of order and disorder, and interconnected diversity. Finally, the chapter examines conceptions of knowledge and learning in complexity theory.[1]

Origins of 'complexity theory'

Alhadeff-Jones (2008) traces three generations of complexity theory. These threads have explored ways to describe and even to generate complex collectives and the ways they change. In the process, they have uncovered new relationships between stability and non-linearity, order and chaos, that coexist in systems. For Alhadeff-Jones, the first generation focused on attempts to describe and map phenomena known as 'organized complexity', observed in a system's ability to absorb external energy or information and convert it into organization or structures. Cybernetics, for example, as studied by von Foerster, von Neumann, Bateson and others, developed the notion of 'feedback': the way in which a system assimilated external information to adapt itself.

In the second generation, the focus was on understanding non-linear and often unpredictable dynamics observed in system behaviour. Artificial intelligence studies attempted to produce symbolic representations of real situations. These incorporated heuristics and reasoning that moved past static algorithmic calculations to describe a system or produce it. System scientists, such as von Bertalanffy using general systems theory, tried to study a system's complexity by examining not just its components, but also the relationships among them, which informed understandings about the importance of the observer's relation to the phenomena observed. Self-organization, a system's ability to evolve as an autonomous structure through fluctuations in the relations among its internal components, as well as environmental influences, had been observed by many of these scientists in various systems – organic, ecological, social and artificial.

Prigogine's introduction of 'dissipative structures' opened new understandings about how change can occur in systems through the amplification of random fluctuations that bring the entire system into a new state of dynamic stability. Chaos theory, with its study of internal attractors around which the elements of a system gather in particular patterns, helped illuminate system behaviour that appears to be random but is actually mathematically calculable. Maturana and Varela's (1987) work on structural coupling and autopoeisis was published in this period, flavoured with Maturana's work in counselling family systems and Varela's infusion of ethics and Buddhist sensibilities into his studies of biological sciences. Fractal geometry showed the phenomena of self-similarity, when tiny parts of a system all appear similar and indeed reflect the same patterns performed by the whole, revealing how order works unexpectedly even in systems appearing as disordered.

In Alhadeff-Jones' story of complexity theory, the third generation beginning in the 1980s saw the introduction of the concept of 'complex adaptive systems'. Research attempted to map a system's variations that caused it to evolve as a self-organizing and complex collective. Waldrop (1994) and others at the Santa Fé institute pushed beyond observing and mapping what *is*, and attempted to simulate what *could be* in social, ecological, artificial and organic systems. In the social sciences, complexity theory has been used to explore phenomena as intertwinings of politics, health, technological innovation, desire and so forth, seeking an expansive approach that sidesteps old subject–object and agency–structure dichotomies (Byrne 1998; Urry 2005; Walby 2009). Walby, for example, uses complexity in her studies of equity and diversity to overcome what she maintains are the analytical limitations of conventional social theory. She analyses social inequalities as separate, but overlapping complex systems (e.g. gender, class, ethnicity) of social and material relations, each with its own non-linear, self-organizing dynamics, and each causally interconnected. For Walby, these systems intersect with institutionalized and sedimented structures of economy, polity, violence and civil society to produce particular actions and possibilities. The point here is that researchers have experimented with various entry points and applications using the theoretical resources offered through a complexity analysis of sociomaterial dynamics. These explorations have proven useful in better understanding issues such as those at the heart of educational processes: change, identities, inequities and social difference, agency, learning and knowing, and the relation of stability with disorder and disruption.

Emergence in complex systems

A central understanding in complexity is *emergence*, the idea that in (complex adaptive) systems, phenomena, events and actors are mutually dependent, mutually constitutive, and actually *emerge together* in dynamic structures. That is, the nature of the system as well as its elements and their relationships – both human and non-human – emerge through the continuous rich and recursive interactions among these elements. This means, among other things, that humans are fully interconnected with many elements of the systems that are constantly acting upon each other. No clear lines of causation can be traced from these interactions to their outcomes. We may try to attribute occurrences to human intention, or to some correlation that we believe we are observing in a system. But often what actually emerges is surprising. It escapes our efforts to represent, model and predict.

Further, what emerges, whether knowledge, identities, practices or symbols, is specific to the system in which it emerged, and therefore cannot exist as an object that can move to another system. In the educational uptake of complexity theory, what is emphasized are the flows and relations *among* things – not the *things* themselves (e.g. see Karpiak 2000; Davis 2004; Laidlaw 2005; Davis and Sumara 2006). The focus is not upon isolated actors and objects foregrounded against some contextual backdrop, but on the dynamic, non-linear actions and connections flowing *between* all these parts. Complexity theory interrupts the natural tendency to seek clear boundaries between figures (objects) and grounds (context), and focuses on the relationships binding humans and non-humans together in multiple fluctuations. Thus the boundaries between self and non-self (nature as well as society) are actually more permeable, and the flow between them more continuous, than we might be prepared to accept.

What, then, constitutes a system? This is a problem for complexity, which understands a system's boundaries to be ambiguous given that any system is comprised of other systems nested within it, and is implicated in other systems that interact with it. Where are the system's edges? Edges are, usually, amorphous. Think of trying to actually distinguish the boundaries of a tropical cyclone from the sea and air currents that sustain it (Osberg 2008) or of trying to separate, at the cellular level, which molecules belong to the system and which to the setting (Davis and Sumara 2008). Yet we engage in setting boundaries all the time in order to talk about and explore phenomena. If we're not careful to remember how contingent they are, such boundaries threaten to produce a thing-ness to a system as though it is an object, inherently distinct, rather than being enmeshed with the systems around it. In the final analysis, a system and its boundaries will be determined according to an observer's choice of focus: what criteria constitute the system, what is relegated to the background as other, as not-system, and what is taken to constitute the edges separating the system from its other.

Within and among systems, then, countless elements are constantly interacting and improvising simultaneously. Uncertainty is a central structural principle within these dynamic processes. So many things are going on all at once, and so many new possibilities emerging, that there can be no reduction of the system's patterns to causes and effects. Thus everything from a weather system to an economic system to a human being is described as a *complex* system, rather than simply a complicated one with a mechanical, predictable system of parts, such as a car or a coffee-maker. A complicated system can be analysed by breaking it into its parts and studying the linkages among them. A complex system resists this kind of analysis because its behaviours *exceed the sum of its parts*.

More to the point, among the possibilities emerging at any given time in the system, it is impossible to predict which will *most influence* what will happen next. This is partly because the principles influencing the system's choices for action and knowledge are *not already given* in the system's present patterns or its parts. They emerge also in the dynamic processes of emergence. Therefore the future of the system can be nowhere evident in the patterns of the present system.

In educational research working with complexity theory, emergence is perhaps the most oft-cited concept. But there are other critical dimensions. Alhadeff-Jones (2008, 2010) draws heavily from the writings of Edgar Morin to show how complexity approaches are useful for educational analyses. Morin, in his considerations of knowledge production, proposed 11 principles to denounce what he characterized as a paradigm of simplification (based on linear causality, reductionism, reliability of logic, universal determinism, and so forth). Alhadeff-Jones offers a translation of Morin's 11 principles for a 'paradigm of complexity':

(1) promoting interpretations starting from the local and the singular; (2) recognising and integrating the irreversibility of time and the necessity to include history in any description or explanation; (3) recognising the impossibility to isolate single elementary units and the necessity to link the knowledge of any elements to the knowledge of the wholes they belong to; (4) the principle that organisation and self-organisation represent problematics that cannot be ignored; (5) the principle of complex causality (including mutual causalities, feedback loops, etc.); (6) interpreting phenomena through the circular logic linking order, disorder, interactions and organisation; (7) the principle of distinction, instead of disjunction, between the object, or the subject, and their environment; (8) the principle of relationship between the observer/designer and the object of study; (9) the possibility of a scientific theory of the self and the necessity to recognise physically, biologically, and anthropologically, the categories of being and existence, as well as the notion of autonomy (e.g., through a theory of self-production and self-organisation); (10) the recognition of the limits of logical demonstration with formal complex systems [. . .] and the discursive principle privileging the association of complementary, concurrent and antagonistic notions with each other; and finally (11) thinking dialogically and through macro-concepts, as a strategy of research aiming to establish and question links and relationships between notions and concepts, and by extension between and beyond disciplines.

(Alhadeff-Jones 2010:480)

These principles of uncertainty, self-organization, time irreversibility, connectivity and so forth have been taken up widely by researchers to explore their implications for educational practice. What we see in this chapter and the next is that these principles pose challenges for educational planning, governance, accountability, professional practices and responsibility, where those involved in such processes seek linearity, predictability and universality, such as through the application of laws and scientific evidence.

Non-linear dynamics and uncertainty

How does emergence occur? The Nobel prize-winning Ilya Prigogine (1997) showed how complex systems, which he characterized as 'far from equilibrium', develop themselves through *non-linear dynamics* of interaction. In observing water heated in a container and changing its states in non-linear ways, he showed that systems such as this cannot be described through linear causality, applying principles that determine natural outcomes from particular inputs. He eventually demonstrated that, within a complex system, choices are continually being made among alternatives that are presented to the system. Many of these alternatives emerge from within the system and seem to be chosen totally by chance, because no possible calculation can demonstrate the system's preference for one or another. As each choice is adopted, the system changes and a new range of choices opens. The system thus unfolds in a series of 'jumps', influenced at each turn by something from within itself that is indeterminate and has no concrete existence (chance), but that irreversibly changes the system and its logic, and expands the possibilities available for its next actions. Important to note about Prigogine's work is that the system moves from near-equilibrium to a complex state far-from-equilibrium through the application of energy: thermal energy, in his own studies. Also critical to note is that in a complex system, large amounts of interacting entities are involved. Prigogine stressed the importance of both interaction and the presence of large numbers to evoke the phenomena of emergence. Within these masses of interaction, the smaller parts of the system become energized and sensitive to even minor fluctuations. The result is a complex system's continuous state of *uncertainty* and surprise, such that chance is always operating in the unfolding configurations, which are always opening a multiplicity of possibilities. Osberg (2008: 150) shows how Prigogine's conceptions are particularly valuable for education, as in complex systems, 'what is already present is reordered or renewed in a way that opens incalculable (and wider) possibilities. In this sense, the non-deterministic "logic" of emergence can be thought of as a logic of renewal.'

In this complexity process of renewal, for Osberg, education is understood to be radically indeterminate. Its trajectory unfolds according to choices continually made among ever-expanding possibilities. Thus complexity allows a vision of curricular spaces actively encouraging the as-yet-unimagined, in Davis's (2004) words.

Positive feedback, coupling and complicity

Positive feedback loops are important in understanding how a system evolves and transforms, often unpredictably and often irreversibly. These are different from the notion of negative feedback, which in earlier systems theories was thought to sense minor deviations and drive a system back to its norm of equilibrium. Positive feedback amplifies particular contingent perturbations in the system, potentially creating a momentum and distribution of small events that give rise to large system effects. Escalating feedback loops mobilize non-linear dynamics that can shift a repeated preference into obsessions or even addictions, or amplify small whorls of warm air and water into extreme weather patterns. With sufficient momentum, a system can pass a particular threshold or tipping point (Gladwell 2002) and shift into a new state. Gladwell compares social phenomena to epidemics that spread in ways that are counterintuitive: such as the apparently sudden galloping popularity of a new toy or shoe design that is otherwise unremarkable, or the ceasing of graffiti sprayed on New York subway cars. These new system states can develop deterministic properties if they become 'locked in' as a particular behaviour pattern or institutionalized convention, which is why institutions are important in understanding the long-term evolution of

systems (Urry 2005). An example is the conventional school classroom archi-
tecture dominated by rows of standard-sized desks for children, which has
persisted for 200 years despite widespread critique on pedagogical, health and
aesthetic perspectives, experimentation with alternatives, and architectural
innovation in school construction since the late nineteenth century (Lawn and
Grosvenor 2005). 'Lock-in' sediments particular paths of development by
shaping opportunity, rewards and knowledge. For example, Walby (2009) shows
that in an economic system which is out of equilibrium, some individuals with
an initial advantage are able to influence a particular direction of technological
development that benefits themselves. In this light, Walby shows that complexity
and the lock-in phenomenon are useful for understanding the emergence of
inequities.

One explanation of the ongoing interactions in complexity is the process of
'structural coupling', offered by Maturana and Varela (1987). When two actors
or systems coincide, the 'perturbations' of one excite responses and changes in
the structural dynamics of the other, which couple with and alter the elements
engaging with it in a new unity. We can observe this phenomenon all around
us. Watch when two friends are engaged together in some activity, like eating
lunch. Their body positions often will continue to mirror one another, even as
they shift position while they are talking and munching. It is difficult to
determine who is leading or following as their positions and vocal tone emerge
together. We could say that they are *complicit* in one another's changes as they
interact, using this word in the sense posited by Stewart and Cohen (1995), who
slid together the terms simplicity and complexity to produce the concept of
complicity. Complicity is when systems do not just interact, but interact to change
one another, and perpetuate something new. Malaria is one example they use,
where the mosquito sucking blood also sucks parasites in someone's blood,
which are then carried to someone else's blood. Further on, we will show how
complicity is argued by Davis *et al.* (2000) to be important for educational
research.

When a group of teachers gather, say, to plan a new teaching unit in social
studies, they enact a collective activity in which interaction both enfolds and
renders visible the participants, the objects mediating their actions and dialogue,
the problem space that they define together, and the emerging plan or solution
they devise. But objects, too, contribute and shape responses in the activity.
Are people hovering together at a whiteboard and pointing to one drawing
representing the curriculum, or are they each seated and peering at a separate
individual diagram? Is a video recorder being used to capture the group's
conversation, such that the conversation shifts slightly as people self-monitor
their performance in front of the camera? Does the meeting get interrupted by
an announcement reminding teachers about the attendance records due?
Perhaps someone shows an animated map that their teenager discovered online
at home, and the meeting is diverted for a while as laptops are opened and the
others figure out how to download and use the map. Perhaps someone else

brings a bowl of fresh berries from their garden to share, and all dig in eagerly. As each person and entity contributes and responds within the activity, she changes the interactions and the emerging object of focus. Other participants are changed, the relational space among them all changes, and the looping-back changes the contributor's actions and subject position. This is 'mutual specification' (Varela *et al.* 1991), the fundamental dynamic of systems constantly engaging in joint action and interaction. The resultant coupling changes or co-specifies each, creating a new transcendent unity of action and identities that could not have been achieved independently by participants. These emergences are recursive, continuing to elaborate what is present and what is possible in the system. Out of these continuous and non-linear interactions emerge dynamic structures that exceed their parts. Osberg and Biesta (2007) call this 'strong emergence': conditions where what emerges is more than the sum of its parts, and therefore not predictable from the ground from which it emerges.

Self-organization and order/disorder

One consequence of this disequilibrium is continuous adaptive change. A complex system is self-modifying in constant dialogue with other systems. Its many components are always alive, always interacting creatively with parts directly around them. These interactions form patterns all by themselves. They do not organize according to some sort of externally imposed blueprint or governing system. Complexity theorists describe such systems as autopoetic (Maturana and Varela 1987) or *self-organizing*. Through the ongoing processes of recursively elaborative adaptation, the system can maintain its form without some externally imposed discipline or organizing device.

This is not to say that the system organizes in complete chaos, with no limitations or direction other than random pursuit of possibilities. What Davis (2004: 151) calls a 'transcendent collectivity' emerges through the bottom–up interactions of multiple agents, with an identifiable unity and coherence. New novel forms of order are continually emerging, but the system usually will continue to maintain its identity except in the condition of severe perturbations. In this condition, the system may tip over a threshold to form a new state.

Throughout its states of change, an interesting aspect that has been observed of complex systems is *self-similarity* in their patterns. A large fern, for example, closely resembles the structures of one branch of the fern, and one single leaf of the branch. A tiny part of a coastline, when magnified, appears remarkably similarly to the pattern of the mapped coastline of which it is part. Thus a system sometimes can be studied by looking closely at one part as well as at the whole body of relationships among parts. One explanation for this is offered through fractal geometry, which portrays the way that repeated iteration of a simple pattern or rule, with just slight variation at each iteration, produces a complex pattern whose bits look like the whole. Davis and Sumara (2005: 309) suggest that fractals are generated through recursive processes——in contrast to Euclidean forms, which are built up through linear sequences of operations. At each stage in a recursive process, the starting point is the output of the preceding iteration, and the output is the starting point of the subsequent iteration. Every stage, that is, is an elaboration, and such elaborations can quickly give rise to unexpected forms and surprising complexity. The sorts of recursive functions that are used to generate fractals are also non-compressible. There are no shortcuts to their final products. A person interested in the eventual product of a fractal-generating function must allow it to unfold.

Whatever its state, a complex system demonstrates spontaneous emergence of order out of disorder. This means there are always disordering dynamics held in balanced tension with self-organizing patterns. A system encounters and contains many forms of limitation that affect its patterns. For example, self-organization is necessarily limited by information such as memory and historical routines, embedded codes such as genetic structures, pre-existing objects and their properties that function within the system, and languages. This information does not predetermine and foreclose the directions of the system, for the information itself is subject to adaptation and shifts as emergence occurs. What it does mean, argue Smith and Jenks (2005), is that a notion of utter contingency is overly simplistic. A system needs different kinds of information and, in fact, a complex system has simultaneous needs for both precise directions and 'loose' contingent information: 'self-organization does not take place against a general background of contingency; rather, chaos and self-organization determine each other *somewhat* in the form of *degrees* or "landscapes" of possibility or impossibility' (Smith and Jenks 2005: 153).

Interconnected diversity

While self-similarity can be detected in complex systems, the possibility of emergence derives from diversity. Whether this is achieved through small variations introduced into successful iterations of a routine, or emerges through perturbations that arise contingently when energy or new information is introduced, a complex system requires internal diversity. Diversity enables the system to generate the possibilities or disorderings required for continual creative adaptation to changing conditions, and diversity enables the resilience allowing the system to sustain itself throughout challenges and losses. Diversity alone is not sufficient, as Prigogine demonstrated: there must be interaction. Thus the key to a healthy (adapting, self-sustaining and emergent) complex system is *interconnected diversity* among its parts. A human body, for example, relies on highly specialized sub-systems that not only each respond to different circumstances and different needs, but also have learned to cohabit and communicate with one another. Another dynamic required in self-organization is redundancy: sufficient overlap among the agents (such as shared texts, language, interests) to enable the interactions that will give rise to the system. There must also be a means by which agents can affect one another, such as proximity, and a decentralized, distributed form of organization that allows multi-directional interactions in networks rather than hierarchies. When these elements are present, a system can emerge with a distinct integrity without top-down control, even as it is continually interacting with the systems surrounding it and embedded within it. As Hesoon Bai (2001: 26) writes, 'changes are the result of our interpenetrating the world', more than of human conscious intentional action to do something.

These concepts of emergence, non-linear dynamics and uncertainty, positive feedback, self-organization, the balance of order and disorder, and interconnected diversity have developed through a heterogeneous trajectory of inquiries and studies in fields that have contributed to complexity, as we saw in the short history provided earlier (Alhadeff-Jones 2008). This heterogeneity is useful to acknowledge again here, to remind us of the ontological roots of complexity thinking in symbolic modelling of whole systems, and to help prevent collapsing the multiplicity of these theories into a few oversimplified or romantic precepts. These multiple explorations point to both the possibilities of complexity theory and its problems for education, such as in its applications to the study of knowledge.

Knowledge and learning

In complexity terms, knowledge and learning are understood as continuous invention and exploration, produced through relations among consciousness, identity, action and interaction, objects and structural dynamics. New possibilities for action are constantly emerging among these interactions of complex systems. Cognition occurs in the possibility for unpredictable shared action. Knowledge is not understood as an autonomous collection of concepts separate from the systems in which these emerge. A 'learner' is not self-evident nor foundational. The learning subject is not clearly distinct from the objects and material flux that are so often relegated to the background in discussions of education. Knowledge, learning and teaching cannot be contained in any one element or dimension of a system, as they are constantly emerging and spilling into other systems. No actor has an essential self or knowledge outside these relationships. In educational applications of complexity theory, attention is drawn to the relationships among learners and the environment.

Edgar Morin (1990/2008) is often credited as one of the first to explore the epistemological implications of complexity. In contemplating the conditions of emergence, Morin noted that we must avoid positing anything like laws of complexity, since its very dynamics defy the reductionist process of deriving laws from observed phenomena to apply to new observations. Further, we must account for our own processes of coming to know emergence at the same time as we engage in those processes. The major problem is one of whole–part implication and mutual looping: coming to know the parts and their relations, while simultaneously coming to know the whole as an organizer and as organized, and the complicity of our knowledge in its organizing. Morin (2007) also identified a major epistemological problem in what he called 'generalized complexity': the inseparable relation between disorganized complexity (irruptions) and organized complexity (understanding how the emergentist organization of complex systems produces complexity). For Morin, knowledge must integrate the complexity of human identity and ethics in a complex science that acknowledges its uncertainty, and the self-organized cycles of knowledge-building.

Turning to the field of educational studies, complexity theorists Brent Davis *et al.* (2000: 74) describe emergence as 'a new understanding of cognition':

> Rather than being cast as a locatable process or phenomenon, cognition has been reinterpreted as a joint participation, a choreography. An agent's knowing, in this sense, are those patterns of acting that afford it a coherence—that is, that make it discernible as a unity, a wholeness, identity. The question, 'Where does cognition happen?' is thus equivalent to, 'Who or what is perceived to be acting?' In this way, a rain forest is cognitive—and humanity is necessarily participating in its cogitations/evolutions. That is, our habits of thought are entwined and implicated in unfolding global conditions.

All complex adaptive systems – forests, weather patterns, stock markets, school districts or groups of students – learn, where learning is defined as transformation that expands the system's potential range of action. Research on HIV-AIDs systems, for example, demonstrates that the immune system remembers, forgets, recognizes, hypothesizes, errors, adapts, and thus learns (Davis *et al.* 2000). A traffic system of roads, vehicles and intersections, car manufacturers and petrol stations, traffic lights that malfunction now and then and unexpected landslides that block passage, continually adapts and reconfigures itself. Human beings are nested within these larger systems that are continuously learning and, as participants in these systems, they bear their characteristics in the ways that the single fern leaf resembles the whole fern plant. Flowing through humans are other systems such as viruses, immune systems, and social panic about pandemics.

Some would call learning the very dynamic of emergence in complex systems. Learning also could be the sudden jumps in the system's phase states, its transformations, as it experiences disturbances and internal fluctuations that can become amplified. Cognition occurs in the new possibilities that are always opening for unpredictable shared action. Some have shown that knowledge in complexity is strikingly similar to Dewey's conception of transactional realism:

> Knowledge *emerges* from our transactions with our environment and feeds back into this same environment, such that our environment becomes

increasingly meaningful for us. This means we cannot have knowledge *of* our environment, once and for all – it is not something we can see, something to look at. Rather, it is something we have to actively feel our way around and through, unendingly. Why unendingly? Because in acting, we create knowledge; and in creating knowledge, we learn to act in different ways; and in acting in different ways, we bring about new knowledge that changes our world, that causes us to act differently, and so on, unendingly. There is no final truth of the matter, only increasingly diverse ways of interacting in a world that is becoming increasingly complex.

(Osberg *et al.* 2008a: 223)

However, complexity leads to insights beyond Dewey's important contribution of the observer as concerned participant in knowledge, because emergence involves elements that are not present in the system. The new forms and characteristics that a system develops arise from things that seem to be introduced into the system, but which are not traceable, representable, predictable, or related to any historical antecedents already at work. These things are chance, they are the 'radically non-relational' elements that somehow become incorporated into the system to produce surprising new configurations:

> The combination of the system's relational past with the totally intractable or unrepresentable to produce new emergent order that supervenes on lower levels *ad infinitum* ensures that the system is never in a state where it is fully actualised, is never fully 'present' at any point in time, because an integral part of it is that which is *not* part of it. It therefore remains always in the process of becoming without being.
>
> (Osberg *et al.* 2008a: 224)

This insight in understanding knowledge as emergentist has excited educational researchers in ways that are highlighted in chapter three. One persistent problem, however, has been the confusion of complexity as a metaphor with complexity as an analytical tool for sociomaterial emergence in education. That is, complexity theory potentially offers a fundamental reconfiguration of investigation approaches in education rooted in an ontology of sociomaterial and simultaneous emergence of knowledge, identities and action. However, when complexity is used as a metaphor, as it sometimes tends to be, its potential is much lessened.

Matter-ings and metaphors

> Matter acquires new properties when far from equilibrium, in that fluctuations and instabilities become the norm. Matter becomes more 'active'.
>
> (Prigogine 1997: 64)

Since the first applications of complexity theory to socio-cultural systems, critics have complained that theories designed to explain phenomena and shifting patterns in the natural world cannot be applied to socio-cultural systems. The claim is that complexity theory has focused on matter – physical movements and links among objects and actors; whereas human systems are very much determined by meaning – interpretive movements among perceptions, symbols, identities and meanings. Therefore relations among humans cannot be explained solely in terms of physical motion and change, because they entail emotion, desire, power and ethics. However, amidst the shift to step away from human-centric preoccupations to embrace the importance of materiality in all relations, there is new emphasis on research approaches and questions that truly appreciate matter in the social and personal. Writers like Barad (2003), Latour (2005) and Sørensen (2009), to whom we will return throughout this book, have worked out detailed analyses of materiality in knowledge, learning and social organization. We might think of these sorts of conceptions as 'matter-ings', following Law (2007), who encourages (re)conceptions of the social whereby *matter*, the material processes of all life, truly matters. However, a concern with matter requires a reconfiguration of ontology and approaches to inquiry in social sciences, where the focus has been mostly so stubbornly centred on human concerns.

In the case of complexity theory, applications to social questions have often been engendered through a *metaphor* of complexity. In other words, the images of emergence, self-organization, connectivity, 'butterfly effects', attractors and so forth can be (and have been) treated as representations of desirable patterns, then projected interpretively onto realist social systems to produce notions of positive human interconnections, inventive adaptation and continuous learning. This approach is both pervasive and limited, argues Byrne (2005). While such metaphors hold a certain romantic appeal, they in fact correspond only faintly either to their scientific progenitors or to the forces that actually influence social systems.

Complexity metaphors have become particularly popular in the field of organizational development, where consultants engaged to facilitate leadership and change in organizations of business and government as well as education have developed 'tools' for these purposes (e.g. Olson and Eoyang 2001; Wheatley 1992). These include a wide range of exercises and activities that are pedagogical, such as 'open space' and 'future search' technologies that are described in the next section on educational change. These tools are in fact metaphors (Eoyang 2004) that can assist participants to become aware of the non-linear dynamics at work in organizational change. Eoyang notes that descriptive metaphors of complexity are easily grasped by people, helping them to notice subtle fluctuations or apparently mundane events, and to begin to understand how these non-linear dynamics interact in their system to create its tensions and its productivity. Dynamic metaphors are manifested in tools used not only to understand, but also to intervene in these dynamics in efforts to shift the patterns. In her survey of such organizational development practices, Eoyang (2004) offers a typology of these practices and pedagogical tools rooted in complexity metaphors.

However, for critics of complexity as metaphor (Byrne 2005; Osberg and Biesta 2007), the problem lies in abstracting concepts of complexity from material dynamics and then applying them as representations to human systems. Such metaphors conserve the very anthropocentric ontology that sociomaterial approaches seek to disrupt, and maintain a divide between social and material/natural reality. They also leave the tools of social science investigation relatively unchanged. In fact, complexity metaphors can be applied to organizations in simplistic ways that can render invisible important dynamics of inequity, exploitation, even violence. In this regard, complexity ideals have been criticized as levers of 'soft management' and control in their usage to prompt employees' continuous learning, innovation and 'systems thinking' in organizations (Fenwick 2001; Mojab and Gorman 2003). More broadly, the problematic tendency to construct a set of rules and then apply them as predictive models for emergence in complex adaptive systems is what Byrne (2005) calls simplistic complexity. In the history of complexity theory, one branch of explorations developed by Holland (1995) and others did in fact focus on creating simulations based on a few simple rules which, through multiple iterations and combinations, could produce complex forms. This approach arises from observing unpredictable self-organizing patterns that arise in natural complex systems, such as flocking birds. Nothing directs the flock patterns other than its constituents all observing a few simple rules: maintain consistent speed and equal distance from neighbouring elements, and move towards the perceived centre of the system. However, this approach, like complexity concepts used as a technology to induce productivity in business organizations, is arguably managerialist and institutionalist: based on a closed notion of the system in question. Boundaries are predetermined and survival as a particular system is an assumed objective, and the inputs and directions for change are manipulated by some external (transcendent) source. For education, which is particularly prone to institutional conservatism and attempts to control, the problems of adopting complexity as a metaphor of rules ensconced in tools and technologies are obvious. As Haggis (2009) shows, historically, even theories intended to signal the highly contextualized indeterminacy and diversity in practices and knowledge, such as situated learning theory, have been interpreted in education to create general principles that become the basis for prescribing universal solutions.

Osberg and Biesta (2007) are among those attempting to counter metaphorical uptakes of complexity. In their writings about education and particularly curriculum, they offer what they call a post-structural or philosophical approach to complexity to open a politically conscious explanation of human systems and relations. In their approach, the focus is not upon patterns of actors and action, but upon enacted knowledge, which is 'neither a representation of something more "real" than itself, nor an "object" that can be transferred from one place to the next [. . .] Knowledge is understood, rather, to "emerge" as we participate in the world' (Osberg and Biesta 2007: 2). The problem is that education has come to treat knowledge as centrally a matter of representations, texts and theoretical models that offer presentations purporting to copy a reality that pre-exists them. Learning is then understood to be a matter of acquiring the knowledge contained in these re-presentations. But complexity refuses to separate knowledge from reality as though they exist in different spheres of participation where mind is divided from the world. Instead, the world and our knowledge of it emerge together. An emergentist epistemology counters the representationalist epistemology of schooling.

In his detailed explorations of craftwork, Sennett (2008) notes the same phenomenon. In the midst of craftwork, of working materially with objects, new problems continually emerge at the point of solving others. That is, problem-solving and problem-finding are intimately curled together in ongoing acts of material practice. Knowing emerges simultaneously with the appearance of distinctions among a solution, a new problem, and the phenomena separated by these distinctions. Barad (2003, 2007) calls this entwining 'intra-activity'. Entities become linked through intra-actions, a term she uses to indicate the mutual constitution that occurs simultaneously with their joint activity. Inter-action suggests that entities are not separate and predetermined prior to their encounter, but in fact all entities (human and non-human) as well as their relata – the nature of the links through which they become related in some way – emerge as identifiable embodied entities through their intra-actions. Working with these ideas through feminist theory and quantum physics, particularly the physics of Neils Bohr, Barad develops a sophisticated conception of complex materiality that she calls 'agential realism'. Here 'the world is an ongoing open process of mattering through which "mattering" itself acquires meaning and form in the realization of different agential possibilities' (Barad 2003: 817). Matter is inherently ontologically indeterminate. But in specific intra-actions, an 'agential cut' is enacted that causes a boundary to appear. This boundary separates matter into distinct entities and identifies some relationship among them, such as causality, or observer and observed – subject and object. An agential cut is realized through what Barad calls an apparatus of observation, which is a specific material-discursive configuration that is exercised in an act of agency. These apparatuses also emerge through other agential cuts. An agential cut is always a performance: the boundaries distinguishing knower, known and knowledge do not pre-exist the cut. Further, an agential cut can be performed only in a local moment and place. Agency is not confined to humans or human-associated desires and energies. Instead, agency emerges through iterative changes that are enabled in the dynamic openness of each intra-action. Thus for Barad (2003: 823), '*matter comes to matter* through the iterative intra-activity of the world in its becoming' [emphasis in original].

For education, this emergentist ontology radically calls into question the material separation of humans, objects and their relations, including the separation of entities and representations, in activities of learning and pedagogy. It also insists that the future is radically open, for at every local performance of intra-action, there is space for material-discursive agency. The emergentist epistemology of complexity, claim Osberg *et al.* (2008), also presents radical challenges to education in its very questions about presence and presenting. They ask, what would schooling look like if knowledge were truly appreciated as unfolding in processes of action that brings forth new worlds? What could occur if curriculum were less concerned with what and how content should be presented, and more focused on being a tool for emergence? Such analysis shifts complexity from being applied to education as a metaphor for desirable forms of systemic collaboration, with its images of interconnectedness and self-organization, to fundamental re-orientation of the matter-ing of education. This is both in the sense of its material matters and the knowledge that emerges within this materiality, and in questions about what truly matters in educative processes.

Conclusion

The concepts of complexity described here are those that appear most frequently in educational writings. They provide useful theoretical resources for understanding, as well as promoting, a healthy uncertainty in educational processes and systems. Understandings of knowledge and learning have been reconfigured by complexity concepts such as emergence, non-linear dynamics and self-organization. These concepts are increasingly useful as computer-mediated networks and virtual spaces proliferate across educational domains. Educational questions about pedagogy and curriculum, such as seeking ways to promote creativity, interconnectedness and even emergence, have turned to complexity principles such as diversity, feedback loops and decentralization. Overall, despite some charges of confusing metaphors with the matter of complexity, and the continuing debates around complexity's engagement with educational purpose, responsibility and power relations, complexity theory has already exercised strong influence on educational research in particular areas. It is to these uptakes that we turn in the next chapter.

Notes

1   It is not the intent in this chapter to debate details of different complexity theor(ies), nor to defend a complexity science explanation of reality, cognition, knowledge and subjectivity. Nor is this an attempt to present a comprehensive view of complexity theory. The many sources referred to throughout this discussion offer further explanations, and readers interested in concepts of complexity theory may find useful the Complexity and Education glossary at the University of Alberta: www.complexityandeducation.ualberta.ca/glossary.htm

Chapter 3

Complexity theory in educational research

In chapter two, we examined the central theme of emergence that pervades the diverse uptakes of complexity theory. We saw that many phenomena of our everyday lives can be appreciated as complex systems, heterogeneous collectivities of constantly interacting entities, that emerge in unpredictable directions and forms through non-linear dynamics.

As complexity theory has moved through various uptakes in social sciences, such as education, it has shifted into new forms and approaches. Thrift (1999) drew attention to this as the inevitable hybridizing of complexity theory. Its ideas have encountered new conditions and communities of thought, and have become adapted to consider new problems. We see examples of this throughout this chapter, where writers have sometimes been deliberately selective in the aspects of complexity that they choose for their analyses of particular educational issues.

What complexity offers to educational research is not unlike other perspectives examined in this volume. It overturns assumptions that a learner is necessarily human, that a subject is separable from an object or a knower from the thing that is known, and that knowledge, learning and education can be understood solely as social and personal processes, without attending to the material that is enmeshed with the social and human. Much more than other perspectives, complexity emphasizes the biological and chemical dynamics in sociomateriality. Further, complexity offers, through its understandings of emergence and non-linear causality, ways to analyse the simultaneous occurrences within and across systems that contribute to the appearance of the messy phenomena of education.

Educationists presented in this chapter have shown explicitly how complexity opens possibilities for renewing educational purposes and practices. This optimism is spreading across the social sciences where, according to Urry (2005: 3), social theorists are using complexity theory to analyse problems in new ways because it enables

> a sense of contingent openness and multiple futures, of the unpredictability of outcomes in time–space, of a charity towards objects and nature, of

diverse and non-linear changes in relationships, households and persons across huge distances in time and space, of the systemic nature of processes, and of the growing hypercomplexity of organizations, products, technologies and socialities.

However, given the rapid uptake of complexity theory in some domains outside education, it is prudent to remain wary of expansive claims and problematic attributions. As Paley (2007) notes about complexity theory in the nursing field, assertions can easily circulate that are just plain wrong: such as that self-organization is inherently a democratic process, that complexity theory distinguishes between competency and capability, or that complexity is a vision for an organization. Like Paley and others who have uttered this critique, we remain cautious about either over-hasty adoption or 'a tendency to get hold of the wrong end of the stick' (Paley 2007: 233) in the wide-ranging experiments with complexity theory in educational processes.

This chapter begins with uptakes of complexity in studies and implementations of curriculum and pedagogy. The second section examines complexity theory in cases of educational change, and the third section turns to professional learning and education, particularly interprofessional education, where complexity theory is increasingly put to use. The final section opens larger questions of power, responsibility and ethics that educators have raised about complexity. The examples and topics selected for discussion here are intended to be indicative, rather than comprehensive or representative, highlighting useful ways in which educational research is employing complexity theory both as analytical strategy and as practice.

Complexity in curriculum and pedagogy

Discussions of complexity in educational research seem to be particularly prevalent in the domains of curriculum and pedagogy. In particular, complexity principles of disequilibrium and amplified perturbation, uncertainty, recursion, and change through unpredictable leaps seem to have resonated with those studying learning activity in children's classrooms as well as university lecture halls. Curriculum writers in the past two decades have suggested language and constructs for studying curriculum and pedagogies that are infused with complexity. Some focus on complexity within the dynamics of the classroom, such as Karpiak (2000), who writes about how teachers can help learners become 'attuned' to the emergent dynamics of the class interactions and knowledge, and their implication in these. Some focus more on large-system reform, such as Morrison (2008), who studies a curriculum renovation across Hong Kong using complexity concepts. While these different uptakes are equally enthusiastic about the value of complexity thinking for practice and research in curriculum and pedagogy, it must be noted that few attend explicitly to materiality and the materializing processes of curriculum. Several work more

with complexity as metaphor rather than as a dynamic that radically reconfigures both education and educational research. Nonetheless, the growing
influence of complexity theories on curriculum reform is undeniable, and
worth examining here.

Among those introducing complexity theory to the study and practice of
curriculum in education, William Doll (1989, 1993) was one of the earliest and
more influential. He called his explorations 'postmodern curriculum', although
his conceptions for curriculum reform were centrally informed by his readings of Prigogine and Stengers (1984). In contrast to the increasing shift to
outcomes-based, scope-and-sequenced prescription and measurement of curriculum, Doll urged an altogether different understanding of curriculum as an
open system with constant flux and complex interactions. In such a system, the
focus is upon students as knowledge-producers, organizing and constructing
knowledge as they interact. Rather than requiring increased control, curriculum
as complexity appreciates errors and uncertainty in learners' actions/inter-
actions. The ensuing patterns of learning emerge in transformative changes that
are neither incremental nor predictable: in individual learners and groups, in the
classroom and in the school.

These understandings emerged at the same time as other curriculum
reformists were advocating greater openness and allowance for uncertainty, a
focus on students' biography and imagination, freedom from linear deterministic
objectives, and curriculum as 'running the course' (Pinar and Grumet 1976;
Slattery 1995). However, complexity theory in curriculum was unique in
offering educators specific tools to understand emergence in learning: the
recursive patterns, weird changes and interconnectivities that constitute their
everyday curriculum work with students. In later writing about curriculum,
Doll (2005) comments that complexity opens ways for educators to explore and
celebrate the interplay among matter and imagination, and to appreciate how
entities emerge along with capacities. For Doll, complexity above all urges
recursivity in curriculum, whereby learners and teachers retrace where they
have been and look at old things with new eyes, always circling while allowing
new patterns to emerge. He wrote of a 'dancing curriculum' of emergent
interactions among teachers–texts, teachers–students, and students–texts (Doll
1993: 103).

A particularly influential move in linking complexity with curriculum and
pedagogy arose in the notion of inducing emergence among a group of learners.
This thinking was inspired by Davis et al. (2000), who have described emergence as fundamentally a learning dynamic, and complex adaptive systems as
learning systems. If emergence is therefore desirable in classrooms, and if we can
identify certain characteristics of emergence in complex systems, then we could
think about ways to promote these characteristics in classrooms. Working from
elements, suggested by Johnson (2001) and others, that create the necessary
conditions for emergence in complex systems, Davis (2004) suggested that
teachers and curriculum designers try to induce certain dynamics of these

conditions. These dynamics include internal diversity, redundancy among agents (sufficient commonality to ensure communication), interaction, decentralized control, and feedback to multiple parts of the system. He added the notion of system constraints, calling them 'enabling constraints', which maintain some kind of system boundaries and facilitate internal interactions, preventing a system's elements from becoming disconnected. He could also have added, from Prigogine's contributions, the notion of external energy applied to a system in ways that create some excitation or perturbation among its elements. Later, Davis and Sumara (2006) suggested that educators consider these conditions for emergence in terms of three complementary pairs: internal diversity and internal redundancy; randomness and coherence; and neighbouring interactions and distributed control.

This research, which focuses on the implications of complexity theory for pedagogical practices more than empirically studying curriculum, has catalysed a range of educational applications to induce curriculum as emergence, as well as studies where researchers have worked with educators to promote emergent conditions in classrooms and trace what happens. Specifically, the educator can focus on initiating what Davis and Sumara (2006) call 'occasions' – events where things fall together – that encourage interaction and have liberating constraints, or some focus and simple governing rules that do not strangle emergent possibilities. Not all events naturally offer occasions for co-emergence. Diversity may be a given but may not be recognized, and diverse individuals may have too little in common to interact. Educators can help amplify diversity, develop sufficient redundancy for diverse individuals to understand one another, and introduce guidelines and limitations for activity that promote organization while encouraging diverse expression and improvisation. Educators also typically promote feedback within a system, which amplifies activities that expand a group's possibilities in healthy directions, and challenges negative loops that threaten to kill a system. Davis et al.'s (2000) conditions for inducing emergence in education could easily become formulaic, centralizing and entrenching a curricular approach that could contradict its own ideals of unpredictability and openness. However, this outline has been used productively by others such as McMurtry (2007, 2010) to reconfigure curriculum, as we shall see in a later section.

One important strand of curriculum and pedagogy research examines the professional development of school teachers. This interest crosses fields of both pedagogy and professional learning research, but we discuss it here because there are so many resonances in approach with the complexity-informed research being conducted in classrooms. One example is a study by Fazio and Gallagher (2009) of two 'teacher development' collectives in Ontario, Canada, one for secondary science teachers and one for elementary learning resource teachers, both of which the authors describe as highly functional. In fact, Fazio and Gallagher had turned to complexity theory *post hoc* to find language and explanatory frames that could help them understand how and why significant

professional learning outcomes had emerged from these collectives. In particular, they were trying to understand how insights emerged within the group
that moved well beyond the individual expertise and experiences of the
contributing members – the phenomenon of 'the sum exceeding its parts' that
is commonly attributed to complex adaptive systems. They found particular
salience in three of Davis and Sumara's (2006) dimensions of complex systems
as learning systems: 'self-organization' (a collective of diverse elements emerging
and arranging itself in unpredictable formations around a clear purpose),
'bottom-up emergent' (no controlling agent or pattern, so that activities are
genuinely emergent), and 'ambiguously bounded' (the bounding of clear purpose unfolds within unpredictable, non-linear and often recursive developments). One especially interesting aspect of this study is the authors' focus on
the tension between the individual teachers and the collective. Teachers each
practised in diverse settings, and were conducting their own classroom inquiries
through action research, integrating new curriculum materials and practices, or
aligning their practices with key elements of scientific literacy. These independent inquiries involved experimenting with all sorts of complex materials
and human intensities, interpreting, self-assessing and so forth. The collective
engaged in a different sort of enquiry of sharing, critiquing and affirming, in
arrangements that progressed in unanticipated ways as splinter groups formed
and as topics emerged and circled back. But overall, what emerged was something different again, something new in the collective as a system and the
knowledge it was producing. This knowledge, of course, looped back into the
individual inquiries, and *vice versa*:

> [T]he independent inquiry feeds back into collective interaction cycles,
> which can continue for several rounds. With each successive round, the inter-
> actions within the teacher development collective become more involved
> and the identities of the individual teachers become further defined.
>
> (Fazio and Gallagher 2009: 17)

What the authors stress, finally, is that these sorts of dynamics do not simply
occur spontaneously. First, the teachers needed to contribute, and to recognize
in themselves and others the distinct specialist identities and expertise that each
brought. This is the diversity required for emergence in complex systems. Fazio
and Gallagher propose that this tension between the independent inquiries of
individual teachers and the dialogue of the collective enquiry in fact helped to
trigger emergence. Second, the qualities of complexity that seemed to produce
the overall group effectiveness and powerful teacher learning needed to be
promoted explicitly. In this case, a facilitator assumed this task, and Fazio and
Gallagher suggest that this role is key in enabling a complex system. The point
is that human beings too often seek order, control, clear direction, strict boundaries and measurable outcomes, and may need external interruption and affirmation of alternative, more emergent and perhaps less comfortable approaches.

Complexity and educational change

In considering the implications of complexity for education and educational philosophy, Mason (2009) concludes that the approaches of complexity are most helpful for analysing educational change. While change is at the heart of learning generally, the focus here is on the broader systems of education – policies, governance, conventions, formal curriculum, collective practices, and education as organizations – to understand how they change and what interventions promote productive change. This literature tends to blur analysis and prescription. This may relate to the rapid proliferation of educational reform implementations, the difficulty of facilitating reform, and the general preoccupation with strategies and leadership for organizational change. In this section, we overview some organizational change research and organizational development literature that has adopted complexity theory, because this has strongly influenced scholarship and practice in educational change. We also describe some technologies for organizational/educational change and development that have been introduced through such literature to illustrate the sorts of change strategies being produced in the name of complexity theory.

In studies of organizational change and learning more broadly, researchers have been drawing upon the analytical resources of complexity theory since the mid-1990s. One summary of this research (Tsoukas 2004) suggests that complexity has helped to transform the orientation of researchers as well as managers to notice small fluctuations or disturbances, and to appreciate how important dynamics of instability and disorder can open into changes that are generative and sustainable. Stacey's books have inspired many studies of organizational learning and knowledge that examine what he claims to be the three key dynamics of complexity in organizations. These are the extent of information flow through the system, connectivity among agents in the system, and diversity between agents' schemas (Stacey 1995). In the field of education, change expert Fullan (2003, 2007) has become an influential promoter of these complexity principles of connectivity and diversity. For leaders facilitating educational change, Fullan offers various 'lessons' premised on embracing uncertainty, nonlinearity and operating at the edge of chaos, but balancing these dynamics with some order, some centralized direction and some clear purposes.

In considering implications for schools of the dynamics of diversity and connectivity in complexity, Stanley (2006) examines health and stress in schools. To remain healthy – capable of sustaining themselves through growth and resilient adaptation to stresses – living systems depend upon the connections that they maintain internally and externally. Connectivity is created through interactions iterated spatially and temporally. Overly tight connectivity produces excessive order that represses adaptability, while overly loose connectivity fails to draw together elements for sufficient interaction, and they drift apart. In schools, as Stanley shows, negative stress and ill health can be created both through insufficient connectivity (e.g. among multiple stakeholders of parents, funding bodies, policy-making bodies, teachers, police services, testing bodies, psychological services, etc.) or overly tight connectivity (e.g. excessive regulation). An optimal level of connectivity in a school is neither too tight nor too loose, where the location and control of knowledge is distributed throughout the school organization, feedback loops maintain knowledge circulation, and elements maintain some autonomy while interacting in relations that are loose and resilient.

As in Stanley's study, complexity has focused researchers' attention on tracking various everyday organizational phenomena that contribute to emerging knowledge and activities. Besides connectivity and feedback, these include such dynamics as:

- time and interactions across timescales;
- information flows and feedback points throughout an organization;
- emergent patterns as well as certain circularities that can be traced in socio-material practices; and
- the question of freedom.

In relation to freedom, the focus is on where it exists in terms of choices available for different agents in the system, where constraints occur, and what mix of choice possibilities and constraints enable optimal emergence and resilience in the organization (Tsoukas 2004; Lemke and Sabelli 2008).

Practitioners in organizational development and community-building, prompted by popular complexity writers such as Margaret Wheatley, Glenda Eoyang and Peter Senge, have created a wide range of educative technologies to help groups and leaders to understand these dynamics. As with some of the work on curriculum, these technologies arise from exploring the implications of complexity for organizational change more than researching change through the framing of complexity. For instance, 'Open Space' was originally developed by Harrison Owen (1997/2008) as an approach to assist a particular community to surface and pursue its own issues requiring dialogue. The guiding principles are:

- whoever comes are the right people;
- whatever happens is the only thing that could have;
- whenever it starts is the right time;
- when it's over it's over (duration is determined by the dialogue, not by predetermined time allotments); and
- the law of two feet (people can leave to join a different dialogue according to their interest).

Participants are asked to think of an issue related to the focus of the meeting for which they feel some energy and are willing to take some responsibility as group leader. Each person who has an issue to bring forward briefly explains this issue to the others in the circle. The issues are given titles and posted on pieces of paper on the walls. Participants are given time to 'sign up' for issues attracting their interest. Group leaders then find a room for discussion from those listed. People go to these rooms and share observations. Group leaders take notes and ensure that participants head back to the plenary room at the completion of the discussion. Results are shared, and the group decides the next steps.

Similarly, 'Future Search' (Weisbord and Janoff 2000) is a complexity-informed pedagogical technology to enable a community to move collaboratively towards helpful dialogue. The difference is in purpose. While Open Space is used to help issues emerge, Future Search is intended to help create a common vision, identify desirable/undesirable practices as defined by the community, and define values for a desired future. Future Search also has become very popular around the world, and has stimulated not only studies of its effects in international communities, but also adoption of the method as a research approach in itself. In a Future Search exercise, the community's focus is not problem-solving, but developing insights across diversity, raising commitment, uncovering new possibilities, and reducing misunderstanding. As many constituents as possible in the community, including various internal and external stakeholders, are invited. The process varies, but often includes the following three movements conducted by an entire community, assisted by a facilitator:

- examining the community's history (identifying different views and meanings defining both successful and unsuccessful events, good and bad trends, weaknesses and strengths of guiding principles, values and actions shaping the community's direction);
- identifying external events and trends affecting the future; and
- generating concrete images for a future, collectively considered the most desirable and attainable actions for self, unit and organization.

Educators assisting a Future Search offer no diagnosis or prescriptions. Facilitators simply set a workable process in motion and allow the system to develop its own directions. Like Open Space, this technology borrows metaphors of complexity but can hardly be described as 'sociomaterial' or even 'emergentist', given its normative assumptions and pedagogical controls.

It is extraordinarily difficult to track socio-political dynamics, let alone their sociomaterial constituencies, through research approaches that are truly 'complexivist' (Davis and Sumara 2006) in orientation. Byrne (2005) suggests working through comparative cases, where each case is understood to be a complex system nested within other complex systems. He recommends that, in each case, researchers attend to the trajectory of the system or the history of the case, the changes in form that it enacts at various times, and the emergent consequences of these changes for other systems, including the global system as a whole, examining multiple and combinatorial causes. Byrne also suggests that, in examining these trajectories, we might look for the qualitative break points that seem to occur as a system shifts into a new phase. These break points can be understood as 'threshold values', at the point or phase reached by a system just before its tipping point (Gladwell 2002), where it transforms into something quite different. These threshold values are not causes, but perhaps can be taken to be indicators of change.

Another educationist who has written much about complexity in educational change is Mason (2008a, 2009). He focuses on the value of feedback, noting that complexity shows how change is mobilized by intervention through deliberate positive feedback at multiple nodes of the system towards a particular outcome. Thus, for educational reform to successfully sustain itself in a given educational system, whether a school, school district or an entire region of networked schools and state education authorities, Mason (2009: 123) recommends:

> [M]assive and sustained intervention at every possible level (including even those factors that, from a knowledge of initial conditions, appear trivial) until the desired change emerges from this new set of interactions among these new factors and sustains itself autocatalytically.

As Mason notes, such intervention seems to require large-scale resources. Yet forms of action research have long been engaged by educators, often without such resources, as a complexified approach to educational change and educational enquiry. While some forms of action research in education follow a more linear problem-solving logic of launching an intervention, then tracing its effectiveness for school improvement, action research as a 'living practice' (Sumara and Carson 1997) affords many possibilities for more complex engagements. In one example, Radford (2007) writes about teachers-as-researchers becoming attuned to classroom events as emerging through multiple non-linear and dynamic elements. As participants in this complexity, Radford recommends that teachers adopt a more open and flexible engagement. In a complexity approach to action research, teacher-researchers would reduce expectations for, and measurement of, particular planned outcomes. Instead, they would focus on describing the information flows and interactional fluctuations that can be observed in particular occasions, including ways in which they adjust their own responses and intentions, and comparing these flows to clusters of consequences that appear to emerge.

Davis and Sumara (1997) have written about complexity in action research as a question of complicity. The researcher is complicit in conversations that occur, questions that are posed, language that may become introduced, objects that may be introduced, and new comings and goings that occur to accommodate research activities, however mundane. There are multiple other ways in which the researcher's presence and interactions begin to generate consequences that reverberate throughout the systems she or he touches. The critical point Davis and Sumara emphasize is that the research process must, as much as possible, find ways to *trace its own entanglements* in the system that it engages. This is not just a question about hypervigilant attunement to one's footprint in the system(s), nor just about recording transactions as observantly and reflexively as possible. It is also about representing the materials and knowledge produced through the research, as well as the process through which they were produced, in ways that clearly delineate the researcher's presence, voice and framing. A narrative is always somebody's narrative.

Complexity theory is also opening ways simultaneously to layer and connect the multiple narratives emerging in any systemic change initiative, such as educational reform initiatives or transnational training. For example, new complexity-based digital tools are now available for scanning and representing small occurrences and fluctuations in large systems, which could prove very useful for studies of educational change. These mappings can occur in real-time, such as data visualizations emerging from 'diggs' or hits on the world wide web that show clusters of topic intensity and frequency as they emerge around the globe. Many of these tools apply aesthetics as well as continuous feed of large amounts of data to illuminate complex relationships with elegant simplicity. As Hall (2008: 134) wrote for an exhibit of technological data design at New York's Museum of Modern Art, 'understanding connections in the vast landscape of information often requires a new way of looking'. One tool Hall describes is 'Rewiring the spy', designed by Lisa Strausfeld and James Nick. Keywords – names of terrorists or terrorist events, in this case – were connected by spring-like links that intensified with their frequency of interconnection in a database, producing visualizations that could be rotated in three dimensions to reveal new viewpoints. Another is the website 'We feel fine' (www.wefeelfine.org), designed by Jonathan Harris and Sep Kamvar. This site searches all global blogs every few minutes for the words *I feel* or *I am feeling* (finding about 15–20,000 per day), tags these along with the blogger's characteristics and geographic location, then can map them along with local weather conditions and news events.

Studies of digital media and learning technologies, and their implications for educational change, are proliferating. While many of these studies draw more explicitly upon theories of virtuality and communication than complexity, they clearly embed complexivist concepts. As new weavings of digital and material life emerge, new possibilities beckon for ways of thinking about knowledge as well as pedagogy. For example, Sterling (2005), a futurist, has coined the neologism 'spime' to refer to things that will increasingly mediate our environments and engagements, but remain speculative. He defines spimes as new forms of intelligent objects that are material instantiations of immaterial systems, such as the iPhones and iPads that have quickly become ubiquitous in some parts of the globe. Spimes require extensive information support, they are identifiable, enhanceable, user-alterable and sustainable, and they contain materials that can fold into production of future spimes. Greenhill and Fletcher (2009) work with this concept of spimes to examine 'blogshops', new forms of interaction appearing particularly among youth that bear some resemblance to a web storefront. However, in a blogshop, materials for sale are embedded amongst personal stories and emotional reflections. While the community engaged with a particular blogshop is continually changing in size and membership, and is widely distributed geographically, periodically it will materialize in a specific time and place to actually complete transactions: things will be bought and sold among those who turn up socially. Blogshops and their participants/authors are often networked so that the sellers and buyers, as well as the locations of transaction, are fluid and unpredictable, giving rise to new material forms of blended social and economic practices. Greenhill and Fletcher speculate about the affordances of such forms of ambiguous computing, suggesting that spimes could be politicized as new democratic possibilities. We might also consider spimes' possibilities for pedagogy, if we return to Sterling's definitions of them.

These new tools are enabling multiple indicators to be employed to examine different emerging patterns in a system, and are positing different ways of understanding relationships among data – seeking beyond more conventional modes of representing tables to show correlation, variance, linked causes, etc. 'Gapminder' (www.gapminder.org) is an example of an educational project promoting sustained global development by using such tools to help online users to see new relations among social, environmental and economic data. The intention is to enable understandings of how patterns of inequity emerge, as well as to promote awareness of intervention strategies and points that can maximize positive change. These complexity-affiliated digital tools for inducing and representing emergence can suggest new approaches and new ways of reasoning in educational research, and possibly even new configurations for understanding educational change. Such change, particularly externally induced change including new technologies, entails what can be massive unanticipated consequences and sometimes frightening personal transitions for both educators and researchers.

Complexity in professional and interdisciplinary education

Education across various professions such as healthcare and social work, as well as teaching, have grappled with the continuous change and growing complexity of practice conditions. Stakeholders have multiple and often contradictory influences on professionals' everyday practice: from parents and patients to policy-makers, funding agencies, scientific authorities producing evidence upon which to base practice, advocacy groups, professional associations and news media. Alongside this complexity is the shift towards multi-professional service, which is by now an established tradition across health and social care, although its influence on school education is relatively recent.

To address these complex patterns of changing professional practice, the concepts of emergence and non-linear dynamics have been employed to understand the patterns better, as well as to suggest actions, including educative action. One example is ISIS, a project of the Tobacco Control Research Branch in the USA (Trochim *et al.* 2006), which uses complexity approaches to develop more effective public health education efforts in smoking reduction. ISIS is a trans-disciplinary group of professionals (systems dynamics, knowledge management, tobacco control, management sciences, health policy) charged with developing a framework for public education aimed at tobacco reduction. They consider questions such as:

> How can the flow in *both* directions between research and practice be optimized?
> How can systems structure and function be best characterized to be useful to the public health community? Which approaches can be used for better understanding and optimization of networks? Through which strategies do information and knowledge become the currency for change?
>
> (Trochim *et al.* 2006: 3)

The group found that tools of complexity enabled flexible mapping of the complex non-linear variables affecting tobacco use, the unpredictable system-wide emergences, and the complicity of planning and action efforts with these emergences. The group also used complexity to explain the intersecting patterns of order and disorder, and to reconcile more reductionist and more expansive patterns and thinking within the system. The project not only applied these concepts to analyse the phenomena of tobacco use, but also used complexity approaches to guide their collective learning and enquiry. Groups were gathered into concept-mapping exercises. These maps were placed in interaction with one another to create systems models, which the group could adapt continually as new information emerged, and as new possibilities became apparent. Four mapping projects were undertaken: mapping the various forms, frequencies, users and geographies of tobacco use; mapping the network of tobacco control organizations; a self-reflexive concept-mapping project to track emerging understandings and to promote better understanding of how to integrate research and practice in tobacco control; and a knowledge map to guide the learning about tobacco control.

In summarizing the utility of complexity theory for examining inter-professional practice and education, Thompson Klein (2004) argues that it affords a new dialogue of science and humanities, new forms of knowledge and problem solving. She analyses a series of interprofessional projects in fields such as medical anthropology, the aerospace industry and environmental research, and suggests the following lessons:

> First in a complex problem domain, the research field is open and ill-defined, and the reality being investigated consists of a nexus of phenomena that are not reducible to a single dimension. Their meaning is context dependent, and the relationship between elements under study constitutes a core concept for complexity. Second, common ground and a more com-prehensive, holistic understanding do not derive from an idealized model

of how the behavioral pattern of the system comes about from its constituent parts. They emerge in the cross-fertilization of multiple methods and perspectives that are adapted to the task at hand. Third, research is multilevel. On the micro-level, research teams must learn to work in inter- and transdisciplinary settings that are inclusive of multiple stakeholders. On a meso-level, the science system is beginning to transform and to create appropriate curricula and institutional surroundings. On the macro-level, political transformations have effects on the science system.

(Thompson Klein 2004: 6)

A key contribution to interprofessional practice and learning offered by complexity, she argues, is its capacity to offer an interlanguage among the disciplines. Emergence is this interlanguage, where the focus is on not analysing independent things, but on tracking interrelationships among biophysical and human dimensions, policy and technology, integrated spatially and temporally 'at the levels of plot, household, and watershed or community' (Thompson Klein 2004: 6).

In both the pedagogical design and the content of interprofessional education, complexity has attracted particular interest, with its focus on diversity and connectivity. A number of educational studies have begun documenting what happens when complexity theory is taught to pre-service student professionals, or used in learning activities. One example at the University of Liverpool, UK, reported by Cooper and Spencer-Dawe (2006), involved 500 students in fields of physiotherapy, medicine, occupational therapy, nursing and social work. Multidisciplinary plenary sessions were held for students, teaching them complexity concepts supplemented with self-directed e-learning. Mixed groups of students also participated in interdisciplinary workshops in issues of clinical practice, facilitated by trained practitioners across the different fields, as well as by service users. Feedback on these various activities was requested at various points and integrated into the unfolding emergent system activities, through students' reflective narratives, practitioners' focus groups, and interviews with service users. Overall, the programme linked explicit teaching of complexity principles to students with an effort to integrate into the overall programme design and pedagogy certain complexity principles of emergence, decentred organization, diversity and multiple feedback loops.

In another, more extended study of interprofessional health education incorporating complexity principles, at the University of Alberta, Canada, McMurtry (2007) tries to analyse how and why elements of diversity and nested systems are so useful in both pedagogy and content. Educator McMurtry worked in a consultative role with healthcare colleagues who were facilitating a mandatory course in interdisciplinary practice for undergraduate students in a range of health disciplines (nursing, occupational therapy, medicine, etc.). His study offers a fascinating close tracing of the process by which these facilitators grappled with the implications of complexity concepts for interdisciplinary health practice as well as for pedagogy in professional education. Important outcomes for interprofessional education of the complexity-infused curriculum included the facilitators' problematization of the notion of consensus, which is often held to be an ideal for interdisciplinary teams. Another was participants and facilitators learning the need not to seek harmony and consensus, but to amplify the diversity of individual elements. Diversity that exists in a system is not always recognized by participants, and complexity emphasizes the importance of recognition. For interprofessional practice, this means professionals learning to make explicit the important disciplinary distinctions among their very different epistemologies, material practices and identities. To contribute to emergence in the sense of a self-organizing learning system, however, this explicit diversity requires conditions that complexity principles refer to as sufficient 'redundancy' (some overlap in purpose and knowledge among the system elements); some central purpose orienting these elements; and sufficient openness to allow the necessary trust and interaction to occur.

Another important outcome for McMurtry was the facilitators' adoption of a new pedagogical framework based on complexity's notion of nested systems, understanding students, patients, system policies and politics, university interests and community resources in nested relations to one another. Thus facilitators learned to design learning activities using nested systems concepts, such as having students work through case scenarios that cut across multiple systems, to prompt student questions rather than solutions, and to foster students' (and their own) awareness of their actions' effects on different systems in which they participated, as well as their interconnectedness with these multiple systems. Nested systems also help facilitators understand, and therefore better assess, the learning that emerges differently for individual students, for interdisciplinary student groups, for the entire student class, and for the larger system of class sections and faculty facilitators. Taken together, these dynamics seem key to fostering the trust, or more precisely the trust-within-diversity, that is critical for productive interdisciplinary teams. The most effective collaborations and the greatest emergence are seen not when large overlaps occur in different professionals' knowledge, but rather when 'specialization is allowed and encouraged, and differing professional specializations are brought together into coherent – if not always internally homogenous – collective plants, treatments or "thoughts" through a different kind of commonality: *trust*' (McMurtry 2007: 91, emphasis in original).

In both of these examples, complexity theory is adopted both explicitly and implicitly. Explicitly, complexity concepts are taught to students and instructors (including non-linear dynamics, self-organization and ways of inducing emergence) in order to understand health issues as well as interprofessional team dynamics. Implicitly, the curriculum design is informed by complexity to get rid of linear frameworks, allow experimentation, watch for and amplify emerging patterns, and focus more on knowledge enacted through participatory action than on the knowledge acquired through predetermined models and representations.

Aside from interprofessional education, complexity theory has been adopted in this combined explicit–implicit approach to specific disciplines of professional education. The rationale for teaching students complexity concepts here is more to help them understand the diverse systems and dynamics in which they must work, rather than learning specifically how to engage productively in inter-professional practice. In social work education, for instance, Wolf-Branigin (2009) shows how complexity can help students to develop capacities such as learning how to find and encourage connectivities among the multiple agencies and emerging social movements in particular communities, or focusing on resiliency in themselves and their clients rather than control and solution. Practices in complexity, where students work on unstructured issues of multiple shifting variables and stakeholders (such as human trafficking, in the Wolf-Branigin example), can be developed within the curriculum. In another example, concepts of complexity theory were taught explicitly to social work students and instructors in the UK. The purpose was to help them adjust to a shift in the practice paradigm from individual client counselling to broad-based community building. This shift entailed new academic and professional require-ments, increased interplay of practice-based and university-based learning, and engagement with multiple stakeholders. Complexity theory was judged as useful by these professionals, who reported that *knowing more about* the dynamics of change and emergence within what felt like a chaotic experience was helpful in *coping with* these changes. Further, learning to recognize and work with complexity dynamics such as self-organization, diversity and feedback loops was helpful for professionals developing new practices of community-building in a highly complex context.

Complexity concepts in all of these examples appear to be useful not only for professionals' own education and development, but also for those facilitating professional learning. In a study of professional learning, Zellermayer and Margolin (2005) use complexity theory to analyse the difficult processes of change experienced by supervisors (teacher–educators) of elementary education student teachers. Unlike the previous examples of professional learning, the facilitator–researchers did not explain complexity principles explicitly to the supervisors featured in this study, although it would have been interesting to see the reaction and results if they had. The externally driven educational changes were multiple, and had terrified many of the supervisors:

- declining student numbers, engendering pressure to reorganize the pro-gramme to be more attractive;
- new curriculum, requiring student teachers to conduct action research;
- new requirements for the supervisors themselves to conduct action research; and
- new expectations for supervisors to establish partnerships across schools.

The researchers were also the facilitators, who gathered volunteers from among these supervisors to meet weekly to learn about action research. What happened is perhaps predictable to any professionals who have worked through major changes to their own practice, knowledge and identity. Some supervisors were curious or even excited about possibilities: one invited two student teachers to assess every one of her classes for a year, keeping daily data on her own teaching throughout that period, to the astonishment of the others. Some felt their authority was undermined, their professional knowledge standards questioned, and their confidence shaken. Others became bitter about colleagues resistant to changing their role.

The study is useful first because the facilitator–researchers identify what they believe to be critical events among these supervisors that catalysed dynamics of emergence leading to productive learning. These critical events were moments of conflict and dissonance, featuring 'dramatic tension among the participants which provides the energy for their interaction' (Zellermayer and Margolin 2005: 1300). This reference to energy recalls Prigogine, who showed that energy is critical to shift a system to a condition far from equilibrium, where it is capable of leaping to a new, usually unpredictable configuration. Further, however, the researchers show that in all the critical events leading towards emergence, participants became attuned to 'the periphery and to the possibility of chaos' (Zellermayer and Margolin 2005: 1300): they actually listened to dissonant views. Within the gap between, for instance, positive innovative views and negative peripheral views, a learning space emerged.

The study is useful secondly because, drawing from knowledge of complexity theory, it highlights key learnings of the facilitators, approaches that they believed supported the professional learning in emergence:

- 'agents may change themselves but are usually unable to change others'
- 'not all participants learn from simply being a part of what is going on around them'
- 'encourage differences of opinion, supporting those who take risks'
- 'provide safe environments to contain the anxiety of those threatened by change processes'
- 'provide opportunities for the participants to "zoom in" on their emotions and to "zoom out" on their learning [. . .] to enable them to see it in a wider theoretical context'
- 'space needs the support of a facilitator who knows how to identify sources of resistance as well as areas of collaboration' enabling 'confrontation between the two that sparks the dissonance for learning and the catalyst for group development'.

(Zellermayer and Margolin 2005: 1304)

Overall, this study focused on ways to hold open the tensions in a system, in order to enable the perturbations and interactions that encourage new relationships and knowledge to emerge. However, the study also begs larger questions of power and politics. Changing regimes for professionals in organizations such as these teacher–educators, alongside corollary technologies of audit and accountability in professional practices, are part of powerful political systems overlapping and nesting the educators' systems of dialogue and learning. In chapter two, we saw that complexity traces the ongoing matter-ing dynamics of the world and its nested systems, dynamics that both reveal and create 'what matters'. But 'what matters' is invariably linked with critical dynamics of power relations, and what matters in education invokes questions of responsibility and ethics.

Power, ethics and responsibility

What does complexity theory say to responsibility and ethics in education? How does complexity address social power relations? Can complexity contribute to analysing how systems perpetuate inequities, exclude participants, consolidate privilege and proliferate misery? Such questions are commonly raised by critical educators drawing from traditions such as emancipatory pedagogies or post-structural and post-colonial theories. Complexity educators offer diverse responses. Here is one:

> Critical theory seems to be structured around desires to extricate and explicate certain categories of intention and the injustices sponsored by those intentions. But complexity theory, while acknowledging that selfish intention can give rise to horrible wrongs, is more prone to regard the injustices of the world as inevitable consequences of complex dynamics. Unequal distributions of wealth and power, argue complexivists, are not only inevitabilities; these are phenomena that are given to self-amplification. Consider, for example the way people aggregate into cities. As insulting as it might sound, the emergent patterns of organization do not depend at all on the fact that humans are doing the clustering. The same patterns show up in colonies of bacteria. In fact, they arise when smoke particles deposit on a ceiling. The rich *will* get richer, the advantaged *will* gain more advantage – not because of intention, but because of the laws of nonlinear dynamics. Such statements are met with knowing nods by complexivists and with indignation by critical theorists.
>
> (Davis and Sumara 2008: 169–70)

A rather different position is presented by Alhadeff-Jones (2010: 487), who works from Morin's (1990/2008) concept of a 'complex way of thinking' to suggest a continuum in critical thinking, education and research. At one end are contributions that are based on 'simplifying' modes of organization, which tend to reduce and fragment a critical system's complex relations (at once both contradictory and complementary, representational and physical/social/material). At the other end are contributions based on 'complexifying' modes of organization. These forms of critique recognize a system's contradictory relations in order to 'rigorously reconceive' their organization; they also respect the uncertainty and openness of such reconception.

However, the question remains of how power flows within a system to enact particular entities, positions and rewards. Power may appear to flow through the system according to how, in everyday interactions, people take up positions and understand others' positions in relation to themselves. The positions are in constant flux, for they change each time someone turns to a new activity or subject. The consequent directions of power and changing locations influence different individuals' ability to participate meaningfully in the systems. Individuals potentially become vulnerable to a few who manipulate the system's activities to sustain their own power, ensuring that their experiences become the most valued knowledge in the collective. We might well ask: What knowledge and activities, among the various relations and processes occurring within a complex system, are afforded the greatest visibility and influence over the movements and directions of the system? Whose interests are most advantaged or disadvantaged by the patterns that emerge? What subjectivities and what possibilities for alternative subjectivities are made available? And for those influenced by more activist concerns, how can better conditions – more generative, open, fair and life-sustaining – be induced in a complex system, or at least be available as possibilities?

Osberg (2008) argues that complexity theory can contribute to understandings of criticality in education by showing how the possibilities for freedom are embedded within the very workings of complex processes. She begins with an exploration of various ideas of what it means to be critical, orienting her discussion in the meaning of freedom, and drawing on writings of Kant, Marx, Gramsci, Habermas, Foucault and Mouffe. As she traces Foucault's conception of freedom as 'a movement which inhabits the interstices of power relations' (Osberg 2008: 140) and Mouffe's portrayal of the political as ineradicable conflict, Osberg sees connections with the emergentist logic of complexity theory.

> The political question is not *how to achieve* or *reach* a pre-defined state of political freedom (in Habermasian style) but *how to guard against the closure of freedom* (including the closure of the notion of freedom itself). In other words we have to guard against the closure of political freedom *without imposing norms*. I believe this is the task of criticism at the *political level*.
>
> (Osberg 2008: 142, emphasis in original)

For Osberg, it is the continual presentation of choices in complex processes, and the continual emergence of different alternatives to choose from in the act of critical choice-making, that can transform the system and its range of multiple new possibilities. This offers a generative way to think about freedom, especially as those choices are not simply human.

Davis and Sumara (2008) also argue that there are certain shared concerns, and even similarities, in the analyses produced through the traditions of critical theory and complexity theory. In particular, Davis and Sumara point to complicity as a notion that they claim is foregrounded in both critical and complexity theories: the understanding that the observer is always implicated in the phenomena being observed, excluding and exploiting in the very act of identifying and focusing. Both critical and complexity theories might enjoin researchers to a mindfulness of this complicity, and both theories might even be characterized as seeking not final truth, but improved conditions for living beings. However in the final analysis, Davis and Sumara conclude that critical theory and complexity theory are best left as autonomous worlds. Each has unfolded as a different world of thought, with different projects producing diverse insights and approaches to understanding the world and generating alternative possibilities. Conversation among their differences can be fruitful, but comparative assessment of their constructs or integration of their views is rather futile.

Fenwick (2009a) has argued that a central problem in applying complexity theory to educational issues remains the question of responsibility. Education is fundamentally about responsibility and purpose, which are both pedagogical and political issues. While complexity may offer important insights for education, it appears to lack analytical capacity to address questions of responsibility or the political. Derived as it was from biological and mathematical sciences, complexity theory as a framework does not inherently offer constructs that speak to questions of educational responsibility. One may manipulate certain precepts of complexity theory to adduce generalizations about responsibility. However, such analyses cannot legitimately answer important educational questions of how one should act, or who is responsible to whom.

The radical ontology of complexity theory can be useful in troubling certain core assumptions of responsibility. Educational responsibility is often driven by moral imperatives and purposes of enculturating human beings or creating social change. But when concepts central to responsibility, such as agency, morality and intentionality, are challenged by complexity concepts of flows, co-specification, self-organization and emergence, the notion of responsibility itself becomes reconfigured. More generative alternatives to moralistic discourses and fantasies of social rescue may be posed by complexity's emphasis on participatory epistemology, mindful engagement, and disruption of certainty (Fenwick 2009a). While the ought of education cannot be spoken through complexity theory, the latter's framework can help to articulate questions and dilemmas of educational responsibility. Bai (2003) asks, what does it mean to be a human being, a person, in a relational universe? How does one being relate to another, and what is it for relational beings to have responsibility towards each other? Bai is one of the few who have undertaken close examination of ethics in complexity theory. She argues that when we view the other as an 'inter-penetrating matrix of relationships . . . an *inter-being* with the self' (Bai 2003: 9, emphasis in original), we think not in terms of controlling the other, but as establishing a union from which a desired pattern of relation for both parties can emerge. These relations are dynamic, non-linear, and hence non-deterministic. In a conception very similar to Varela's, Bai describes being as an 'inter-penetration' of elements and forces that cannot be considered as separate or separable. This conception implies that there is no distinct other to which a subject responds, and therefore no singular subject that discerns distinction and need, and formulates a response.

Some have pointed to the alignment of complexity with writings of, for example, Paulo Freire (Davis and Sumara 2008; Gilstrap 2008). Freire was a passionate advocate for educators' responsibility in transforming patterns of inequity and oppression in the world. He adjured educators to eschew 'banking' education, which simply presents preconceived ideas of what the world is and how it works, and instead to participate with learners in educative processes that interrupt existing relations. His suggested methods of problem-posing, where groups of learners connect their own particular experiences to wider systemic patterns through dialogue, and together experiment through active participation to invoke and amplify changes, appear to reflect a complexified understanding of how systems become transformed.

The notion of emergence also invites considerations about what sorts of responsibility might arise out of entanglement in volatile processes, and what forms of novelty and surprise might arise out of response and responsibility in emergent processes. We may need an ethics to negotiate and regulate conditions of uncertainty. This may be particularly pressing when we believe all of our actions are so interconnected as to pose profound implications for the system's emergence. If actors simply respond spontaneously, care for the vulnerable may or may not emerge: indeed, social history has proven quite the opposite. And accountability, which rests on notions of personal and collective responsibility, remains an important, if currently over-rationalized, dynamic in educational purpose and delivery. What are the implications of responsibility when causes cannot be disentangled from effects?

Conclusion

Both educational researchers and practising educators have adopted complexity in eclectic ways to understand and reconfigure various educational processes. As we have seen in this chapter, these tend to have focused on activities associated with curriculum and pedagogy in different contexts: schooling, higher education and interprofessional education. A growing body of literature has also applied complexity concepts to the study of educational change. Some have worked with complexity to transform fundamental educational assumptions, such as representational views of knowledge (Osberg and Biesta 2007, 2008) or the role of a classroom teacher (Davis and Sumara 2006). Others have adopted certain principles of complexity to formulate models for pedagogical action, some more helpful than others. There is no shortage of prescriptions, ironically, attempting to turn complexity theory into formulaic models of practices for classroom, leadership and change implementation. There is also no shortage of educational writings in the name of complexity that remain at the metaphorical level; or worse, that simply borrow and romanticize a few appealing concepts such as flow, emergence and co-participation. While the complexity approaches most influential in educational research are fundamentally material in their disciplinary origins, ranging from Prigogine's thermal dynamics to Varela's evolutionary biology, the material dimensions seem to shrink or even disappear in many educational studies employing complexity analyses. For some reason, these studies tend to take more inspiration from how complexity speaks to phenomena of group dialogue, consciousness and human organizational behaviour than for its invitation to analyse, for example, a classroom pedagogical event as a co-mingling of ideas and frustrations and desires and curiosities with electric grids, databases and buzzers, bubblegum and broken pencils, health-and-safety policies and so on. The sociomateriality of pedagogy and learning, through such complexity concepts as nested systems, bottom-up emergence and feedback loops, could reveal a far greater range of triggers and amplifiers of emergence than are currently appreciated when the focus remains on human and social elements of education.

In these ways, complexity theory arguably offers much greater analytical power, and more challenging strategies and languages for analysis, than educational research is currently accessing. However, as argued in this chapter, education raises serious questions about power, purpose and responsibility to which the framework of complexity may not offer completely satisfactory responses. This is not to deny the importance of complexity's possibilities for educational research. Perhaps we might, as Byrne (2005) suggests, consider the task not as importing complexity models and analytical approaches from without (e.g. the 'hard' sciences), but as reconstructing social science from within, with the sensibilities of complexity. This involves:

> [T]hinking about the social world and its intersections with the natural world as involving dynamic open systems with emergent properties that have the potential for qualitative transformation, and examining our traditional tools of social research with this perspective informing that examination.
>
> (Byrne 2005: 98)

Chapter 4

Contradiction and expansion

Understanding cultural historical activity theory

> Activity theory seeks to analyse development within practical social activities. Activities organize our lives. In activities, humans develop their skills, personalities and consciousness. Through activities, we also transform our social conditions, resolve contradictions, generate new cultural artefacts, and create new forms of life and the self.
>
> (Sannino *et al.* 2009: 1)

Cultural historical activity theory (CHAT) includes a host of principles that have been painstakingly established over the better portion of a century. Both theoretically and empirically, many of these principles continue to be debated and modified. What is clear, however, is that these principles bloomed from a dialogue. On the one hand, this dialogue involved a variety of European intellectual traditions, notably dialectical philosophy and Marxism. On the other hand, the dialogue included an emergent version of psychology that challenged the very meaning of the discipline, then as now. It is partly for this reason, inter-disciplinary dialogue, that aspects of CHAT have been so readily recognizable to so many other disciplinary traditions.

However, at the centre of it all is CHAT's core concept of *activity* itself. This is a technically precise term. As we will see, it involves a series of more elementary concepts such as object-relatedness, contradiction and, perhaps above all, artefact mediation. The concept of activity is premised on an understanding of learning, human development and education, as a matter of what, why and how people do things together, either cooperatively or conflictually, over time; mind as a thoroughly *social* and *material* as well as historical phenomenon. Simply put, CHAT persistently and forcefully directs attention to the importance of the form through which people's social creation and use of tools/artefacts (culturally) successively over time (historically) explains learning and development.

In this chapter, we will encounter concepts that speak to virtually every aspect of the learning and developmental process. We will see how this approach addresses the roles of materiality, the symbol or sign, consciousness, thought, meaning and communication. We will see how these things relate to context-dependent operations and goal-directed action, and how broader shared purposes, that are called objects and motives, culminate in an activity analysis that inextricability ties individuals–groups–society together as dimensions of learning and change. Likewise, we will see how change is understood within the tradition of dialectical thought and dialectical materialism, highlighting how contradictions within complex sets of relationships both mutually define and undermine these relationships as part of the learning process. Learning, development and change emerges here as a unity of individual and societal, the symbolic and material, the present and the past.[1]

In terms of research, CHAT analyses argue vigorously that education, learning and human development are rooted in active, living, contingent and contradictory, social and material relationships. In education research, CHAT has been enormously important in shaping approaches to constructivist teaching and learning. It has illuminated aspects of school organizational change, professional development, the learning across multi-professional groups and so on. These and other educational applications of CHAT are discussed in chapter five.

Our attempt to provide an overview of CHAT is pre-dated by a variety of important monographs and collections that serve as invaluable, diverse predecessors (Daniels 1996, Chaiklin *et al.* 1999; Engeström *et al.* 1999; Chaiklin 2001; Robbins and Stetsenko 2002; Kaptelinin and Nardi 2006; Sawchuk *et al.* 2006; Van Oers *et al.* 2008; Sannino *et al.* 2009). In these sources, one can find primers and synopses as well as critical observations and advancements. All of these are further supplemented by several notable special journal issue collections in the field of education specifically (Daniels and Edwards 2004; Williams *et al.* 2007; Martin and Peim 2009).

In this chapter, the focus is on understanding the concepts of CHAT, *how* these concepts developed, and *why*. Arguably, CHAT research has the longest continuous intellectual lineage amongst those we consider in this book. For this reason, our approach is to deal with significant CHAT discussions within contemporary research, but also to register its origins and seminal research. This chapter begins with a brief recovery of the basic origins of CHAT that, among other things, will emphasize its inherently interdisciplinary orientation. Next, we address some of the core, ontological elements of education and learning processes, as well as the criticisms of mainstream learning theory, through the lens of CHAT in order to ground the core preoccupations of the tradition that continue to live on today. We then take some time to discuss the original work of the founder of CHAT, Lev Vygotsky, to obtain a glimpse at the transition from elementary dimensions of human thinking, learning and development toward the concept of activity as we would recognize it today. Following this, we outline many of the core theoretical concerns and innovations of contemporary CHAT. By way of conclusion, we summarize fundamental points but also provide a discussion of CHAT's future; a discussion framed first by the contrasting ways in which CHAT researchers have sought to understand its past.

Chat: origins and resemblances

From its inception in the works of Vygotsky (1896–1934), Luria (1902–77) and Leontiev (1903–79), all the way to today's contemporary expressions of the tradition, CHAT has remained highly interdisciplinary. At first generated from readings by the originators in psychology as well as philosophy, linguistics, history, biology and social theory, CHAT has come to attract the attention of anthropologists, sociologists, political scientists, socio-linguists, communications studies scholars, ergonomists, computer design engineers and so on. It is amongst educational scholars, however, that CHAT has found one of its most significant followings. This is understandable. As we will see, Vygotsky and colleagues, as well as many of those they directly trained and influenced, often had educational applications explicitly in mind. However, this orientation to interdisciplinarity shines through strongly in the original work of Vygotsky and others. In contrast, for example, with Piaget's concern to maintain the scope of psychology, we find in the writings of Vygotsky (e.g. 1987) an equally persistent concern to read across a variety of disciplines to think of human life more broadly.

According to some contemporary researchers, the topic of activity demands such interdisciplinarity. Holzman (2006a, 2006b), for example, has argued vigorously that CHAT should encompass a wide range of intellectual inspirations and disciplinary approaches. Others, such as those in Martin and Peim (2009), suggest connections to postmodernist and other European traditions that were unheard of in Vygotsky's day, but that may be as important as they are overlooked. As it did amongst the originators of CHAT, this diversity has challenged people's thinking considerably in an extremely productive way. So much so, in fact, that cautions about 'eclectic combinations of ideas' undercutting CHAT's development as a distinctive approach have occasionally been issued (e.g. see Engeström 1999b: 20). For these CHAT researchers, the concern is rooted in the potential to lose sight of the original 'germ cell' of the tradition – the activity itself. Sannino *et al.* (2009) have likewise defended the primacy of core principles even where other perspectives are engaged.

Questions regarding interdisciplinarity aside, perhaps the best way to begin to understand CHAT is to discuss the reasons why this theory, and related schools of thought, emerged in the first place. What were the critiques of theories of education and learning that gave rise to it, both in the past and today? By way of introduction, we begin with contemporary critiques that may be more familiar to the reader, working our way back toward the work of CHAT's originators in the 1920s and 1930s.

Looking carefully across contemporary educational, learning and developmental theory, researchers have noted a number of limiting tendencies. In Sawchuk (2003), these tendencies are summarized from the perspective of CHAT as a set of four interlocking biases: individuation; universalization; ahistoricism; and pedagogization and acquisition. These form what was said to be a hegemonic block of principles because of their mutually supportive character which, together, produces broad societal effects across many institutions. For example, we see the importance of the credentialization of *individuals* for the functioning of labour markets, career and paid work relations, and we can see that a guiding principle of liberal democracies is the concept of the autonomous *individual*. The legitimacy of state institutions – schools, but also those related to health, social services, criminal justice and so on – depend enormously on an ideological presumption of a type of *universalized* treatment that sometimes denies social differences of background, and the personal as well as collective *histories* of specific social groups. Knowledge production and distribution, the legitimization of authoritative forms of knowledge, revolves disproportionately around the sciences and biases of mainstream *pedagogy*, the notion of individual *acquisition*, and the possibility of decontextualized learning transfer. We also see that at the heart of this block of principles lies what is known as the Cartesian bias. This, CHAT researchers have argued, ratifies a series of separations – between mind and body, between internal and external life, and between the subjective and objective.

Working backwards, we can easily see that this type of critique is not very new. Since the 1980s, a range of critiques of mainstream approaches to educational theory have continuously emerged, many of which depended upon CHAT specifically (Rogoff and Lave 1984; Engeström 1987; Lave and Wenger 1991; Salomon 1993; Cole 1995; Hutchins 1995; Stetsenko 2008, 2009; Niewolny and Wilson 2009). Emerging in the late 1970s and 1980s, these criticisms are easily traceable to earlier ones. In relation to the dominant psychological theories of the early twentieth century, many of the same elements are seen in Vygotsky's original critique of Piaget, Freud, various gestalist theorists and others. Both Luria and Vygotsky critiqued the Cartesian bias of theories of thinking, learning and development (e.g. Luria 1976: 19). But what exactly are the similarities and differences among these earlier anti-reductionist and anti-Cartesian approaches, and specifically, what is it that sets CHAT apart?

Taking the example of three seminal figures in learning theory, Stetsenko (e.g. 2008) summarized the relationship between Piaget, Dewey and Vygotsky, beginning with some strong family resemblances in terms of a 'relational ontology' of learning and human development: 'the notion that social and psychological phenomena are processes that exist in the realm of relations and interactions – that is, as embedded, situated, distributed, and co-constructed within contexts while also being intrinsically interwoven into these contexts' (Stetsenko 2008: 477). For those who see few differences between, for example, Dewey and Vygotsky, here is one of two main reasons why. However, a second family resemblance relates to education, learning and social action and their relation to active engagement. This is something Stetsenko refers to as action-centredness. What we see is that education, learning and development – for Piaget, Dewey and Vygotsky – implicate increasing elaboration of successive practices in which learning is an active endeavour rather than passive trans-mission of knowledge. Each theorized learning in this way: people learn as active agents in the world. What this meant was that practice – that is, *doing* – is not ontologically separable from learning and human development, but rather is the very substance of them. It was this perspective that placed these three in direct opposition to the powerful common sense views, then as today: mind as container.

This departure is summarized by Stetsenko (2010: 8) which, in turn, leads us to a final point related uniquely to the CHAT tradition.

> Lev Vygotsky laid foundations for a theory that potentially represents the next step after establishing the situated and active nature of development and learning because development, in his approach, can be conceptualized as the transformation of socially shared and fully contextualized activities into internalized processes without positing any ontological breaks between internal and external, social and individual, and continuity and change (or transmission and transformation). He understood all of these putatively dichotomous constructs as interrelated (opposite but not disjunctive) poles on one continuum of a unified reality of collaborative transformative practice.

In this excerpt, we see a discernible break between CHAT and the other approaches to learning. It revolves around the question of the relation between adaptation and transformation, and quickly spirals into a concern for the social *and* material dimensions of learning. To deal with these in turn: in educational thought, the ontological presumption regarding education and learning *as adaptation* can at times be overwhelming in its ubiquity. Of course, in schools it is difficult to deny that the primary institutional goals revolve around student adaptation. Likewise, in the context of forms of adult training, for example in the workplace, the same can be said. However, for Vygotsky, education and learning are not ruled strictly by adaptation. While Vygotsky, Dewey and Piaget oriented toward a social relational ontology and action-centredness, Dewey, and in particular Piaget, can be characterized as offering primarily adaptive rather than transformational perspectives. This is so whether we look toward Piaget's dominant concern for principles of equilibration and assimilation; or, alternatively, if we turn to Dewey's culminating concerns for highly naturalistic, genetic and transactional arcs of development. Preoccupations with social change, which appear so relevant in today's globalized world, are marginal in the conceptual frameworks of both Dewey and Piaget. Not so with Vygotsky, and this is where his willingness to entertain broad, historical perspectives on social and material bases of human change played such a powerful role. Piaget referenced no political theory, Dewey a form of liberal democracy; Vygotsky, on the other hand, explicitly oriented to the possibilities of more fundamental societal transformations, and the role of human learning and education with them.

Vygotsky wrote of the social transformation of human life, although he is most often associated exclusively with processes of sign-mediation. But framing of his work as strictly oriented to symbols, meaning and sign-mediation can be misleading. How social transformation was related to education and learning was, for him and collaborators, historical, symbolic *and* material. Using dialectical materialist thought, Vygotsky and followers interrogated the inseparability of adaptation and transformation – both individually and collectively – in the world around us. Adaptation and transformations of the world were accomplished through signs, material tools, interfunctional psychological systems, meaning and communication. Under specific concrete historical conditions, human needs, objects and motives, forms of mediation, are reorganized by, and in turn reorganize, concrete social relations and interactions. The materialist and, more broadly still, the realist (as opposed to the idealist) impulse in Vygotsky's work was explicitly and deeply interwoven with specific empirically grounded research.

> ideas readily live in harmony with one another, yet they violently collide in space. Therefore, when a child begins to think in a given situation, this not only means that the situation changes in how it is perceived and interpreted, but above all, that the whole dynamic changes. The dynamics of a real situation, when converted into the fluid dynamics of thought, reveal a situation's new features, new opportunities for movement, association, and communication among sub-systems. However, this direct motion of dynamics from the actual situation to thought would be quite useless and unnecessary, if the reverse, the backward transition from the fluid dynamics of thought into rigid and firm dynamic systems of real action also did not exist. The difficulty of implementing a set of intentions is directly related to the fact that the dynamics of an idea, with all its fluidity and freedom, must be transformed into the dynamics of real action.
> (Vygotsky *Collected Works*, Volume 5, as quoted by Zinchenko 2002: 19)

Inspired by what is arguably Vygotsky's (1987) master work, *Thinking and Speech*, but for those interested fleshed out and significantly extended across the breadth of the volumes of the *Collected Works* series as a whole, these are the precise points that would later become elaborated in the work of Leontiev, Luria, Galperin, Davydov, Engeström and many others.

It is also, however, in this sense that, according to Stetsenko (2008: 471, 474), this Vygotskian-inspired perspective – social relational, action-centred, transformational, dialectical and materialist – explicitly represents an 'ideology of empowerment and social justice'. In this formulation, learning theory is rooted in the 'collaborative purposeful transformation of the world [as the] principled grounding for learning and development'. Much more than simply a statement of political commitment, this approach is also a reflection of specific ontological and, in turn, analytical terms of reference for a critical approach to education and learning such as CHAT.

Seminal conceptual departures: from mediation to activity

To better understand CHAT research in the context of this book's themes as a whole, it remains important to explore the seminal concepts that helped establish the tradition's potential overall. In this brief section, we begin with the analytical break in understanding thinking, learning and human development afforded by one of the most basic ideas of CHAT – *mediation* – and discuss how it, and a series of other ideas flowing from it, eventually culminated with the concept of activity.

For Vygotsky, and others since, the principle of mediation directs our attention to a basic fact. People always interact with, think about, feel, adapt to and transform themselves and the material world around them through social practice that is mediated by artefacts. These artefacts can include virtually everything: from physical tools and technologies to spatial or temporal properties of the environment; from language, narrative and non-narrative aspects of discourse or ideology to organizational rules, divisions of labour, social norms, specific cognitive or affective schema, desires, fears or other elements commonly associated with personality, subjectivity or identity.

The historical dimension of CHAT, however, makes additional demands of this concept of artefact mediation. CHAT requires attention to the history of artefacts in order to, in turn, understand their effective tendencies of mediation. Specifically, all artefacts come from somewhere, were made under certain conditions, and emerged from specific sets of goals and purposes. Obvious at first glance, its implications are considerable. It was a point Vygotsky took time to emphasize explicitly in his concern for an historical approach (i.e. historical in terms of an individual, their learning and development, as well as for a human group or humanity as a whole). The histories of human changes (i.e. learning and development) were inseparable from the histories of production of the things that mediate their ongoing practices, goals, interests and energies. And, just as we might say that our prior learning experiences can either expand or limit our future horizons, so, too, the historical features embedded in the symbolic and material artefacts that surround us are central for understanding how human practices are expanded and limited through processes of mediation. *Vis-à-vis* the histories of artefacts, history can be seen to live within and around people, in the present.

How did Vygotsky and colleagues arrive at such claims? An answer to this question requires some attention to how Vygotsky worked. This involved extended and detailed criticism of existing theory, and, importantly, it built upon extensive empirical work with children and, to a lesser extent, adults. Vygotsky's approach in fact rejected the belief that the study of child learning cannot contribute to a general theory of human learning. In part, this allowed his early work to demonstrate how *adaptation* (what he called turning or interiorization) described a moment of the learning process through which external social and material relations – the things happening in the world around a person – become the roots of learning and development. That is, the inner world of cognition, emotion, learning and development was premised on the structure and dynamics of the outer world. Here, for example, we find detailed arguments for the development of meaning that grows in people, not from part to whole, but rather from whole to part (e.g. Vygotsky 1987). And here we also encounter Vygotsky's discovery of the special role of play. Play is one of several key terms, along with the concept of 'task', for example, that seemed to have led him toward the activity concept that we know today (e.g. Vygotsky 1987: 124, 126). Importantly, Vygotsky would later attend to studies of externalized (mediated, indirect) semiotic-materialized memory; perhaps the most often-cited example being his attention to the significance of strings tied on one's finger, or knots in a handkerchief. It was this type of empirical exploration that, in turn, initiated his concept of the mind as not simply an internal phenomenon, but an externalized one, dependent on mediations by external symbols and material artefacts.

Vygotsky's original work on child learning concluded that *sign*-mediation was primarily, though not exclusively, inwardly directed; involved most intensely in the moments of learning and development characterized by adaptation or interiorization. Signs were later realized to mediate social relationships, which can be considered an important exception in this regard. And, as this became more clear, his thinking increasingly turned toward the idea of communication rather than meaning. In contrast, *material* artefacts, for both Vygotsky and Leontiev, were linked primarily to the moments of learning and development characterized by transformation of the 'dynamics of real action'. Thus, while the initial concern for sign-mediation and then the mediation of practice by material objects was Vygotsky and colleagues' initial challenge to the dominant role of stimulus and response psychology, they discovered that a theory of mediation in itself was inadequate to the task of providing an adequate account of learning.

Already expanding rapidly in terms of its implications in the work of Vygotsky himself, the concern for mediation became more elaborated still in the work of his colleague Leontiev. CHAT approaches understood that all social action and, in turn, all practices of learning and education were mediated. In fact, it is this basic concept of mediation that establishes the triangular model of social (inter)-action so prominent in certain schools of CHAT analysis today (Figure 4.1).

But associating a theory of activity strictly with later CHAT researchers such as Leontiev may not be all that accurate. While certain aspects do seem to have been more explicitly the focus of the work of colleagues, nevertheless, with reference to Vygotsky's own work, Minick (1987) summarizes the type of transition from early concerns with sign-mediation to the concept of activity. He explains, for example, that following Vygotsky's work between 1925 and 1930 on sign-mediation, by 1933–34 Vygotsky announced that the explanatory

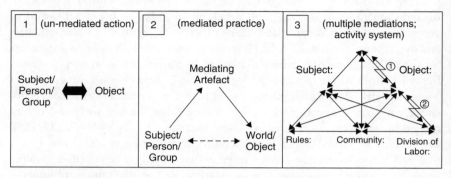

Figure 4.1 CHAT Analytic Progression – Mediation Concept

principles of psychological functions were 'social systems of interaction and action' (Minick 1987: 17–18). This shift was expressed, for example, in the way that the concept of communication (a contextualized social interaction) came to envelop his earlier concern for the principles of word meaning – '[i]t may be appropriate to view word meaning not only as a unity of thinking and speech, but as a unity of generalization and social interaction, a unity of thinking and communication' (Vygotsky 1987: 49). It was this type of shift that was responsible for several of Vygotsky's most widely recognized conceptual points, including his idea of zone of proximal development and the distinctions between everyday and scientific concept formation. Our point here is that it was through this shift in thinking that Vygotsky arrived at the conclusion that mediation was necessary but insufficient for understanding learning, development or education. E.g. *'Activity and practice* – these are the new concepts that have allowed us to consider the function of egocentric speech from a new perspective, to consider it in its completeness' (Vygotsky 1987: 78, emphasis added).

Amidst some of the detail that we have introduced in this section, it is perhaps equally important to note the breadth of the theory that Vygotsky and colleagues set in motion. As Jerome Bruner (1987) recognized explicitly, Vygotsky's radical approach eclipsed psychology and learning theory. Vygotsky was, in Bruner's words, a visitor from the future who incorporated psychology into a theory of cultural change, and the role of education and learning within it providing an invitation to explore the unity and wholeness of thought, speech, cultural and historical as well as material practice. This wholeness of thought, its simultaneity, and eventually the inherently *sociomaterial* notions of meaning and communication correspond directly to the dialectical whole that, for Vygotsky and CHAT researchers, is *activity*.

Key concepts of the CHAT tradition

This backdrop, establishing both the adaptive and the transformative dimensions theoretically inherent to CHAT, provides us with an entry point into many of the key concepts of the CHAT tradition. We begin with the concept of *activity*, drawn from the work of Leontiev:

> The minimal meaningful context for understanding individual actions [. . .] In all its varied forms, the activity of the human individual is a system set within a system of social relations [. . .] The activity of individual people thus depends on their social position, the conditions that fall to their lot, and an accumulation of idiosyncratic, individual factors. Human activity is not a relation between a person and a society that confronts him [*sic*] [. . .] a person does not simply find external conditions to which he must adapt his activity, but, rather, these very social conditions bear within themselves the motives and goals of his activity, its means and modes.
>
> (Leontiev 1978: 10)

Amidst the contingencies and complexities of the flow of social life, the CHAT concept of activity, motive (or rather object/motive), goals and so on play a central role in the active, social structuration of practice. The concept of object/motive forefronts the mutuality of collective, un-self-conscious as well as self-conscious purpose. In this context, the term *object* in object/motive should not be seen as simply either a thing (Russian word *objekt*) or even the general notion of a personal objective. Rather, it takes a more expansive, specialized meaning in CHAT expressed by the Russian word originally used in Vygotsky's work, *predmet*. In this latter meaning, the object/motive relates to a broader social need, sense and relevance. The object/motive includes, but is not reducible to, individual intentionality. The object/motives of activity are, in essence, chunks for units of actively, symbolically and materially produced social concerns; the object/motive generates and focuses individual and collective attention, efforts, meaning-making and of course interaction. A CHAT perspective suggests that where we find patterned human practice, we find people adapting to and transforming the object/motives of activity. Where we find the activity of people interlinked across not just time but locales, places, spaces and scales, from a CHAT perspective, we find some modicum of shared (even if conflictual and contradictory) object/motives.

Beyond these general comments, what does this concept of object/motive refer to, and how does it relate to other key CHAT concepts? As Leontiev (1978: 62) put it, '[i]t is understood that the motive may be either material or ideal, either present in perception or existing only in the imagination or in thought'. Need, as such, does not play a role in isolation and thus, paraphrasing Leontiev closely, Miettinen (2005: 54) is more concise still: 'need becomes a motive capable of directing actions only when it finds its object'. Kaptelinin (2005) explains it further, noting the object of activity is both a projection of the mind onto the world *and* vice versa. It is, in his phrase, 'the sense-maker' which demands 'anchoring and contextualizing subjective phenomena in the objective world' (Kaptelinin 2005: 5). And this is so both in practice and in the practice of CHAT analysis.

Building upon this concept of object/motive and the object-relatedness of all other dimensions of activity, we can see more clearly how CHAT analysis distinguishes first between *action* and *activity*. An action is conducted by an individual or group to fulfil some *self-consciously held goal*. In short, this refers to intentionality; what people explicitly understand themselves to be doing. But the point of CHAT analysis is that this intentionality in itself cannot generate an analytically meaningful understanding of what is in fact going on, what people are learning and how. Thus, while people have intentions and goals, these actions take the form they do in relation to an activity which is undertaken by a social formation of some type (e.g. a class in a school room, a community, a group, a work team in an organization) involving some form of division of labour oriented by a purpose, a sense-maker, or *object/motive*. A third basic term is, in turn, necessary for us here. *Operation* is distinct from activity and action as a habituated – that is un-self-conscious – practice in direct response to conditions. Leontiev's (1981) oft-quoted heuristic of the primeval hunt is still the classic illustration of these differences: for example, there are those who beat the bushes and scare the game toward others; here the *object/motive* of *activity* is the provision of food and clothing even while the *action* and *goal* for the bush-beaters themselves is to actually drive game away, involving certain *operations* undertaken in response to given *conditions*. In education, we can think how for teachers (a collective subject) the actions of preparing students for a test, for example, are highly goal-directed. In the course of pursuing this goal, these teachers need to carry out a series of operations attending to the available resources (classroom space, supplies, etc.), and the type of student population and surrounding community, which corresponds to conditions. Finally, we might think about how the actions and operations of these teachers make sense only as a whole, as activity, for example in terms of what educational attainment means in our society, how educational credentials are (or are not) valued in communities, households and labour markets, how testing operations structure the meaning and content of education, and so on. Such object/motives are rarely intentional; that is, conscious dimensions of their practice. Throughout it all – whether we are looking at actions, operations or activity – specific symbolic as well as material artefacts mediate teachers' practices in specific ways. Likewise, throughout it all, there are contradictions within operations (e.g. uneven avail-ability of resources), actions (e.g. differing conscious attitudes and goals related to 'teaching to the test'), and activity (e.g. school success seems to be reproducing social differences, there are few jobs available).

In many ways, the heart of the matter is not the individual, elementary concepts themselves, but rather what Galperin referred to as the elusive 'blue bird of psychology' (quoted in Arievitch 2003: 283), and what Leontiev (1978:

67) indicated remains too often concealed: the internally related way that the processes of transformation of object/motives express a series of constantly emerging forms as well as specific projects expressing what people think they are doing (goals), how they go about doing what they do (operations), and the myriad mediating artefacts involved in each instance.

> An analysis leading to an actual disclosure of sense cannot be limited to superficial observation [. . .] After all, from the process itself it is not evident what kind of process it is – action or activity. Often in order to explain this, active investigation is required: substantiating observation, hypothesis, effective verification. That to which the given process is directed may seem to be inducing it, embodying its motives; if this is so, then it is activity. But this same process may be induced by a completely different motive not at all coinciding with that to which it is directed as its results; then it is an action. [. . .] In spite of what it seems to be from the superficial point of view, this is a way that confirms the objectivity of its bases to a high degree inasmuch as this way leads to an understanding of the consciousness of man [sic] derived from life, from concrete beginnings, and not from the laws of consciousness of surrounding people, not from knowledge.
>
> (Leontiev 1978: 173–4)

Emerging from the work of Vygotsky, Leontiev's conceptualization of activity furthered the possibility of systematic analysis of the entire realm of education, learning and development with reference to both consciousness and tacit dimensions of practice. In turn, this provided a means to appreciate the patterned, meaningful, political, historical, yet vast and otherwise chaotically complex flow of experience that people make themselves. Thus CHAT analysis suggests that learning is defined by the contradictory yet relationally patterned ways (the form) in which a relational configuration of actors and artefacts mediate interaction with the world, all the while producing a shifting kaleido-scope of object/motives. Most importantly for our purposes here, what expresses the action-centred transformational ontology of CHAT is *this pro-duction process*: what in CHAT theory is understood as the dialectical unity of processes of *both* internalization *and* externalization. In turn, this draws our attention toward not simply the limitations of the world around us, but the degrees of freedom afforded by specific meditational processes (e.g. people may appropriate artefacts and use them in unexpected ways) and, more broadly, the freedoms afforded by the shifting organization of meditations – shifting configurations of actors and things – and thus form of activity. In other words, learning is never limited merely to the moments of internalization and adap-tation. People actively produce and transform the form of activity. The suggestion from this approach is that learning limited to adaptation is not only partial and misleading, but fundamentally flawed.

Related to these discussions of mediation, activity and transformation, as suggested above, is the relationship between CHAT and dialectical thought. Among other things, this relationship is central to the idea of mutually constituting and undermining relationships of activity (and overlapping activities). From a dialectical perspective, the relationships that constitute activity never work simply unidirectionally, but rather are reciprocal and historically evolving. It is this point that separates dialectical logic from other forms of logic (Bakhurst 1991; Ollman 1991; Ilyenkov 2009).

Both theories of activity and dialectical thinking have as their purpose the description and explanation of the complexity of change processes. They highlight the way that *contradictions* express a unity of opposites locked together in a series of mutually supportive *and* mutually undermining relationships. Contradictions in activity, and their partial or complete resolution in the course of adaptation to and transformation of activity, explain why and how change erupts both in large-scale social transformations, group or organizational shifts, as well as in ways that are more intimate and personal. Roth and Tobin (2002: 115) summarize the concept with reference to the work of Ilyenkov and Engeström, establishing its implications and origins while adding parenthetical comments to place it in the context of educational activity specifically.

A crucial Marxist insight was that the changes are driven by contradictions within and between activity systems (Ilyenkov 1977). In fact, the study of contradictions allows us to avoid dualism and subjectivism. Contradictions are developmentally significant and exist in the form of resistance to achieving the goals of the intended activity and as emerging dilemmas, disturbances, and discoordinations (Engeström 1999c). Engeström identifies four different types of contradictions. Primary or inner contradictions are located within each constituent component of the central activity (e.g., when intended object, student learning, has been substituted by 'doing fun [activities]'). Secondary contradictions exist between the constituents of the central activity (e.g., when the language [tool] used to teach is in conflict with the students' primary language [object]). Tertiary contradictions arise from the differences between the object/motive of the dominant form of the central activity and the object/motive of a culturally more advanced form of the central activity (e.g., learning in school science vs. scientific laboratory). Quaternary contradictions arise between a constitutive component of the central activity and a component-producing neighbor activity (e.g., a teacher, as the object of research on teaching feels like a 'lab rat' or 'guinea pig').

Translated further into the language of CHAT researchers, such changes and resolutions are practically achieved moments of externalization and transformation. They are themselves linked to the earlier moments of internalization or adaptation of social relations. In other words, CHAT allows us to address here not simply the unity of opposites in general (i.e. as provided by a general theory of dialectical materialism), but also the unity of internalization and externalization processes as the basis of how learning, training and education transpire. Likewise, rooted in this matter of internal and external contradictions of an activity, are the contemporary conceptual terms *expansive* versus *contracting* activity. An expansive cycle of learning and development, for Engeström (1987), involves individuals or groups who in some way question, re-mediate, re-instrumentalize her/their activity. Whether it is through creating new artefacts or putting existing artefacts to new use, expansive activity is meant to refer to the way people move beyond existing forms of practice. New patterns of individual participation, and new patterns or forms of activity, or even new forms of relations between systems of activity, are produced. Involving the many elementary concepts we have discussed in this chapter – from sign-mediation, thinking, speech and communication, concept formation all the way to adaptation and transformation *vis-à-vis* operations, goals, object-relatedness and activity – contradiction and expansion can be seen as something of a summary phrase for how learning, development and change transpire from the perspective of CHAT.

Where, we are now in a better position to ask, does contemporary CHAT research stand in relation to these basic concepts? Several authors have attempted summaries of contemporary concerns in CHAT. These include active research seeking to take up established concerns anew, as well as many others who are seeking to explore underdeveloped questions involving issues such as the role of authority, identity, human agency and affect (see Engeström 2009). However, perhaps the most widely pursued contemporary concern involves an interest in accounting for the effects of articulating or overlapping activity systems on learning and change in activity. Following this, we see elaborations on how a 'multi-dimensional network of activity systems' interact, support, destabilize and interpenetrate (Engeström 1992: 13, see also Engeström *et al.* 1995). This concern expresses many of those held by the originators of CHAT, including Vygotsky, who sought to grapple with the enormous complexity of not simply isolated psychological functions, but mental life in dialectical relation to the concrete world as well as historical change. Contemporary research has developed terms such as poly-contextuality, knot-working and so on to begin to account for this complexity. And, as we see in chapter five, such concerns have become a staple for many educational researchers. A second important conceptual concern is the issue of the 'heterogeneity of expertise' or 'multi-voicedness' which researchers such as Wertsch (1991), Engeström (1992), Holland *et al.* (1998) and others have attempted to understand to explain more coherently alternative – cooperating and conflicting – perspectives within activity. Alongside these additional lines of inquiry in the CHAT tradition, however, people's active-centred doing and the expansion of activity appear to have remained central to empirical research as well as theoretical debate. Likewise, issues of change and transformation discussed in relation to the contradictory and changing nature of the object/motive of activity is widely shared by CHAT researchers, confirming the expression of Lektorsky's (1999: 67) that 'in order to create or change "inner" or subjective phenomena, it is necessary to create some objective thing'. We suggest that these and other insights provide important entry points into explanation of the specific modes of thinking, feeling, talking and acting by individuals and their non-human actants, by and across groups as well as across organizations, regions, countries, places and spaces, which, in turn, demands an interest in the complexity that such situations entail. In these terms, we find a variety of points of contacts with other traditions of sociomateriality discussed here.

The past, present and future of CHAT: critiques

As we see in chapter five, prominent amongst educational researchers are attempts to use CHAT to analyse and make changes regarding not only pedagogy and curriculum, but also school-based organizational change initiatives and school–community relations. We can see that researchers today are developing new applications, extending and creating new conceptual terms, as well as generating new and often productive criticisms of CHAT. Reflecting on both contemporary CHAT research and criticism of CHAT, how can we make sense of where the approach may be headed in the future? This is a question that we return to again in chapter five, but for now it seems clear that to understand the future better, it is important briefly to take a moment to reflect on how CHAT scholars have sought to construct its past. And in these terms, we can begin with the dominant construction of CHAT's history: the 'three generation' model (e.g. Engeström 1987, 1996b). What does this image of the past say about future concerns? Is there a need for alternative or additional perspectives on the past? And do formulations of the past perhaps hold a key to better understanding contemporary criticisms of CHAT?

CHAT's past, according to the three generation model, begins with Vygotsky. His argument regarding mediation and consciousness, particularly though clearly not exclusively semiotic mediation, frequently bound with his concept of zone of proximal development, is typically presented as the starting point for the tradition. In turn, the second generation of CHAT research is associated with Leontiev, and is said to revolve around the elaboration of the concept of activity, with special attention to social relations, divisions of labour, and material conditions. Indeed, the idea of these two generations offers a highly accessible outline of the origins of the tradition. As we arrive at the present (third generation), authors such as Engeström, Cole and others have regularly affirmed the relevance of the prior stages and added several new conceptual concerns, as noted above. The chronological basis to understanding CHAT in this way seems clear.

However, framing the development of CHAT as a generational model probably comes with several unintended consequences, and these consequences include certain modes of criticism that bear on the contested future of the tradition. There are at least two related ways in which this is so. First, the generational model, while useful, probably encourages a reading of first-, second- and third-generation scholars in isolation from each other. This is a problem we have sought to address through the foregoing discussion of original CHAT research. As is well known (though still too often ignored, it seems), the so-called troika of Vygotsky, Leontiev and Luria produced works that were highly co-dependent. In fact, they were largely dialogical. The generational model probably encourages a consecutive rather than a dialogical reading of these sources. Second, and closely related, in presenting the CHAT tradition as a consecutive and successive trajectory of development, the presumption is that the latest generation has built successfully on the past, effectively subsumed the tradition, and can stand in for it as a whole. While clearly advances have been made, just as clearly engagement with prior literature outside of some of the most recognizable voices in the tradition is uneven. Among the results is a tendency amongst critics to ignore this dialogical and co-dependent nature of CHAT, particularly amongst the earliest scholars, which provides the opportunity to make individual 'third-generation' scholars attractive targets for criticism of the tradition as a whole. For this and other reasons, an alternative formulation of CHAT's lineage may therefore have an important role to play.

Stetsenko (2008, 2009, 2010), for example, sees the CHAT lineage not as a series of successive and coherent intellectual steps or generations, but rather as an ongoing contestation – a to-and-fro swing – between canonical and non-canonical CHAT. From this perspective, canonical approaches are rooted in the westernization of the Vygotskian tradition and include a more limited concern for broader forms of social transformation. Approaches that deviate from this established canon emphasize this more far-reaching, often politicized, dimension of activity. For us, this alternative formulation suggests the history of CHAT as a type of *paradigmatic tension*. This tension revolves around the waxing and waning of transformational, social change and social justice orientations. In either case, whether one views CHAT lineage as a series of generational developments and/or a paradigmatic tension between more adaptive as opposed to more transformational orientations, it seems that how we construct the past shapes the basis for future conceptual, empirical and methodological choices.

However, do these different formulations of the past and future of CHAT help us in some way to understand better the range of contemporary criticisms? Some researchers, for example, maintain that contemporary CHAT offers an overly structuralist analysis (e.g. Garrison 2001; Davis 2007; Williams *et al.* 2007). It may be sensible to see the prevalent use of triangle diagrams (e.g. Figure 4.1) in this way, especially where they are left to stand in for the complexity inherent in the activity concept as a whole. Others see a radical localism in CHAT that eschews broader structural effects (Peim 2009). A host of researchers have sought to show how contemporary CHAT research demonstrates a lack of appreciation for the influences of, or inherent linkages with, other European traditions:

for example, Spinoza (Jantzen 2002); Derrida (Flint 2009); Heidegger (Peim 2009); Hegel and Goethe (Blunden 2010). Perhaps most broadly of all, there are those who argue that CHAT analyses offer little if any explanatory value (e.g. Toolmela 2008, Bakhurst 2009). Differently focused, not infrequently warranted, even if occasionally somewhat contradictory when taken together, our point is that, with very few exceptions, these criticisms are almost exclusively oriented to third-generation CHAT research. It is in this sense that we wonder whether a generational model has unintentionally provided the conditions for this type of reading, even if it remains unlikely that every criticism would be resolved by such an appreciation.

Alternatively, we can ask how contemporary criticisms relate to the canonical/non-canonical formulation, or rather the paradigmatic tension view, of CHAT's development. Contemporary CHAT is noted by some for a less critical, less socially transformative and non-Marxist orientation (e.g. Newman and Holzman 1993; Langemeyer and Roth 2006; Avis 2007, 2009; Warmington 2008; Jones 2009; Niewolny and Wilson 2009). The work of Engeström is a common focal point, but even CHAT researchers (old and new) oriented explicitly by Marxism, for example, are not excluded from such critiques (see Jones 2009). Other critics have argued that the work of some contemporary CHAT researchers expresses a managerialist ethic of improvement (e.g. Flint 2009), or produces inadequate analyses of power relations (e.g. Blackler and McDonald 2000, Hartley 2009). In an interesting way, paired with a very different example of criticism that disputes the Marxist influences ascribed to Vygotsky and subsequent research (e.g. Kozulin 1990), it is possible to see terms of debate expressing and affirming the type of ongoing canonical/non-canonical tension across the tradition. In this context, the canonical/non-canonical tension would seem to explain a good deal about how CHAT's past, present and future is debated.

Conclusion

In our view, understanding alternative formulations of CHAT's past is at least partially suggestive of distinctions between the terms of debate that continue to shape the tradition. However, what is clearer is that constructive critics and purveyors of CHAT alike have regularly offered valuable grist for its future development. Our view is that the concepts of the CHAT tradition continue to provide viable and invigorating resources for better understanding the relationship between mind, society and materiality as well as adaptation and transformation. In terms of educational research, broader CHAT debates offer important theoretical resources. These bear directly on how researchers understand operations, actions and activity, as well as types of contradiction and the role of artefact mediation. As we have tried to emphasize above, the tradition rests on a dialectically unified set of social, material, semiotic and psychological processes rooted in fundamental questions about the relations of thinking and concrete social practices. Mediations, and specifically the way that artefacts – a history in the present – shape but do not necessarily determine practice, and the way that practical and mediated resolutions of contradictory relations transform activity, likewise remain central. Shifting systems of activity are complex systems in themselves. In recognizing mediated forms of human agency within them, they are perpetually undergoing specific forms of transformation that in many instances are unpredictable. Activity analysis inevitably becomes ever more complex when we turn our attention toward the articulations, overlaps, inter-actions and, in particular, contradictions between the wider array of activities that constitute society more broadly. Many such systems are at play in education, to which we now turn.

Notes

1   We are aware of the history of debates regarding the naming of this tradition (e.g. cultural historical activity theory, socio-cultural activity theory, the activity approach, activity theory, etc.). The resolution of these matters is not an issue we pursue here. We use the term 'cultural historical activity theory' throughout to simply reflect a basic level of continuity between Vygotsky and collaborators through to contemporary research (for further discussion see Kozulin 1990; van der Veer and Valsiner 1991; Stetsenko and Arievitch 2004).

Chapter 5

Cultural historical activity theory in educational research

Beginning from Vygotsky's early work with elementary school children, as well as through his work at the Gomel Teacher Training School (Yaroshevskij 1989), we find that practical educational processes were an important preoccupation. This concern both for education as well as for the general mutuality of theory and concrete institutional change were central to his approach. These were concerns that shaped the CHAT tradition from the beginning, and they were also concerns shared by his closest collaborators. Leontiev, for example, spent considerable time on the question of medical rehabilitation, intertwined with theoretical development. Luria's work attempted to deal with literacy, learning and developmental changes associated with farm collectivization policies in Central Asia, while his applied research on criminal rehabilitation pioneered a unique qualitative interview method. Amongst later CHAT researchers, this pattern of engaged practical–theoretical development is repeated, and again there is a special place for matters of education specifically. Prominent CHAT researchers such as the philosopher Ilyenkov worked closely with special needs students in school settings even while developing sophisticated philosophical treatises. Davydov's research was intensively guided by focused collaborations with working teachers, through which was produced arguably the first comprehensive application of CHAT thinking to pedagogy and curriculum studies.

We begin this chapter in this way in order to register the fact that the roots of CHAT are found in the challenges of concrete realities, the solutions to which were frequently sought through analysis and intervention in terms of learning and education. From the very beginning, the CHAT tradition has oriented to the problems and needs facing thinking, feeling and acting people, often in the context of educational sites. The resulting tradition of practical–theoretical development continues today.

Facing difficult challenges in many countries, the institution of education remains a fertile ground for this approach to research, and thus it is hardly surprising that CHAT has increasingly flourished amongst educational researchers. Moreover, CHAT is also well suited to education research, since it is virtually impossible to understand and engage it without the categories of education, learning and development. It inherently includes the category of education even in Vygotsky's original theories on thinking, speech and concept formation, for example. The concept of zone of proximal development (ZPD) is a direct tool for understanding pedagogy both in the classroom and beyond it. Compared with other traditions reviewed in this book, CHAT is somewhat unique in its explicit relationship with education, learning and development.

The myriad forms of educational research associated with CHAT reflect a series of differences, often overlapping, in the tradition. For example, some research is oriented more to description and modelling, other research more to analysis and explanation. In focus, some research is more logocentric or semiotic in its interests, other research concentrating more on social relationships and/or sociomaterial issues. In emphasis, some research is more concerned with how actors adapt to normative practices, while other research seeks to explore transformation of such practices. To us, these three sets of distinctions are helpful in identifying the preoccupations and strengths of various applied, critical and theoretical research in the CHAT tradition.

Despite the challenges of sorting out the distinctions, overlaps and contradictions amongst CHAT educational research, building on themes introduced in chapter four, we maintain there is an underappreciated departure shared by the most developed work in this area. It is rooted in the notion that people, individually and collectively, can and do change; people can and do *learn* to become authors of their own lives and authors of the world around them. In short, they do not strictly recreate and adapt to the situations with which they are presented. Moreover, this change process, this individual and collective authoring process, is both symbolic and material. It depends upon the individual and collective mind as constituted actively and transformationally amidst the concrete symbolic and material arrangements of things – artefacts, in CHAT language. For these and other reasons, CHAT appears to have encouraged both intellectual excitement and creativity amongst recent generations of educational researchers.

This chapter introduces the issues and approaches of CHAT research in education. Our review aims to reveal not only the basic insights CHAT has to offer on educational processes and systems, but also the types of questions about education that CHAT research tends to suggest. The focus here is on contemporary empirical studies associated directly or indirectly with schools. Necessarily, the review is indicative rather than exhaustive. Below, we organize the review into five sections. First, we begin with early research in the CHAT tradition that demonstrates several key ideas that appear to emerge again and again in contemporary research. This is followed by a brief examination of the sorts of methods that have been adopted in CHAT-based educational research. In the third and largest section, attention is devoted to research exploring the basic dynamics of pedagogy and the intra- and inter-institutional dynamics of schools. We then turn to research that forefronts somewhat broader social themes of equity and power in education. We conclude with a brief discussion of challenges in understanding the broad range of CHAT educational studies.

Early educational research in the CHAT tradition

Clearly, one of the significant contributions of CHAT is that external relations – thoroughly and inextricably social, historical as well as material – lie at the root of what we think of as individualized thinking, meaning, sense, emotion and, in general, higher mental functions of people. In other words, these are the relational origins of what ultimately appears as the final individual *learning and change* accomplishment. The CHAT perspective in turn says that the resultant formations of personality, identity, subjectivity, behaviour, comportment, values, orientations, styles, skills, knowledges and so on shape those same social, historical and material relations. Thus an alternative condition is produced, a new configuration of these relations and their mediations emerges, and human learning and development proceeds. From its earliest days, CHAT elucidated these exact processes through direct experimental and non-experimental empirical research. It was not a tradition that progressed simply through theoretical speculation. This strong empirical commitment began, but did not end, with Vygotsky. It is notable in the works of Leontiev (1978, 1981), Luria (1976) and Galperin (1992) in particular. These were path-breaking programmes of research and theoretical development. Some, such as Elhammoumi (2006), go so far as to describe these early works of CHAT research as amongst the most profound intellectual achievements available addressing the dynamics of mental life (e.g. the relationships between sound, word meaning, experience and consciousness), social life (sociomaterial interaction) and history.

In terms of pedagogical research, some of the most foundational are found in the works of Galperin and Davydov. Stetsenko and Vianna (2009: 46) describe the way that the work of Galperin, and later Davydov, expanded directly upon the work of Vygotsky in the area of school, teaching and learning studies.

> [T]hey focused their efforts on exploring and conceptualizing the links among the process of teaching, learning, and development, while working in the midst of classroom practices, actively shaping and transforming these practices and drawing theoretical implications from these transformative engagements – thereby putting forth, with unusual clarity, the message about theory and practice being intertwined.

Each provided highly specified developmental and learning approaches that would shape teachers' work directly. Davydov, for example, emphasized interventions based on CHAT principles including 'everyday' and 'scientific' concept formation. Building from Vygotsky's (1987) work, we see the term 'everyday concepts' meant to indicate ideas that tended to remain involuntary in the sense that they would be used/applied without conscious awareness of their meaning, and were not linked to a logical discursive, ideational or organized knowledge system. Everyday concepts emerge spontaneously out of concrete practices in the learner's immediate, individual experience (they are a reflection of practical action). In contrast, the term 'scientific concepts', closely associated by Vygotsky and Davydov with forms of instruction, tended to be applied independently of individual experiences, were more self-consciously available to the learner, and in this sense were linked to matters of conscious volition (acceptance as well as resistance). According to the work of Galperin (1992) and Davydov (1990), it was scientific concept formation that held the key to the most crucial accomplishments of higher mental functioning. Moreover, in this process of learning, we encounter the CHAT axiom of instruction leading development and how this generates the capacity to reconfigure the learner's reflection of reality which, in turn, allows engagement in transformations of that reality. Connected with this notion of transformational potential, Davydov (1990) was careful to distinguish between different types of instruction. For him, authorized or closed instruction utilized disassociated facts and pieces of information and resulted in *empirical generalizations* that did not encourage transformational potential in students. This type of instruction was contrasted with the development of new discursive tools that allowed for active recon-struction and transformative engagement in the world. These tools were what Davydov referred to as *theoretical generalizations*. This formulation provides one of the strongest analytical departures from generalized theories of acquisition in education, which we discussed in chapter four as an interlocking block of presumptions that often continues to live on in educational practice today. It also provides a conceptual means for educators and researchers to distinguish different types of educational practice they know to be more and less pro-gressive. Along the way, it also affirms the core CHAT principle that social and material relations are central to understanding the mind.

> [T]raditional instruction typically includes the requirement to teach young children in a 'piecemeal' fashion, whereby they are exposed to small bits of information supported by concrete illustrative examples, with no attempt to reveal the general rules and connections that lie behind these examples. As a result, children indeed do not develop the ability to operate with abstract (i.e., generalized, systematic) concepts. In contrast, research findings by Vygotsky and his colleagues demonstrate that when knowledge is taught as tools that stem from meaningful practices and can be used in solving practical tasks [. . .] there are spectacular development changes, including process in abstract reflective thinking, self-regulation, and cognitive control [. . .] In this sense, then, the traditional instructional restrictions thought to be grounded in inherent limitations of children's minds in fact themselves produce these limitations!
>
> (Stetsenko and Vianna 2009: 52)

The roots of Davydov's conclusions in this area are found in the dialectical materialist orientation outlined in the previous chapter. Davydov's (1990) work affirms, for example, the centrality of dialectical materialist thought by drawing heavily on the philosophical works of the philosopher Ilyenkov (e.g. 1982) cited in the introduction to this chapter. For example, the instructional processes and concept formation are shown to be driven by contradictions of activity. Closely associated with these ideas, we find additional insights related to Vygotsky's concept of the ZPD (Davydov 1988). In Vygotsky's (1978: 86) original work, we find the oft-quoted formulation that the ZPD refers to 'the distance between the actual developmental level as determined by independent problem solving and the level of potential development as determined through problem solving under adult guidance or in collaboration with more capable peers'. Or, rephrased for broader application, the ZPD is defined as 'the distance between the present everyday actions of the individuals and the historically new form of the societal activity that can be collectively generated as a solution to the double bind potentially embedded in the everyday actions' (Engeström 1987: 174). Here we find another crucial conceptual tool for educators that extends the basic CHAT principles more deeply into concrete educational practices of all kinds.

Methods in CHAT educational research

The character of educational research methods in the CHAT tradition shows considerable variation as well as recognizable trends. A great deal of the original CHAT research, including the pedagogical research introduced above, was based on experimental and quasi-experimental design. For example, we often find specific classroom-based tasks were designed by researchers and educators beforehand and then tested. Control groups were often utilized, and participants carried out these tasks while researchers carefully analysed and drew conclusions. More broadly, Luria's (1976) famous studies of change in rural life involved specific types of tests for inhabitants as well as general observational methods. The changes in state policy and programming (the collectivization of farming) offered a notable source of systematic variance to be analysed. Not without their own limitations, of course, these methods may have been crucial for the conceptual precision associated with CHAT. Moreover, in recognizing the limitations of these methodologies, as Vygotsky did explicitly, it is likely that earlier research set the stage for later, more naturalistic methods which encouraged additional and broader sociomaterial as well as historical perspectives that have come to characterize the CHAT tradition.

Further review of the materials we discuss below (and those we did not have space for) shows that today, forms of naturalistic, qualitative research are dominant. Many studies now use ethnographic and participant observation as well as interview research techniques. Given the centrality of the historical approach to activity in CHAT, including the history of specific artefacts, we also tend to see a great deal of documentary analysis to establish the historical origins of a particular classroom or school procedure, an occupational role, a technology, a policy, a curriculum document, and so on. Still, forms of survey research, participant self-report tools and other quantitative methods can also be found. Not surprisingly perhaps it seems, however, that these are rarely used in isolation from some form of qualitative analysis or prior researcher experience in the specific area of inquiry. Case studies are frequently seen, although many researchers also generate comparative insights as well (e.g. across different classrooms, schools, school districts and countries). Usually linked to specific projects, a variety of researchers have offered useful reflection on methodological issues in CHAT educational research (e.g. van der Aalsvoort and Ghesquiere 2004; Beauchamp et al. 2009; Jaworski and Potari 2009), while Koszalka and Wu (2004) offer a comparative analysis of the unsuitability of standard research methods in CHAT analysis.

Building upon the history of the CHAT tradition in many ways, we can also see a strong and sustained attraction to applied and interventionist research methods (see Cole and Engeström 2007; see also Sannino 2008). We see this, for example, in work such as the 5th Dimension research on educational change (e.g. Blanton et al. 1997) as well as in the workplace learning research carried out or inspired by Engeström's interventionist method (through the use of his Change Laboratory; see Engeström 2007). In general terms, interventionist strategies are framed by detailed research linked to close, ongoing, participatory consultation with research participants. They are consulted first in the meaning of the research, and second on ways to experiment actively with changes in the environment of interest, for example through the introduction of new key mediating artefacts. Such interventionist research strategies and methods have explored pedagogical change, school organizational change, curriculum and learning technology implementation, for example.

There are good number of examples of interventionist studies in CHAT-based educational research. Roth and Tobin (2002) offer a good case in point. They report on the development of a new urban teacher education programme in the USA, and specifically generated a new activity analysis of co-teaching across actors (student teachers, instructors, school-based supervisors). Specific techniques included peer debriefing, monitoring emergent collective descriptions of events and situations, validation of descriptions by the actors and so on. The general lesson gleaned was that CHAT offers a conceptual approach 'commensurable with [an] epistemology of praxis [. . .] [and] consistent with an interventionist approach in which research and theory are in the service of practice in order to bring about changes as part of theory development' (Roth and Tobin 2002: 113; see also Roth and Tobin 2001; Tobin and Roth 2002). Others examples of interventionist CHAT educational research in terms of co-generative dialogues with students (e.g. Stith and Roth 2008), school–university partnerships (Yamagata-Lynch and Smaldino 2007).

A more recent set of educational studies in the UK adapted Engeström's Change Laboratory method in an interventionist approach called Developmental Work Research (DWR). Arguably a key example of analysis across educational and other forms of activity (health, social services, etc.), and remarkable for its substantive contribution with an explicit interventionist perspective, is found in the British 'Learning in and for Inter-agency Working' (LIW) project (e.g. Leadbetter 2006; Daniels and Warmington 2007; Daniels *et al.* 2007; Leadbetter *et al.* 2007; Martin 2008; Daniels 2009; Edwards *et al.* 2009). Unique in its own right, with a focus on experience of professionals working with at-risk students across several institutional sites, the work extends and elaborates on the work of Leontiev and Engeström – utilizing some of the latter's key concepts such as co-configuration, knot-working and boundary-crossing. Beyond the descriptions provided by Engeström himself, the LIW research provides one of the clearest outlines of how interventionist research is organized and carried out. And – while more effective, critical historical models of changes in forms of employment can be found elsewhere – it nevertheless provides among other things a high-quality exemplar of education-related, overlapping object/motives of activity and the processes of object formation discussed in chapter four.

In the LIW, six workshops were held with professional team members. In the workshops, practitioners begin by discussing the object/motive of their professional activity, facilitated by a researcher. Together they analyse traces of experiences from their work practice (narrative accounts, photographs, video-taped work episodes, etc.), looking particularly at critical incidents such as disturbances or problems as well as solutions. This analysis employs the conceptual tools of CHAT to reveal the implicit in narratives, examining the systemic roots of the situations: not only the complex objects centrally directing the activity system(s), but also the history and contradictions at play, the role of particular mediating artefacts, the rules and division of labour, and so forth. Of particular interest, for example, was the relationship between roles of rule-bending, shifts in object, and, *vis-à-vis* CHAT analysis, their ramifications for new practices, learning and development.

> Their practice was driven by expanding the object of their practice in an 'ideological' sense, so that the 'well-being' of the 'whole child' became their object, rather than just attendance issues (her absence from school). The well-being of the child, rather than the process rules of the school or local authority, was the key driver.
>
> (Daniels *et al.* 2007: 534)

Later, the workshops focus on collaboratively envisioning ideas and tools for concrete changes that can productively expand their practice. In a dialogue situation among different professions, the very terms through which such discussion and analysis proceeds, and the categories and values that frame these terms, are objects for negotiation. These also turn out to be important sites for learning. Edwards and Kinti (2009) highlight the 'relational agency' (capacity to work collaboratively to respond purposefully to complex problems) that was strengthened through this CHAT-based interventionist approach. They argue that practitioners' exchange and analysis of their own narratives in DWR sessions helped to reveal each others' different categories, values and motives, and to engage with these differences towards negotiating action to expand the object of activity.

In another analysis of the (inter)professional learning process that emerged through this project, Daniels (2009: 106) focused on the institutional structures themselves as 'cultural products that serve as mediators in their own right':

> My suggestion is that there is need to analyse and codify the mediational structures as they deflect and direct attention of participants and as they are shaped through interactions that they also shape. In this sense I am advocating the development of cultural historical analysis of the invisible or implicit mediational properties of institutional structures that themselves are transformed through the actions of those whose interactions are influenced by them.
>
> (Daniels 2009: 107)

As Daniels notes himself, this analysis expands a Vygotskian focus to integrate it with a sociological institutional analysis of learning in and through work activity. The LIW research publications clarify and extend a number of CHAT principles. They clarify the importance of contradiction in overlapping activities and divergent objects of these activities; they confirm and extend CHAT analyses of (professional) identity; and they shed new light on divisions of labour across groups of workers dealing with at-risk youth speaking directly to the emergence of new knowledge forms (and the challenges to existing ones). In relation to education, the researchers put considerable flesh on the bones of what in chapter four we defined as the possibilities of complex, expansive learning environments. In fact, inclusive of the LIW project and a number of others (see Edwards and Fox 2005), in contemporary CHAT educational research the diverse set of contribution of British researchers has stood out. Overall, this project illustrates not only the different kinds of work that CHAT-inspired methods can do in educational research, but also the diverse departure points that educators have taken, which in turn contribute to CHAT's key conceptions.

Chat educational research on pedagogy and schools

Building on the introduction to analysis that we began in our discussion of methodology, in this section we examine research that makes up by far the bulk of CHAT educational research, focusing on pedagogy, curriculum, programmes and organizational change. Additional CHAT research focused on learning related to the workplace, professional identities more broadly, and so forth must be left aside. Perhaps the first observation that can be made about CHAT educational research is that it is vast and deep.

The way that students form everyday and scientific concepts in the classroom has continued to be the subject of research from a CHAT perspective. For example, CHAT research on meaning and algebra learning, specifically the way in which scientific concept meaning emerges in classrooms (Radford *et al.* 2007), demonstrates the ongoing relevance, or continuing analytical resonance of these original Vygotskian, and later Davydovian, ideas. Others, building on the influential work of Galperin, have pushed the question of meaning further by focusing on the distinction between verbalizations versus image-based internalization (Feryok 2009). Like Feryok, a distinct treatment of imitation in the educational process is addressed by researchers such as Arievitch (2003). He highlights sequential imitation, which is not a matter of simply reproducing a specific performance, but rather is understood as an instance of appropriation and change. It is a learning process that facilitates a step-wise teacher learning strategy, in the case of Feryok's research amongst science and math teachers reflecting on issues of language.

Introduced above, a particularly significant line of CHAT analyses of education has also emerged from the work of Roth and colleagues. This work has spanned wide conceptual foci and empirical contexts with particular attention to science educational practices. Notably, its attention to emotion into CHAT analysis is innovative (Roth 2007; Roth *et al.* 2009; see also Daniels 2001). Emotion had for some time remained obscure in CHAT studies, finding expression unevenly amidst psychological discussion of personality. Incorporating earlier insights on emotions, Roth *et al.* (2009) found that it was necessary to recognize an enormously wide activity system if one was to analyse effectively a specific curricular change initiative. Their project used an interventionist method that involved the town council, farmers, environmental activists, professional biologists as well as students and teachers. It legitimized broader collective object/motives of activity (environmental health in the Hagan Creek area community), and changes in divisions of labour. Among other things, the project showed the shifts in emotional energy and participation levels significantly depending on the structure of activity, and so on.

> [I]n the Hagan Creek project, students are not treated as individual learners but collaborators with peers, scientists, teachers, parents and researchers as community learners. What is significant is the changes that the group as a whole can bring about in the part of the world that matters to them.
>
> (Roth *et al.* 2009: 152)

Paralleling the types of concerns that we discussed earlier in terms of Davydov's seminal work, CHAT educational research in this context puts meat on the bones of an otherwise vague notion of authentic curriculum. Their studies confirm, in the context of science education, a core preoccupation with sociomateriality:

The nature of the *material object and concepts cannot be articulated independent of concrete, practice activity* – including the work of mathematicians and theoretical physicists, who, in communicating what they do/think always and already draw on material signs and human bodies.

(Roth *et al.* 2009: 143; our emphasis)

At the same time, researchers have also moved beyond a focus on theories of either concept formation or activity-based analysis of curriculum to understand what goes on in the educational processes more broadly. They have more and more frequently sought to combine these with an even wider menu of CHAT analytical terms. In particular, a number of studies have examined overlapping activity systems; that is, activity systems understood as mutually constituted by related activity systems. For educational research, the concept of overlapping systems helps to break free from container-like notions of the classroom as a bounded context or a particular activity. The overlapping also shows how learning often occurs at the boundaries of different systems, where objects of activity are shared yet have distinct effects. A recent example of this can be found in Kelly (2008), who shows that student inquiry and concept formation in high-school science classrooms cannot be understood in isolation from the broader systems of argumentation of science in general. Here there is specific emphasis on the principle of overlapping systems of activity, but also how they must be supported by specific teacher interventions (see also Joung 2008).

Likewise, a host of researchers have effectively applied CHAT perspectives to classroom communication in similarly expansive ways. Recent examples of this include Barowy and Smith (2008), who combined CHAT with ecological psychology to explore meaning-making. The core CHAT principle explored is the role of material mediations of communication (i.e. not simply specific artefacts, but artefacts in space and time). Supported by a rich array of data, Barowy and Smith address the processes through which a sense of coherence and contextual cohesion (meaning) is generated in a classroom. They argue that a sense of coherence and meaning is most effectively understood in light of, among other matters, artefact-mediated processes. In a first-grade class, for example, different coloured rugs, the use of a reading bin, the use of louder or quieter voices, the orientation of a student's and teacher's body, glances, and so on mediate practices within a coherent activity system. Williams (2009) establishes additional insights in the context of mathematics teaching with an emphasis on pedagogical gestures to generate objects of activity/meaning. Here again, we find reference to the importance of multiple activity systems in interaction with one another. Similar research on the relevance of overlapping activity systems focusing on classroom writing has been done (e.g. Russell 1997). This work is complemented by that of Jaworski and Potari (2009), who demonstrate the analytical (and practical pedagogical) power of examining overlapping activity systems, i.e. how classroom learning is linked with broader social frames outside schools. Importantly, they show how traditionally underachieving students' attainment or lack-thereof can be explained by tensions across multiple sets of mediating artefacts (within and beyond schooling). They present, for example, a theory of classroom resistance that explains how and why student orientation to affective object/motives of activity (e.g. having friends, being accepted, not being judged) relates to mathematics learning. The teachers in the study re-orient their pedagogy with a new recognition of student classroom activity systems and the overlapping systems that inform it.

The work of LIW project researchers discussed above has solidified the current state of the art in CHAT-based multi-activity analysis. However, in Roth (2005) we see a CHAT perspective that further deepens understanding of the broader complexities and effects of overlapping activity systems. Each activity system is seen to function with different collections of object/motives and related artefacts (with special attention to temporal orientations). The contradictory relations (disconnection) across activity systems of professional science, phenomena in the surrounding community and science in the classroom are shown to result in negative effects on student learning. In a similar way, analysis of curriculum (e.g. van Eijck and Roth 2008) has placed the representations of scientific practices in a new light as an extended, mediating process as well. In terms of learning activities outside the classroom, studies by DeWitt and Osborne (2007) show how field trips, for example, bring into motion overlapping learning systems. In essence, they provide a systematic language for explaining what many educators sense intuitively. Overlapping systems can explain the social and materially constituted nature of students' motivation to learn in these different settings, the mediational effects of non-school artefacts (e.g. museum artefacts and texts from outside the school curriculum), how such artefacts establish boundary objects (i.e. objects that are shared by school and non-school activities that in turn shape learning), and how the border-crossing activities of students facilitate better educational experiences and outcomes.

This strong interest in the way the activity systems interact and mutually constitute one another has been a staple in other areas of CHAT educational research. Here we refer specifically to research on school-to-work transitions. Miettinen and Peisa's (2002) research recognizes the problem of adequate vocational curriculum and dynamic overlapping activity systems, and has gone on to study the use of an 'alternative firm' project, which aims at establishing a new ZPD ultimately to increase the relevance and success potential of transitions of students to paid work. Young (1998) also takes up the issue of overlapping spheres of activity and curriculum related to school-to-work transitions, highlighting the importance of connective specialization. Similarly, these are issues that Guile and Young (2003), among others, have discussed in terms of consequential transitions (i.e. the dimensions of activity relating to vital life transitions). These school–work transitions have also been analysed with CHAT to highlight the importance of connectivity and the processes of re-situation as young people try to relocate themselves in systems of activity with different objects, rules, divisions of labour and related artefacts (Young 1998; Guile and

Griffiths 2001; Griffiths and Guile 2003). These works can be linked with that of Engeström (1996b, 2004), who explicitly challenges the separation of spheres of organized school-based learning and informal work-based learning experiences or learning sites. School-to-work transitions, in other words, require attention to skills that function across and join multiple spheres of activity: 'the aim is to develop polycontextual and connective skills which enable "boundary crossing" by students, that is, the ability to work in changing and new contexts' (Guile and Griffiths 2001: 144). Overlapping, knot-worked activity, boundary-crossing and connectivity are central to the research analysis of learning and education in this context.

A different but equally well developed stream of CHAT-based educational research has explored learning technologies in schools (e.g. software applications in the classroom, student use of text messaging related to portfolio development) and beyond them (in terms of e-learning for distance education and training). Educational researchers have explored the roles of mediating tools and signs in classroom computer gaming projects (e.g. Barab *et al.* 2005; Krange 2008), showing, for example, how new gaming artefacts or new computer mapping tools mediate new forms of activity and have the potential effectively to link learning across multiple sites (e.g. classroom and community). Hardman (2005) shows how mathematics teaching seeking to make use of new computers and software tools produces contradictions within and between activity systems (e.g. of a classroom and the computer lab). These contradictions, in turn, help to explain (and change) teaching practice *vis-à-vis* a shift in the object of teaching practice (see also Roth *et al.* 2000; Roth 2002 on how contradictions drive teaching as well as curricular change in high-school classrooms). Other analyses of the use of technology in the classroom show similar effects (e.g. Lim and Hang 2003; Plessis and Webb 2008). Jacobs (2006) offers a careful analysis of the different roles and ways in which text messaging is used, emphasizing how this artefact/technology generates distinct modes of participation in activity – students are producers, collectors, assemblers and distributors of information as well as consumers *vis-à-vis* text messaging. Hence new modes of activity and learning are produced that may be more than simply a distraction in the classroom, but in fact may be ideally suited to a rapidly changing economy and society. Murphy and Manzanares (2008) offer a strong examination of virtual education teaching/learning, focusing on technological artefact mediation and contradictions. Their study shows how 'innovation [. . .] emerges not necessarily because it is planned or intentional but because it is actually a response to the tensions between two [activity] systems' (Murphy and Manzanares 2008: 1070). In research on this topic, there has sometimes been a call for renewed attention to the taken-for-granted tools associated with a teacher's physical presence (in a virtual classroom there is no physical presence and the teacher cannot rely on visual cues and interaction to control attention). This attention turns to new ways of communicating and shifts the object of activity, as Murphy and Manzanares found, from centralized control to one preoccupied with distributed engagement. Kang and Gyorke (2008) offer a concise theoretical comparison of traditional transactional distance-learning theory and CHAT, arguing that the latter incorporates a much needed social relations perspective fundamental to understanding the distance-learning process. CHAT's highly developed conceptual views on artefacts (much broader than seen in the traditional approach), as well as the interconnection between a range of activities that make up the distance-learning process, are said to offer fundamental improvements for analysis.

Bridging the themes of learning technologies, school policy and organizational change is another related cluster of research. These studies are not limited to compulsory education. CHAT researchers have shown how the process of ICT adoption in university chemistry courses is differentiated (and occasionally frustrated) by university policies which, in turn, shaped teaching strategies and effectiveness. The theme of the relationship between teaching practice, learning and school-based policy is also examined by Demiraslan and Usluel (2008). These authors outline contradictory relations amongst purposes (object/motive) and goals on the one hand, and key mediators (e.g. administrative oversight protocols, timetabling and curriculum) on the other. Here CHAT analysis demonstrates how and why, far beyond apparent financial supports and organizational motivations, expansive learning processes can remain highly elusive in school environments. In other words, such research addresses the ways that key artefacts, or boundary objects, proved very difficult to produce, resulting in the failure of many school change initiatives. It is also the case that CHAT has been applied to the study of school administrators (e.g. Spillane et al. 2004). In Ritchie et al. (2007), for example, we see among other things the powerful effects of artefact production in an interventionist attempt to create new roles for students and teachers in order to bring about greater shared responsibility in a school.

In post-secondary education, recent studies have been undertaken in medical education (e.g. Wearn et al. 2008) and graduate studies training for university teaching (e.g. Hopwood and Stocks 2008; Beauchamp et al. 2009). While these studies of post-secondary schooling tend to provide only introductory and/or initial exploratory applications to this point, nevertheless CHAT appears to be posing new questions, specifically identifying new objects of inquiry around matters of contradictory relations. These in turn illuminate how educational practices in these diverse settings both flourish and, more often, flounder. Wearn et al. (2008), for example, addressed the contradictions emerging between, on the one hand, peer examination exercises, and on the other, those that used volunteer patients. On the surface, the scenario appears almost identical, yet they showed how the differences in rules and the multiplicity of roles (e.g. students were both fellow student, sometimes friend, as well as 'doctor' to the peer-patient) and, ultimately, the different objects of activity that were produced (despite virtually all the same mediating artefacts otherwise) created difficulties for student learning.

CHAT analyses have also explored formative and summative educational assessment (e.g. Habib and Wittek 2007), where evaluation instruments are conceptualized as key mediating artefacts in addition to functioning as goals, and occasionally as the object/motive of activity. Here we can begin to perceive how assessment artefacts can even be seen as actors within activity. While the non-CHAT literature on educational assessment is large and seemingly exhaustive, in many ways it is the identification of multiple functions of evaluation in this dialectical way – and specifically the processes through which these functions are transformed – that seem to have allowed CHAT to offer some unique, explanatory commentary. As Habib and Wittek (2007) argue, CHAT (as well as actor-network theory) provides a grounded way of understanding the conditions under which evaluation becomes overzealous and dominates the learning process – a matter with which, no doubt, many educators identify.

We began this chapter noting how closely many of the originators of the CHAT tradition and subsequent researchers have attended to teacher practice and teacher education. Contemporary research has maintained this interest. CHAT has been used extensively in analysis of initial teacher education and ongoing professional development. Yamagata-Lynch's (2003) exploration of teachers' learning in the area of new education technology deals with, among other matters, the effects of multiple activity systems from many perspectives (i.e. those of teachers, teachers-as-students, students, administrators, etc.) and how the recognition of what many contemporary researchers have referred to as multi-voiced-ness helps to explain the challenges, contradictions and new possibilities for learning and education. Later work by Yamagata-Lynch and Haudenschild (2009) offers analysis of additional types of contradictions of professional development activity where competing value systems clash. These clashes have an impact on, and not infrequently detract from, teacher development. Yamagata-Lynch and Haudenschild conclude, as with many of the researchers discussed above, that attention to joint (that is, overlapping) activity and the contradictions (and learning) it initiates is central to future research as well as successful intervention.

> For future professional development efforts to succeed, the tug-of-war between teachers and professional development coordinators must be addressed. One method to minimize this struggle is for teachers, school districts administrators, and universities faculty to acknowledge that they are participating in a joint activity. This requires engagement in a discussion to identify what the joint professional development activity is and how the activity affects the individual teacher activity and institution school/university activities. Activity systems analysis can take a role in this process to help researchers and practitioners identify joint activities and what specific aspects need to be changed or monitored to minimize

tensions that impede the progress of individual and institutional professional development activities.

(Yamagata-Lynch and Haudenschild 2009: 516)

What becomes clear in these educational studies is that core ideas initiated in the earliest CHAT research are being tested and reproduced effectively in new environments. These ideas have proved particularly useful for understanding taken-for-granted aspects of educational practice. Concept formation, artefact mediation, zones of proximal development, the contradiction-driven nature of learning, and the more contemporary and increasingly prominent concern for overlapping activity systems have retained a good deal of relevance.

CHAT educational research on difference, equity and power

In the previous section we briefly registered the concept of multi-voiced-ness in CHAT analyses of education. This was a conceptual theme noted in chapter four as a critical contemporary concern amongst CHAT researchers generally. However, this brings up a point that deserves some expansion. Although original CHAT researchers explored how, for example, disability shapes learning and development for children (e.g. Vygotsky); or how relationships of social class, literacy and education level, religion as well as rural production methods, shaped learning and development in adults (e.g. Luria), a gap is apparent in this earlier research. This gap has been its capacity to take up issues of social difference in education more broadly and in a more sustained way. Far from simply a matter of recognizing different perspectives and experiences, this is obviously also an important bridge to questions of marginalization, equity, power, resistance and social justice.

The recent work of Stetsenko offers a relevant starting point on this issue. Stetsenko's work, mentioned earlier, distinguishes between canonical (mainstream, westernized) and non-canonical (critical, transformation-oriented) approaches to CHAT. Stetsenko (2008: 471, 474) describes CHAT's orientation as 'underwritten by [an] ideology of empowerment and social justice' and an orientation to the 'collaborative purposeful transformation of the world [as the] principled ground-ing for learning and development'. This perspective, summarized as a 'transfor-mative activist stance', emphasizes that teaching/learning practices cannot, according to Stetsenko, be fully understood as simply *participation*, but rather must be understood as a process of construction, or rather *contribution*. In this sense, educational processes from the original CHAT perspective offered by Vygotsky, Leontiev and Luria, partially revived by Stetsenko, emphasize an analytical shift from participation in social life, to individual contribution to social life, and finally to collective contributions to transforming social life.

Stetsenko, however, is hardly alone in this perspective. Several researchers referenced in the previous section (e.g. Roth) offer similar views. Also offering, in this sense, a more politicized CHAT perspective on education, we can look towards the work of Murphy and Carlisle (2008), for example. These authors apply an activist/transformative perspective to the matter of teaching, co-teaching and the need for co-generative dialogue. Understood through the lens of CHAT, this refers directly to education, learning and development as a collective process of shared contributions; a process dependent on specific mediational artefacts and processes arranged and evolving through a particular form of activity.

Other educational researchers working with CHAT have also taken this type of politicized stance in their choice of method, research focus and conceptualization. For example, Cole (1996) established the importance of activity analysis in terms of diversity and education by introducing a method he called the 'Fifth Dimension' approach, which has since inspired a significant amount of applied action research (e.g. Blanton *et al.* 1997; Blanton *et al.* 2003; Lecusay *et al.* 2008). Fifth Dimension approaches seek to generate interventionist research engagements in curricular and extra-curricular educational activities through an after-school programme using special computer-mediated software. This software is designed to radically expand the opportunity for students to engage in a ZPD related to basic and advanced education skills. The approach is presented by researchers as *expansive* in that it requires including the broader partners of the educational enterprise (e.g. community service providers, teachers, students, academic researchers). In fact, it emerged out of the broader need (contradiction) of the increased experience of youth as 'latch-key kids' (often working-class children whose parent or parents work late and are not at home for them after school). Recalling our comments about Vygotsky's treatment of play in chapter four, a sense of educational play orients this system. Through a specific computer artefact (a complex system including task cards, weblinks and a host of thematic streams), students are given control of virtually all dimensions of activity (operations, goals, object/motive of activity) in the Fifth Dimension system. 'Fifth Dimension citizens' (students) have been shown to increase school performance enormously through participation in this programme. In North America, this has become the largest research-based attempt at CHAT application in education for the purposes of increasing equity and challenging socially reproductive tendencies in educational life.

Equally relevant here is the work of Gutiérrez and colleagues in illuminating cultural practices in the classroom itself. This research opens another important entry into teaching/learning processes of schooling by examining equity in terms of micro-cultural production/social construction (e.g. Gutiérrez 2002). CHAT analysis in this research emphasizes how classroom literacy learning, for example, can and should meet the challenges of analysis across classrooms and other additional spheres of development that always, necessarily, overlap and mutually constitute one another. Gutiérrez summarizes an equity evaluation of literacy learning in the USA in the following way.

[. . .] recent educational reforms restructure literacy activity and limit the use of mediational means available to English language learners. Most notably, learning oral English fluency is the primary target of instruction and the use of the students' complete linguistic and sociocultural toolkit is no longer a viable (legal) resource in meaning-making activity [. . .] [R]ich learning contexts [on the other hand] are characterized by dynamic participation structures and the strategic use of a wide range of mediational tools, including hybrid language practices.

(Gutiérrez 2002: 317–18)

In other work, Gutiérrez *et al.* (2002) show how English-only instruction in urban schooling (the elimination of teachers' use of student's first languages in California), in conjunction with the introduction to classroom practices of other specific mediating artefacts, explains the reproduction of the *status quo*; in fact, how particular hierarchical relations of schooling amongst linguistic/racially minoritized students are created and recreated. Gutiérrez *et al.*'s notion of 'back-lash pedagogy', specifically how such back-lashes function in schools, depends on the fundamental points of departure provided by CHAT. Such research makes it clear how and why, for example, research into the self-conscious intentions of teachers and school administrators simply cannot explain such outcomes on their own. It also shows how the analytical potential of approaches like CHAT do explain such outcomes specifically in terms of the power of mediational relations within specific activity systems.

Although exemplary work such as that of Gutiérrez *et al.* focuses on issues of racial, ethnic and linguistic phenomena, other contemporary, critical perspectives on education have explored additional social differences. The work of Davis (2007), for example, has highlighted how gendered discourses of reading in primary schools – applied by teachers and students alike as a key mediation – must be understood in relation to the non-school community. Specifically, she explains how students' gendered reading practice outside school configures their reading practices in school (overlapping activity systems) to a significant degree *vis-à-vis* the shared boundary object of student discourses about reading. Likewise, studies of disability and special education (e.g. Gindis 1999; van der Aalsvoort and Ghesquiere 2004; Spinuzzi 2007) have been undertaken echoing and advancing several concerns of CHAT originators such as Vygotsky. Such studies have addressed issues of teaching method, classroom and learning technology design as well as curriculum development. Gindis (1999), for example, problematizes not the individual differences of students and their relation to their learning, but rather the 'handicapping conditions' of education – what in contemporary disability studies is typically referred to as the social model of disability – that shape activity and continue to reproduce contradictions that, in turn, reconstitute what could be called *ablest* societal relations of schooling. Given its close association with Marxist thought originally and Vygotsky's (1994) own specific commentary, class differences have also been dealt with, although sometimes in more diffuse ways; a point alluded to by, amongst others, Young (2003) as well as Avis (2007). Nevertheless, CHAT has served to explore issues of social class in education (e.g. Panofsky 2003; Portes and Vadeboncoeur 2003) and in adults' learning in relation to past experiences of schooling (e.g. Sawchuk 2003, 2006). Here we see instances of class biographies, formed to a significant degree during school ages, continuing to produce various trajectories of learning and development in the context of (shifting) mediational processes within and across different forms of activity (Sawchuk 2006). These learning trajectories implicate various forms of class consciousness as mediated activity.

Contemporary challenges in CHAT educational research

A scan of the educational research cited in this chapter, as well as the bulky weight of additional materials that we had no space to address properly, shows that crucial concerns of CHAT researchers include mediational processes, concept-formation processes, ZPD, the role of contradictions in activity, different perspectives in activity (multi-voiced-ness) and, in the past decade or so in particular, a concern to explore overlapping activity systems, co-configuration, poly-contextuality and their effects within and beyond the classroom. These studies exemplify the analytical power of a particular sociomaterial approach to education that extends, and in several instances departs from, the confines of earlier CHAT research.

As one of the most popular sociomaterialist perspectives used in educational research, CHAT offers strengths in analytical clarity and an enormous range of applications. Representing this range is difficult for two reasons. First is the persistent – and often highly productive – combining of CHAT with other theoretical resources. A significant proportion of the studies cited here include reflections on the relationship between CHAT and at least one other theoretical tradition. In some instances such researchers maintain few definitive boundaries between CHAT and these other theoretical approaches. In fact, for many researchers the differences between CHAT and other theoretical schools of thought, including the potential ambiguities and occasional incompatibilities, are typically not as relevant as the exciting potential advances of combining ideas that have not been brought together before to respond to concrete educational problems. These more eclectic approaches bring with them other challenges. Occasionally researchers leap to new theoretical resources without registering – where applicable – those resources already available in the existing tradition, and particularly the often underappreciated original research that we have taken time to summarize in this and the previous chapter. This may in part be a reflection of a non-dialogical reading of the CHAT tradition as a whole; a point we emphasized in the conclusion to chapter four.

A second challenge in the diversity of CHAT-based educational research can be thought of as related to, yet distinct from, this first one. It involves the uneven application of core terms. There remains significant dispute over how terms are understood and applied. For example, in some instances the concept of ZPD appears to have been applied in a somewhat generic way. Likewise, it seems that a good deal of contemporary CHAT educational research struggles to express clearly the meaning of object/motive as something including and oriented beyond school success. In other instances, the dialectical unity of activity (operation, goal, object/motive) appears to slip from consideration. In such instances, the results can sometimes be a relatively mechanical, deterministic analysis of activity – one that has not infrequently spawned criticism.

Another notable case in point is the concept of contradiction. Here unevenness in definition, application and general appreciation have provoked far-reaching critical observations of contemporary CHAT research. As is pointed out, for example, by Avis (2009) (see also Sawchuk 2006; Sawchuk and Stetsenko 2008; Niewolny and Wilson 2009), the central notion of contradiction in activity is sometimes ignored entirely. In other instances, recognition of the full range of contradictions in activity – as well as their broader social and political implications – is uneven. Clearly, sustained analytical attention to the notion of contradictions in activity is marginal in certain clusters of educational research. Amongst others, while referenced, the concept of contradiction appears to be underdeveloped conceptually and, as such, unsustained analytically. Avis (2007, 2009) argues that even amongst some leading proponents of CHAT research, the term is not infrequently narrowly construed. In turn, this tendency and/or the perception of it has provoked the claim that CHAT tends to express socially reproductive rather than transformational learning dynamics (e.g. Martin and Peim 2009); a matter that researchers simply cannot afford to ignore.

These challenges are implicated when CHAT theory as a whole becomes generic. This results in statements such as that learning or development is socially constructed; or that people learn with the help of a more experienced other; or that 'context' matters, and so forth. In this vein, it is also not unusual to find instances of unwarranted conflation, for example, of the works of Dewey, Lave, Leontiev, Engeström and Vygotsky. Generic appreciations of CHAT probably represent a source of limitation for the tradition's development in educational research, as well as a source of difficulty for researchers attempting to make clear sense of its contribution. Challenges such as these underscore the purpose of paying close attention to the key examples of research that we took time to dwell upon earlier.

Conclusion

These difficulties and unevenness aside, what seems clear in looking across CHAT educational research is that it offers a powerful and sustained intellectual lineage. Increasingly, researchers in curriculum and pedagogy, children's learning, educational technology, higher education and interprofessional learning draw upon CHAT to understand the dynamics of activity and mediation in educational processes, and the effects of sociomaterial connections and mis-connections. CHAT features detailed technical studies of these specific socio-material dynamics of learning, as well as broad analyses of the interconnections between life within and beyond the classroom and the school, which introduce the dynamics of equity, social justice and social transformations. Attention to material artefacts (as well as symbolic ones), and in some instances matters of space and time, continue to play a strong role in CHAT educational research. Despite the seemingly natural pull of educational researchers to focus on student learning and development, we nevertheless see a persistent appreciation of both the social relational and specifically materialist dimensions of practice. A somewhat more radical approach to materiality is presented in actor–network theory. Although ANT has been compared with activity theory, it is arguably very different in its origins and analyses, as we see in chapter six.

Chapter 6

Translation and network effects

Understanding actor-network theory

Actor–network theory (ANT) can be traced in a lively trajectory through the social sciences, from its emergence in the early 1980s at the Centre Sociologie de l'Innovation of the École Nationale Supérieure des Mines de Paris, to its current profusion of highly diverse practices and assertions. Largely associated with its progenitors in science and technology studies, including Bruno Latour, John Law and Michael Callon, ANT has catalysed analytical approaches that rupture central assumptions about knowledge, subjectivity, the real and the social. ANT's analyses trace how all things – natural, social, technical or, more accurately, the messy mix of these – become assembled and enacted in networked webs, how they associate and exercise force, and how they persist, decline and mutate. Nothing is anterior in ANT approaches. That is, what we think of as the human, the social, subjectivity, mind, the local, social structures and other categories common in educational analyses are not accepted as given. All of these things are, in ANT readings, *effects* of particular assemblages and enactments. ANT traces how these effects arise through network processes that manage to gather and *translate* or transform human and non-human elements so that they link together to act.[1]

Since the 1980s, ANT studies and debates have figured prominently in research published in sociology, technology, feminism, cultural geography, organization and management, environmental planning and healthcare. Within educational research, ANT has been introduced through influential studies such as Nespor's (1994) *Knowledge in Motion*. Nespor showed how the learning of American undergraduate physics students was radically different from the learning of management students precisely because of their different material realities, produced through micro-connections that translated behaviours, identities, ideas and things. In another important study, Verran (2001) used ANT to explore *Science and an African Logic*. She traced the material connections at play to show how Nigerian science knowledge functions as a different ontology – a different way of being – from those assumed in Western science and in the curriculum presented to Nigerian students. Mulcahy (2007, 2010) has been analysing standards of accomplished teaching in Australia to examine the multiple, often contradictory enactments of standards, how these are produced through networks of texts, desires, things and other vast assortments, and the ways that teachers juggle these enactments of teaching standards. These examples and more are described in further detail in chapter seven. We believe they indicate the ways in which ANT offers important insights and questions about the processes and practices of education.

Like all theoretical resources, ANT has its limitations and its excesses, which we outline below. Overall, however, for educational researchers ANT's approaches offer fine-grained ways to recognize the materiality and material-izing processes that are central to understanding learning and teaching, edu-cational policy, curriculum and implementation, school reform, and a host of other educational issues. ANT allows us to explore how education is assembled as a network of practices, appreciating the multiple overlapping worlds that may be lashed together as temporary stabilizations in the process. Further, ANT offers a language and conceptual resources with which to understand difficult ambivalences, messy objects, and apparent contradictions that are embedded in so many educational issues. Finally, ANT is attuned to the politics through which networks become assembled: many ANT studies in particular have focused on investigating how certain networks become mobilized and sustained to produce powerful effects, and how particular sites become the confluence through which powerful networks intersect.

The risk in trying to explain ANT is to treat it as an 'it' that can be known and contained. Its own key commentators refuse to call it a 'theory', as though ANT were some coherent explanatory device. It may be more accurate to think of ANT as a virtual 'cloud', continually moving, shrinking and stretching, dissolving in any attempt to grasp it firmly. ANT is not applied like a theoretical technology, but is more like a sensibility, a way to sense and draw nearer to a phenomenon.

Those familiar with ANT debates will know that many speak of 'after-ANT' or 'post-ANT'. Some avoid using explicit ANT terminology, preferring terms such as complexity, material semiotics, or science and technology studies. The frustration expressed by the most prominent ANT commentators is that many past uptakes of ANT reified concepts such as networks, solidified particular models of analysis, and colonized their objects of inquiry in representational ways that ANT approaches were intended to disrupt. A landmark volume of essays entitled *Actor Network Theory and After* (Law and Hassard 1999) was premised on the assumption that ANT ideas proliferating throughout the 1990s in various studies had largely run into an impasse. At that time Law (1999), for example, worried that ANT's topological assumptions had come to homogenize the possibilities of understanding complexity in spatial and relational socio-material events. Other authors suggested eliminating or replacing naturalized ANT language and models, delimiting ANT's claims and opening its conceptual scope.

However, we believe that it is more helpful here to use one term, 'actor-network theory', to refer to the wild constellation of ideas that have associated themselves with ANT at some point, rather than to attempt problematic periodizations of early-ANT, after-ANT, ANT-diaspora and so forth. In this way, we think of ANT as a marker – perhaps contingent and precarious – for all approaches that share notions of symmetry, network/webs broadly conceived, and translation in multiple and shifting formulations.

In a recent mini-history of ANT's development, Law (2009a) emphasizes the openness, uncertainty and revisability of ANT-inspired studies. In fact, he suggests that we talk of 'material semiotics' rather than ANT, and offers a stark warning: 'beware [. . .] of any text about actor-network theory that pretends to the objectivity of an overall view' (Law 2009: 142). Approaches and explorations that can be linked to ANT offer an array of tracing practices, but it is not a totalizing theory of the world and its problems. Nespor (2010) puts it well when he describes ANT ideas as undermining reductive explanations and pushing us towards engagements with evidence. Here we describe briefly certain well known ANT ideas that have been taken up in educational research, including symmetry, translation, network ontology, network effects, (im)mutable mobiles, obligatory points of passage, and scale play. Terminology like this is useful for pointing out what may be radically new ways of thinking for some educators, although it's important to treat such language lightly and provisionally, as openings rather than doctrines. We also introduce further critiques of ANT and 'after-ANT' conceptions such as ontological politics. While this is an expository discussion, we endeavour to avoid re-establishing and imposing a purity of ANT-ness that Law (1999: 10) has warned against: 'only dead theories and dead practices celebrate their identity'.

Symmetry: human and non-human elements treated equally

ANT studies treat all human/non-human entities as effects performed in relations, thereby decentring human intention and agency as the engine of society and history. The objective is to describe the specificities of *how* these things come together – and manage to *hold* together – to assemble collectives or networks that produce force, agency and other effects: knowledge, identities, routines, behaviours, policies, curricula, innovations, oppressions, reforms, illnesses and on and on. ANT thus helps us to ask, what are the different kinds of connections and associations created among things? What different kinds and qualities of networks or webs are produced through these connections? What different ends are served through these networks? A key assumption is that humans are not assumed to be treated any differently from non-humans in ANT analyses. This assumption, elaborated by Latour (1987), is called *symmetry*. Everyday things and parts of things, memories, intentions, technologies, roads, bacteria, texts, furniture, bodies, chemicals, plants are all enacted in a web of relations. All things are assumed to be capable of exerting force and joining together, changing and being changed by each other. The networks thus formed can keep expanding to extend across broad spaces, long distances or time periods.

Of course, networks can also break down, dissolve or become abandoned. ANT seeks to show how things are attracted to, gathered in, or excluded from these networks, how some linkages work and others do not, and how connections are bolstered to make themselves stable and durable by linking to other networks and things. In particular, ANT focuses on the minute negotiations that go on at the points of connection. Things persuade, coerce, seduce, resist and compromise each other as they come together. They may connect with other things in ways that lock them into a particular collective, or they may pretend to connect, partially connect, or feel disconnected and excluded even when they are connected.

Latour (1999) protests the separation of materiality and meaning as forcing a rupture between an object and its sign, which are part of each thing. He considers a central problem to be the 'circulating reference' between words and world that attempts to transform matter, the objects of knowledge, into representations, as though there were justifiable anterior distinctions between mind/matter or sign/object. He, like Barad (2007) and others, is therefore critical of social constructivists as well as realists in assuming that materiality and representation are entirely separate realms. They may be separated but they are not inherently separate. The important point is that ANT focuses not on what texts and other objects *mean*, but on what they *do*. And what they do is always in connection with other human and non-human things. Some of these connections link together to form an identifiable entity or assemblage, which ANT refers to as an 'actor', that can exert force. 'Playground', for example, represents a continuous collaboration of bats and balls, swing installations, fences, grassy hills, sand pits, children's bodies and their capacities, game discourses, supervisory gazes, safety rules, and so on. This playground is both an assemblage or network of things that have become connected in a particular way, and an actor itself that can produce fears, policies, pedagogies, forms of play and resistances to these forms – hence, actor-network. And the things that have become part of this actor-network are themselves effects, produced by particular interactions with one another.

ANT tries to faithfully trace all of these negotiations and their effects. In the process, ANT shows how the entities that we commonly work with and often take for granted as categories in educational research – for example, classrooms, teaching, students, knowledge generation, curriculum, policy, standardized testing, inequities, school reform – are in fact assemblages of myriad things that order and govern educational practices. These assemblages are often precarious networks that require a great deal of ongoing work to sustain their linkages. ANT can show how such assemblages can be unmade as well as made, and how counter-networks or alternative forms and spaces can take shape and develop strength.

Debates have centred around the absurdity of ANT's notion of symmetry. How can human subjectivity and meaning-making be set aside to consider humans as entities on par with non-human elements? How can humans speak for non-humans? How can you interview inanimate things? ANT researchers often find themselves in a paradoxical situation in field studies, charged to genuinely represent human and non-human entities as ontologically equivalent in potential power and importance in their connections and effects. However, this has to be done without erasing distinctions, flattening political hierarchies and inequitable distributions, or failing to account for interests, imagination and subjectivity. In choosing a focus for study, ANT researchers confront McLean and Hassard's (2004: 516) challenge

> to produce accounts that are sophisticated yet robust enough to negate the twin charges of symmetrical absence or symmetrical absurdity [and] to understand the paradoxical situations in which ANT researchers find themselves in conducting field studies and producing accounts, notably in respect of notions of power, orderings and distributions.

Translation: how change occurs at connection points

From its early stages, ANT has been described as a sociology of translation. Translation is the term used by Latour (1987) to describe what happens when entities come together and connect, changing one another in the process of forming links. At each of these connections, entities work upon one another to *translate* or change to become part of a network of coordinated things and actions. Entity is a loose way to refer to various things that can be entanglings of human and non-human, including different kinds of material things and immaterial (conceptual, moral, virtual) things and actions, that are not pre-given, essentialized and defined. As Law (1999) explains, an entity is more than one and less than many, not a multiplicity of bits nor a plurality, a division into two or more others. In traditional ANT language, while the working entity is called an 'actor', the worked-up entity is referred to as an 'actant'. In other words, according to Latour (1999: 18), when the actant becomes translated to become a performing part of the network, the actant behaves with what appears to be particular intentions, morals, even consciousness and subjectivity. In other words, when translation has succeeded, the entity that is being worked up is mobilized to assume a particular role and perform knowledge in a particular way. It performs as an actor.

Translation is not deterministic nor linear, for what entities do when they come together is unpredictable. They negotiate their connections, using persuasion, force, mechanical logic, seduction, resistance, pretence and subterfuge. Connections take different forms, some more elastic, tenuous, or long-lasting than others. Translations may be incremental or delayed. Entities may only peripherally allow themselves to be translated by the network. In Latour's (2005) ontology, entities undergo myriad negotiations throughout the process of translation. For Harman (2007), this is an important contribution of ANT to education: tracing exactly how entities are not just effects of their interactions with others, but are also always acting on others, subjugating others. All are fragile, and all are powerful, held in balance with their interactions. None is inherently strong or weak, but each only becomes strong by assembling other allies. Translation is the only encounter between them.

In one example of cement workers learning safety skills, Gherardi and Nicolini (2000) used ANT to examine how knowledge is translated at every point as it moves through a system. Safety knowledge was embedded throughout the system: in safety manuals, protective equipment that workers were required to wear and use, signs that reinforced safety rules, and inspectors with lists of specific safety practices. However, at each node within this system, safety knowledge was continually being modified or even transgressed. One workman might show another how to change a new safety procedure or modify a tool to make a task easier. When the cement mixer's steering wheel was redesigned to include a special disc to avoid catching a worker's arm in its spokes, it translated workers' practice to different rhythms – except when a worker removed the disc, translating the wheel to make it easier to use. The worksite safety inspection represented a series of translations. Workers translated visible objects: 'making the site look in order' so as not to attract the critical attention of the inspector, but leaving certain minimal details so that the inspector would have something to write about. The foreman translated the meanings of what was visible: 'Inspector: This parapet is out of order [. . .] it's too low. Site foreman: You must be joking [. . .] Aw come on, its five centimetres' (Gherardi and Nicolini 2000: 342). Deadlines and weather conditions invoked different safety knowledge and even different standards of safety. The crew's culture embedded a history of use possibilities for their tools that translated their performance of safety skills.

Eventually, these dynamic attempts by entities, which are themselves network effects, to translate one another can become stabilized. The network can settle into a stable process or object that acts as if it has inherent properties and maintains itself. Like a black box, it appears naturalized, purified, immutable and inevitable, while concealing many of the negotiations, connections and messiness that brought it into existence. Education is filled with examples, such as mandated curricula, lists of teaching competencies, classrooms filled with desks, or the school timetable and its regulating buzzers. Each entity also belongs to other networks in which it is called upon to act differently, taking on different shapes and capacities. An employment contract, for example, is a technology that embeds knowledge from both networks that produced it and networks that have established its use possibilities and constraints. In any employment arrangement, the contract can be ignored, manipulated in various ways, or ascribed different forms of power. Thus no agent or knowledge has an essential existence outside a given network: nothing is given in the order of things, but performs itself into existence. However stable and entrenched it may appear, no actor–network is immutable. Counter-networks are constantly springing up to challenge existing networks. Continuous effort is required to hold it together, to bolster the breakages and counter the subterfuges. However, too often an assemblage or network is taken as fixed and inevitable, the process of its emergence long forgotten. Nespor (2002) has pointed out that this is particularly true in education, where so many practices have become deeply entrenched and prescriptive, creating inequities and exclusions. ANT unpicks the history of negotiations that built the networks that are producing the practices, and the different kinds of work holding them together. This not only exposes the lumps, tangles and patches that had been smoothed over to appear impenetrable, but also points out openings for alternatives.

Networks: beyond the chain-link metaphor

If translation is what happens at the nodes of a network, how does a network actually grow? Callon (1986) offered what has become a much cited conception of networks assembling and extending themselves through four moments of translation. Over time there have appeared formulaic applications of Callon's ideas as a fixed model, even a managerial tool, which distort the complexity they were intended to liberate. This is undoubtedly as true in educational research as it has been in other fields of social science. However, there also exist educational studies showing the utility of Callon's moments of translation in illuminating why certain networks become so durable and apparently powerful in education, exerting influence across far-flung geographical spaces and time periods. Callon (1986) proposed that some types of network begin with *problematization*, where something tries to establish itself as an obligatory passage point that frames an idea, intermediary or problem and related entities in particular ways. For example, a teacher's mathematics curriculum guide can function as an obligatory point of passage. Her lesson plans, her choice of texts and assignments must all at least appear to be aligned with it, and are at least partially translated by its prescriptions. Thus this teacher's knowledge and activity, along with all the other mathematics teachers and classes, the consultants who assist them, the administrators who supervise them, and the textbook publishers preparing materials for them, must pass through this obligatory point, this curriculum guide, to form their own networks. The translations whereby separate entities are somehow attracted or invited to this framing, and where they negotiate their connection and role in the emerging network, Callon called *interessement*. This functions as a selection process determining not only those entities to be included but also, importantly, those to be excluded. Those entities to be included experience *enrolment* in the network relations, a process whereby they become engaged in new identities and behaviours and increasingly translated in particular directions. When the network becomes sufficiently durable its translations are extended to other locations and domains through a process of *mobilization*.

In ANT terms, a network is an assemblage of materials, brought together and linked through processes of translation, that together perform a particular function. A textbook or an educational article, for example, each bring together, frame, select and freeze in one form a whole series of meetings, voices, explorations, conflicts and possibilities explored and discarded. Yet these inscriptions appear seamless and given, concealing the many negotiations of the network that produced it. And a textbook or article can circulate across vast spaces and times, gathering allies, shaping thoughts and actions and thus creating new networks. The more allies and connections, the stronger the network becomes. Law (1999: 7) explains that in a network 'elements retain their spatial integrity by virtue of their position in a set of links or relations. Object integrity, then is not about a volume within a large Euclidean volume. It is rather about holding patterns of links stable.'

ANT's network ontology is particularly useful for enabling rich analyses of contexts, which have become increasingly important in educational studies of pedagogy, curriculum and educational change. Contexts such as schools, lecture halls and workplaces are created and continually shaped through social and material processes – the folds and overlaps of practices. These folds and overlaps are very much about network relations. In fact, human geographers have long worked with ANT, applying its ideas, critiquing and extending them, to understand social space as a multiplicity of entities engaged in fluid, simultaneous, multiple networks of relations (see Murdoch 2006 for a review).

Power is central to any understanding of context as enacted through networks of sociomaterial relations. Bosco (2006) credits ANT for drawing attention to how highly diverse different entities emerge and become positioned through these relations, and how they come to enact different forms of power. ANT also can trace how assemblages may solidify certain relations of power in ways that continue to affect movements and identities. Perhaps particularly in educational spaces, as Nespor (1994) has shown in his study comparing undergraduate physics and management students, the sedimentation of power relations and their effects on human identities, knowledge and behaviours are ubiquitous.

In ANT's early years, the term 'network' was employed to suggest both flow and clear points of connection among the heterogeneous entities that became assembled to perform particular practices and processes. However, with the proliferation of technological network systems and the concomitant ubiquity of the network metaphor to represent such phenomena as globalization and social capital, the term has come to problematically suggest flat linear chains, enclosed pipelines and ossified tracks. Educators, points out Frankham (2006), have particular reason for caution when networks are everywhere invoked to represent idealized learning communities that are homogeneous, apolitical and closed in ways that prohibit dissension, discontinuity and difference. ANT-associated writings have explored alternative metaphors of regions and fluid spaces (Mol and Law 1994) to approach the complexity of sociomaterial events and avoid imposing a linear network model on the ineffable and imminent. Some have explored ways of retaining notions of network by refusing pipeline associations and showing diverse shapes and forms that a network can assume. Some networks are provisional and divergent, while others are tightly ordered, stable and prescriptive.

One problem with this network conception is what and where one should focus in conducting research. Miettinen (1999) makes this point in his critique of ANT, arguing that the network ontology is infinite and therefore unworkable for researchers who need to bound a unit of analysis. Indeed, 'cutting the network' (Strathern 1996) has always been deemed a necessary aspect of using ANT in research, but this requires researchers to be explicit about how that enacts the effects of their own research in certain ways. Wherever and whenever one puts boundaries around a particular phenomenon to trace its network relations, there is a danger of both privileging that network and rendering invisible its multiple supports. Critiques of ANT studies have noted their fondness for examining powerful, visible networks, and their tendency to reproduce network participants' views of their reality (Hassard et al. 1999). Representations of networks are themselves concrete, implying the realities to be far more stable and durable than imminent precarious shifting sociomaterial relations ever can be. Familiar issues of reflexivity are no less problematic in ANT accounts, which can objectify networks as something produced solely in the eye of the researcher, and simultaneously forget to paint the researcher's representations into the portrayal of network translations, thereby leaving the entire analysis in control of the researchers. This not only turns a supposedly heterogeneous, symmetrical perspective into a decidedly human-centred one, but also pretends to honour uncertainty and messiness in what is, in effect, a predetermined account.

Hetherington and Law (2000) argue that the metaphor of the network can presume to colonize all dimensions, elements, layers and spaces of a phenomenon, as though everything that exists is drawn somewhere, somehow, into the relentless knots of networks extending infinitely. A network reading potentially 'leaves no room for alterity and allows for nothing to stand outside the relations that it orders through its descriptions of the word' (Hetherington and Law 2000: 128). This problem extends further than colonizing or speaking for marginalized humans and things. The problem is also about dividing space and action according to issues of relation and difference: what becomes connected and mobilized into a network, and what remains different according to that network's terms and relations. What of alterity that is blank, unexpected, novel and ambivalent? What of otherness that lies within or flows across network alignments, that is incoherent or non-representable? These questions warn the ANT analyst from presuming to offer any single account of events, and alert attention to spaces and discontinuities that may be enacted through certain conventional network readings.

Network effects: re-imagining agency and learning

The overriding insight of ANT views of the world is that all objects, as well as all persons, knowledge and locations, are relational *effects*. We may represent individual objects, such as cups, as having particular capabilities, such as holding hot coffee, but this is to miss the practices through which the cup has been gathered materially in space–time as a thing. Thus the teacher is an effect of the timetable that places her in a particular room with particular students, in a class designated as Social Studies, amongst textbooks, computers, class plans and bulletin boards and stacks of graded papers with which she interacts, teaching ideas and readings she has accumulated in particular relationships that have emerged with this year's class of children. In the pedagogical practices of her work, she is a 'knowing location'. In one example, McGregor (2004: 366) traces how the teacher as knowing location is produced in science classrooms through

> the laboratory, with its electricity points, water and gas lines. The Bunsen burners and flasks set up by the technicians, who have also ordered and prepared the necessary chemicals according to the requisition sheet, the textbooks and worksheets that the students are using. Mobilized also are the teacher's experience and education. These are further affected by networks of activity that composed and timetabled the student group in a particular way and allocated the teaching assistants.

These things that act at a distance – buzzer, database, textbooks – are what Latour (1987) originally called *immutable mobiles*. These are only visible within a particular network of relations. They can be silent, ignored, or overridden by other active objects. However, like a ship, they have developed enough solidity to be able to move about and still hold their relations in place. In effect, they function as the delegates of these other networks, extending their power by moving into new geographical spaces and working to translate entities to behave in particular ways. Law and Singleton (2005) explain that whether a thing is more or less abstract (a pedagogical idea compared with an instrument) is not the point. The key feature is how it is identified, how it is made real, in particular networks of historical, cultural, behavioural relations that make it visible. However, immutable mobiles are often not terribly immutable, but break and shift, grow and adapt and mutate as they travel.

Returning to the teacher as a knowing location, what of her agency and subjectivity? She is planning lessons, choosing particular pedagogical approaches, deciding whether to solve the myriad classroom problems that emerge in this way or that. How does ANT avoid casting her as determined and recognize her own force exercised through her pedagogical participation? How does ANT understand the sources and effects of her intentions, her desires, and the meanings she makes of her pedagogical encounters with students? Certain critiques of ANT have accused it of failing to appreciate what is fundamentally human and subjective in flows of action, suggesting that perhaps it ought to modify its stance of radical symmetry to admit that humans are different because they make symbolic meaning of events and exert intentional action (Murdoch 1998). However, ANT's ontology of folding and unfolding networks is incommensurate with any agency/structure dualism. Nor does ANT conceptualize agency as an individuated or collective source of empowerment rooted in conscious intentions that mobilize action. Instead, ANT focuses on the circulating forces that get things done through a network of elements acting upon one another.

> Action is not done under the full control of consciousness; action should rather be felt as a node, a knot, and a conglomerate of many surprising sets of agencies that have to be slowly disentangled. It is this venerable source of uncertainty that we wish to render vivid again in the odd expression of actor-network.
>
> (Latour 2005: 44)

What appears to be the teacher's agency is an assemblage of energy. It is an effect of different forces, including actions, desires, capacities and connections that move through her, as well as the forces exerted through the networks of texts, technologies, built environment, educational prescriptions and so forth that circulate through the teacher's practices. This is not to say that her own actions and desires are simply determined by the network. Rather, these emerge through the myriad translations that are negotiated among all the networks – movements, talk, materials, emotions and discourses – making up the classroom's everyday encounters.

Pondering ANT's utility in overcoming the limitations of intersubjective or humanist conceptions of agency in education, Leander and Lovvorn (2006: 301) warn that 'removing the agency of texts and tools in formalizing movements risks romanticizing the practices as well as the humans in them; focusing uniquely on the texts and tools lapses into naïve formalism or technocentrism'. Agency is directly related to the heterogeneity of actors in networked relations. These are not actors plus fields of forces or contexts, but actants which can only proceed to action by association with others who may surprise or exceed. As McGregor (2004: 367) concludes from her study of teachers in science education, 'knowing is a relational effect where pedagogy is a collective accomplishment and learning a situated activity'.

The network effects that produce immutable mobiles and obligatory passage points are important dynamics in the power relations circumscribing actions. The circulation and effects of these objects and things can assemble powerful centres that accumulate increasingly wider reaches of networks to hold them in place. *Delegation*, the ability to act at a distance through things, is one way that power circulates through a network. How fast these immutable mobiles move, their fidelity or how immutable they really are as they move through diverse networks, and what barriers they encounter or damage they sustain to their internal network relations, are questions worthy of exploration in different interests.

Scale is another important area for consideration in ANT. In fact, as Law and Hetherington (2003) note, if space is performed, if it is an effect of hetero-geneous material relations, then distance is also performed. What makes near and far, here or there, is not a static separation between two points that is travelled by some object. Instead, these concepts of distance are created by relations that are always changing. For instance, we may sit in a chair and feel as though we are still, but that might only be in relation to the room we are in. In relation to the Earth, we are spinning. When multiple points are linked together through actor-networks, the concepts of micro- and macro- do not hold. The teacher planning Tuesday morning's class and the final meeting of the mathematics curriculum developers simply represent different parts of a net-work that has become extended though space as well as time. They do not exist as separate spaces of local and global, as though these are identifiable and distinct regions. Instead, these are scale effects produced through network relations. A series of intricate links runs among the different enactments of, for example, an educational policy, whether visible in OECD (Organisation for Economic Co-operation and Development) documents, school district-wide databases, parent discussions, or a teacher's correction of a student. ANT resists a conception of scale as ontologically distinct layers or regions, and thus helps to penetrate some of the more nuanced circulations of power in practices and knowledge-making. Notions of social structure, ideology, powerful agencies and so forth, in ANT logic, are not overarching 'big' entities that pre-exist the actions they appear to influence. Rather, they are traceable as multifarious webbed nets of local, mediated conduits. While these nets often become stabilized and far-flung in their enactments, they require continual effort to hold together their links, and continual action to come into presence.

As much as network relations are useful to trace these dynamics of delegation, immutable mobiles, obligatory points of passage and scale play, the temptation to collapse all interactions and connections into networks needs to be avoided. While most entities and forces are usefully viewed as effects within an ANT-ish arena, not all relations that contribute to producing these effects will be net-works. There are other types of regions, other kinds of connections, other forms of space and foldings of space that work alongside and through networks (Hetherington and Law 2000). In analysing the enactment of public policy, Singleton (2005) argues that the relative stability of certain networks occurs not through their coherences, but through their incoherences and ambivalences. An overly narrow preoccupation with network relations speaks to a bias that will inevitably banish from sight some of the more interesting or puzzling messiness of educational phenomena. This is not to downplay the importance of under-standing entities and forces as effects. It is to encourage more open and rich exploration of the multiple forms, lines and textures of materials that come together in different ways to produce these effects.

Similarly, learning in ANT logic is not a matter of mental calculation or changes in consciousness. Instead, any changes we might describe as learning, such as new ideas, innovations, changes in behaviour, transformation, emerge through the effects of relational interactions that may be messy and incoherent, and spread across time and space. This conceptualization, described in more detail in chapter seven, offers a way to think about education which steps outside the enculturation project that typifies pedagogies ranging from the emancipatory to the transmissive. Regardless of ideological persuasion or educative purpose, such approaches support education's infliction of some future ideal on present human subjects and activities with the objective of developing learners' potential to become knowledgeable, civic-minded, self-aware, and so forth. However, since ANT views all things as emerging through their interconnections in networks, where their nature and behaviours are never inherent but are produced through continuous interactions and negotiations, an imagined future, if any, would be treated as yet another actor. It would not be simply imposed to shape the present. This is a powerful counter-narrative to the conventional view of developmentalism that dominates the pedagogical gaze, positioning learners in continual deficit and learning activities as preparation for some imagined ideal. ANT's ontology, like all sociomaterial arenas, forces attention on all the work that is too easily swept away by such neat developmental teleologies.

Multiple worlds

Like many others, Law and Singleton (2005) argue that the epistemological issues to do with knowing, or knowing well, are bound up with the ontological question of what exists. What is, and the knowledge of what is, are enacted together. Yet in education there is much emphasis on learning as knowing through (re)presentation of the world 'out-there' to the mind 'in-here'. In conventional enactments, it is often suggested by realists and social constructionists alike that there is one world about which humans can have one or diverse perspectives. This assumption underpins a certain common form for education, and in so doing, enacts what it assumes.

Certain strands of ANT, however, suggest that we do not simply have multiple perspectives, but that we are part of multiple worlds that coexist and overlap, often in the same material spaces. Mol (2002) was one of the first to propose that researchers need to appreciate how different objects and different worlds – multiple ontologies – can be enacted together in the name of one practice. This would include the reality of the account being enacted by the researcher to represent any of these ontologies and their intermeshing. In her study of physicians' diagnoses and treatment approaches for lower-limb atherosclerosis in different locations, such as the pathology laboratory, the radiology department, the surgical theatre, the physician's clinic and so forth, she shows how very different methods and practices were being employed in each environment.

Each was enacted through unique assemblages of instruments, routines and language. In each situation, Mol (2002) concludes, atherosclerosis itself was enacted as a different thing. In the laboratory, it was a slide under a microscope showing a section of artery with thickened intima. In radiology, it was a set of X-ray pictures compared for percentage of lumen loss. In surgery, it was a rubbery piece of theromatous plaque to be surgically removed and discarded. In the physician's office, it was enacted as a disabling condition, with discussions about lifestyle modifications. Each region of practice, with its own reality and distinct enactment of atherosclerosis, had to communicate with one another and with the patient, and they had to somehow create passages for the patient from one region to the next. How can one transcendent medical concept provide valid unity to these different things? Even something represented in a canon of medical knowledge is yet another enactment, another different thing. Mol (2002) argues that these examples illustrate multiple (coexisting) ontologies. She suggests that the practical problem is one of patching together the different things to achieve some coherence in order that a medical intervention can be determined.

In analysing Mol's work and its implications, Law (2004b: 55) writes:

> And this is where the question of difference, of multiplicity, raises its head: when medicine talks of lower-limb atherosclerosis and tries to diagnose and treat it, in practice *at least half a dozen different method assemblages* are implicated. And the relations between these are uncertain, sometimes vague, difficult, and contradictory. [. . .] We are not dealing with different and possibly flawed perspectives on the *same* object. Rather we are dealing with *different objects produced in different method assemblages.* Those objects overlap, yes. Indeed, that is what all the trouble is about: trying to make sure they overlap in productive ways.

Imagine the educational implications of this. For example, negotiations of educational curriculum, pedagogy or policy among wide ranging stakeholders could be conceived as fragile enrolments and assemblages of multiple ontologies, rather than multiple perspectives framed within a single ontology. The problem of difference in knowledges of the same thing across different regions is not particularly new. But to acknowledge different *worlds* being enacted simultaneously in any negotiation, whether educational policy or teaching–learning transactions, as far more than just different *views* of a common world, is to open important questions about the complexity of communication – and especially about what to do. Should different worlds be mediated? Adjudicated? Combined? Juxtaposed? The dynamics of difference, its problems and its enactments, become increasingly important to understand as globalizing production processes attempt to enforce universal standards of knowledge (definitions, competencies, practices, league tables) in vastly different circumstances, where they are performed alongside competing knowledges.

For example, in one study of agricultural extension, traditionally an important area of adult education, Coughenour (2003) examined the introduction of no-tillage practices among US farmers. Such developments are often approached through a model of external agencies imposing innovative technological knowledge on farmers. In this case, Coughenour (2003) traced the contestations among the knowledge networks of local indigenous farmers, farm advisors, agricultural scientists and farm supply representatives. The process was lengthy and potentially fragile, a case of coalitions gradually forming through the discovery and translation of certain common goals as well as some congruence in the technological developments of the separate innovation networks. The process was also enhanced by extending the local network through extra-local linkages that enrolled actors and mobilized networks well beyond those in the same region, while maintaining the power of the immediate networks and the importance of individual participants as innovators. Network participants – not just farmers, but scientists and everyone else involved – eventually had to allow themselves to become translated into new relationships between farming and soils. These new relations also translated their former roles and reputations as farmers or professionals. In these ways, the new no-till cropping practices developed through reconstruction of both indigenous and professional knowledges. This entailed neither a blending of the two nor a colonializing attempt by one to dominate the other, but a patching together of different ontologies.

Clearly, as ANT explorations have shown, knowledge cannot be viewed simply as coherent, transcendent, generalizable and unproblematic. These studies also show that knowledge and the real emerge together. The thing is not separate from the knowing that establishes it as a thing. Furthermore, a thing can be enacted through multiple knowings or ontologies that coexist, in a contentious and discontinuous dynamic. This has implications for education and educational research. Fountain (1999: 355), for one, adopts an ANT approach to challenge conventional science education that

> privileges detached, scientific reasoning [and] will fail to recognize the complex interpenetration of the various factors which make up these issues. It will also mean taking a political position which often denies the involvement, interests, and complicity of science in the issue in question.

In education, conflicting powerful practices from government, industry, parents, students and professionals entangle with every major thing, from what counts as scientific knowledge, to methods of reading instruction or purposes for a university education. It is commonplace to assume the problem to be one of managing these diverse perspectives or even reconciling them. The recent ANT switch to understand practices as multiple simultaneous ontologies opens a rich approach to appreciating the fundamental differences afoot, and for patching them together without attempting to impose false coherence.

Conclusion

In its insistence on attending to these minute interactions, the precise ways in which they occur as well as their effects, ANT challenges many assumptions underpinning certain educational conceptions of development and learning, agency, identity, knowledge and teaching, policy and practice. ANT's analyses make visible the rich assortments of mundane materials at play in events and how they are connected. ANT's examination of the different processes and moments at work in translation, in particular, extends beyond a simple recognition that artefacts and humans are connected in social and cognitive activity. It also does not take contradiction as the fundamental relationship from which change arises. In Latour's (1999: 17) summation, ANT's main contribution is to 'transform the social from what was a surface, a territory, a province of reality, into a circulation, where time and space are understood to result from particular interactions of things'. ANT's conception of symmetry unlocks a preoccupation with the human, the intersubjective and the meaning, and refuses a rigid separation between the material and immaterial, human and non-human. In tracing what things do and how they came to be gathered, ANT offers a method for picking apart assumptions about categories and structures in education, some of which appear to exert power across far-flung distances and temporal periods. ANT's notion of immutable mobiles offers an approach to understand and challenge the strategies of powerful networks that work to authorize, control, compel and measure practices and knowledge. For analysing politics and policy in educational research, Nespor (2002: 376) argues that ANT raises important questions about 'how and in what forms people, representations and artefacts move, how they are combined, where they get accumulated, and what happens when they are hooked up with other networks already in motion'. ANT analyses not only perform the shifting locus of power, how different actors are dominant at different times within different networks, but also show the nuances and ambivalences within this performance of power. In attempting to enrol and mobilize ANT into educational research, we would expect parts of that research to become translated into something other than it now mostly is. There is the presumption that this other would also be better, because of, rather than despite, the messiness it enacts. Obviously any such translation is incomplete and fragile.

Note

1   This chapter presents material that is more fully explicated and developed in Fenwick and Edwards (2010).

Chapter 7

Actor-network theory in educational research

Imagine [. . .] a university student working in a dormitory room on a physics problem [. . .] The space of the classroom is extended into the student's residence, and the student's out-of-school time is synchronized not just with the professor's pacing of course materials, but also to an institutional calendar, which organizes 'learning' into arbitrary units of time like semesters, and semesters into multi-year programmes of study. There are also links between the space–time of the problem-solving and anticipated evaluated events elsewhere in the future. At the same time, insofar as the problem solving is part of a 'course', there are connections to previous physics or math courses the student has taken where similar problem forms, tasks, and concepts were encountered. There are also connections to disciplinary sites where 'physics problems' are constructed and warranted [. . .] and to physics courses around the world where the same or isomorphic problems are assigned [. . .] The physics problem is not so much an 'articulated' moment as a moving articulation, the translation of a succession of place-makings, enrolments, decontextualization and recontextualization, temporally unfolding from secondary school onward.

(Nespor 2003: 94–95)

It may be fair to say that educational researchers did not rush to embrace actor-network theory (ANT) when it was first being taken up more widely in organizational studies and other studies of professional practice. In its first educational uptake, ANT studies were published by a few science educators as well as by researchers tracing technology innovations in education. This is perhaps not surprising, given ANT's early focus on the assemblage of scientific knowledge and innovation practices (Latour and Woolgar 1979) and its roots in science and technology studies. Perhaps some educators found it difficult to connect with a theory whose constructs of actant, network, translation and intermediaries may sound too mechanistic for questions of learning, meaning and humanity. Nor has ANT tended to align itself with education. The major European association devoted to science and technology studies since 1981 did not include a stream for education until 2010 (EASST 2010).

However, with the publication of some major works in education using ANT (e.g. Nespor 1994; Verran 2001) and the emergence of feminist writings that opened out ANT approaches to address multiplicity, ambivalence, otherness and equity (e.g. Mol 2002; Singleton 2005), more educational researchers have turned to ANT's resources (Fenwick and Edwards 2010). These are used selectively, eclectically and with wide variation. They illuminate aspects of educational problems and generate strategies for ways forward in education.

In this chapter, we outline the major elements of ANT's conceptions that appear to have inspired educational researchers, as well as the methodologies that they have found useful. The first section focuses on how educators have examined materiality and materializing processes drawing from ANT, particularly in terms of how these processes help to configure educational actors, subjectivities and knowledge. The second section turns to educational policy and politics, showing where researchers have used ANT sensibilities to analyse policy as assemblages, and to highlight strategies for intervention and influence. The third part presents conceptions of learning and change that educators have proposed in working with and through ANT ideas. The final section highlights specific aspects of method in ANT research, to which educational researchers have made important contributions.

Materiality and materializing processes in education

One of the most important contributions of ANT to educational analysis has been to foreground the significance of materiality in educational processes. With their tendency to focus on the human, intersubjective, interpretive, discursive and meaning-centred, educational analyses rarely attend to the behaviour of things that are so ubiquitous in all aspects of educational activity. While all sociomaterial theories as a whole attend to the material relations that interpenetrate the social, ANT is particularly provocative with its insistence not that non-human entities are simply important, but that they are *equivalent* in importance to human elements in educational transactions.

A recent uptake of ANT's view of materiality in education is by Sørensen (2009). She deplores a history of educational research that she claims virtually ignores things – or, more important, materiality and material relations – in ways that ensure a blindness to critical aspects of patterns we are trying to discern in education. As she explains it, ANT can help move beyond simple acknowledgement of physical objects to analyse materiality as a distributed effect, among both physical presences and social entities.

> [W]e may understand materiality as *the formed pattern in which a particular entity takes part and which allows it to relate in particular ways to (an)other particular entity(ies)*. With this definition, we can talk about the materiality of materials as well as about the materiality of social entities. Materiality is, notably, not an essential property of an entity, but a distributed effect.
>
> (Sørensen 2007: 10; italics in original)

In examining precisely how and why linkages came to be among human and non-human elements in order to produce something that appears to be an entity – whether a playground, a blackboard, a curriculum policy, or an activity such as grading student papers – ANT shows how the entity is a hybrid assemblage of heterogeneous materials. Further, as Sørensen stresses, this assemblage or pattern is fundamentally material in ways that define its internal relations among the parts, its possibilities, and its overall effects. Not only are the material linkages traceable, but so also are the politics through which their various nodes of connection (or partial connection) are negotiated and sustained, or interrupted, reconfigured or even dissolved. Agency, in this view, as explained in chapter six, can be understood as distributed. As a force of flows, agency is not an essential property of one actor but emerges through micro-negotiations at the various nodes connecting entities. Landri (2007) argues that these attachments are woven with emotion, even passion – not driven by human sources, but emerging as effects of the network negotiations in materialities of learning. His research focuses on the materializing of learning and knowledge in virtual and disembodied spaces of e-learning, where emotion is inseparable from knowing. This focus on distributed and relational materiality potentially opens a wider-angled view of educational processes than the resources offered by social constructionism or the post-structural analysis of discursive practices.

For example, we might return to McGregor's (2004) description of a teacher as a material effect, mentioned in chapter six. From an ANT perspective, what appears to be the teacher's agency is an effect of different forces, including actions, desires, capacities and connections that move through her, as well as the forces exerted by the texts and technologies in all educational encounters. Yet, while networks and other flows circulate through the teacher's practices, her own actions, desires and so on are not determined by the network, but emerge through the myriad translations that are negotiated among all the movements, talk, materials, emotions and discourses making up the classroom's everyday encounters. Agency is directly related to the heterogeneity of actors in networked relations. Within such a view, it no longer makes sense to target educational reform upon (re)training the individual teacher and her practices alone. Instead, researchers can attempt to disentangle the network(s) of connections and other relations that together produce particular effects in educational innovation, classroom activity or children's engagement and learning.

Another aspect of ANT's approach to tracing materiality that has inspired educators is its attention to the material details that comprise the most mundane everyday activities. The injunction to look critically at the taken-for-granted is difficult for many to undertake – where to begin? Gough (2004: 258) shows how ANT approaches can reveal the 'banal structures and simplistic textual practices' of education. He suggests that we should start by unpacking mundane, everyday tasks to trace the seemingly infinite interconnectivities among things and people that hold together any action in a particular place and moment. Making a cup of coffee, for example, connects water from a tap pipelined to a reservoir miles away, to an electric kettle plugged into a plastic plate on a tiled wall into a complex grid and flow of electric power, poured into a coffee pot holding together bits of plastic, glass, screws, then to an aluminium mug with Starbucks stamped on it, attached to an arm then lifted to a mouth containing a new dental crown [. . .] and so on. Gough draws upon Angus *et al.* (2001: 195), who suggested the need for a 'cyborg pedagogy', engaging students in mapping such myriad details 'between heres and theres, between humans, between humans and non-humans, between non-humans and non-humans'.

Another science educator mentioned in chapter six, Fountain (1999: 355), contends that with these approaches ANT moves education 'from a rhetoric of conclusions towards a rhetoric of contentions'. ANT challenges conventional science curriculum that presents received explanations, and instead advocates children's experimentation with the mundane to examine and intervene in the complex interpenetration of the various factors that make up these explanations and science's interests in sustaining them. Fountain suggests a range of instructional approaches integrating ANT, such as having children map the associations that are employed to produce and to represent a particular scientific explanation, and then to examine what associations in an educational context enable or constrain particular points of view. Learners can trace what and who have been mobilized to uphold particular concepts, but also the associations that do not appear, the things that are not mentioned or are discredited, the things that are not yet imagined but may be at work.

These educational researchers argue for adopting ANT's close attention to the material connections which bring about and hold together events, people and ideas. Their work shows how ANT's approaches can assist in two key activities for educational practice and for research. One is in interrupting or deconstructing *what is*, to ascertain the minute connections and the ongoing work (as well as complicity, negotiations and translations occurring at these connections) holding it together. This enables not only understanding authoritative knowledge and entrenched practice, but also identifying the most opportune points for intervention, dissolution or transformation. This approach has been followed to suggest alternative approaches to pedagogy and curriculum-making, as in the Gough and Fountain examples here, as well as in activities of educational assessment (Fenwick 2009b). The other is in following new unfolding directions, so as to appreciate the dynamics and energies that can perform the possible, and to participate in bringing it forth.

Researching educational policy and politics

While there is ongoing debate about the extent to which ANT can speak to the political, educational researchers have shown its value in many questions of educational politics, power relations and policy. ANT's sensibility focuses upon the politics of negotiation occurring at each connection of any assemblage. ANT helps show how a confluence of practices can be aligned together and mobilized to order far-flung materials, ideas and desires, as in initiatives for educational accountability (Fenwick 2011). An example of this can be seen in standardized tests of student achievement. Increasingly mandated across states and provinces in North America, such tests help to link together massive networks through the movement of the test as an immutable mobile. Nespor (2002) explains how the fixed items of such tests work to translate complex learning practices into limited categories, the calculation of which translates year-long and vastly different educational processes around the state into numeric scores. Teachers are bypassed as mediators of pedagogy and knowledge, and students are directly enrolled into subject matter that has been translated into the test's limited forms of knowledge. Because the stakes are high in the calculative process (schools scoring less than a certain percentage lose their accreditation), Nespor shows that the test mobilizes a whole series of events and people to align with its forms. Administrators force curricula to conform to the test's demands, teachers drill classes in test preparation, remedial classes are arranged to improve students' test achievement, and fear is mobilized among all. The result is a

> funnelling, hierarchical network in which the state becomes a centre of accumulation collecting standardized representations of all the students in its political borders. The state can then summarize and compare students as a class, and more importantly speak for and act upon them.
>
> (Nespor 2002: 375)

In these extended networks of evaluation, certain kinds of materials and people are assembled and translated to become aligned with the standardized form, while others, such as the testers, supervisors and the state, are not. However, these actors also are effects of network processes. They are combined with other forms, representations and artefacts. They are 'hooked up' with other networks already on the move: 'historically and geographically stretched out in materially heterogeneous networks that overlap and interact with one another' (Nespor 2002: 376).

As Latour (2005) points out, a war room can command and control anything only as long as it maintains connection with distributed sites of action through continuous transport of information. Evaluation and accountability 'is made only of movements, which are woven by the constant circulation of documents, stories, accounts, goods and passions' (Latour 2005: 179). What the ANT perspective contributes is much greater focus on the objects and texts that mediate these evaluative processes, and the diverse and unpredictable negotiations that occur as these things intermingle with teachers and learners, even become part of them, in everyday micro-interactions. For Nespor (2002), this insight gives rise to important questions for educational policy research. Is it practical, or politically effective, to segregate educational issues from the other materials and networks (community, housing, health, etc.) tied to them? And

how can actors mobilize politically effective networks, mindful of the importance of artefacts in directing these networks, to engage school change issues
such as standardization?

Given the diverse forms proliferated through standards in practice, ANT also
helps illuminate the multiple heterogeneous possibilities embedded *within*
any formal iteration of educational standards that are inscribed in these texts,
these immutable mobiles. In practice, these possibilities emerge and jostle in
unexpected ways. The possibilities emerge as different elements are introduced
into practices of standards development and their usage, different material
limitations and cultural expectations contribute to and resist the ideas contained
within written standards, and as one set of written standards collaborates with
other forms of standards at play in any region of educational practice. Thus what
may be characterized in certain analyses as local resistance to standards is viewed
by ANT as one visible instantiation of a whole series of possibilities and transgressions. ANT shows that these are not added to the list of standards by particular people, but hetereogeneity is contained within the standards themselves.
The mobile is not so immutable as it appears, but is capable of multiple unfold-
ings. Every artefact at play embeds so many mappings of memory, association
and performativity that immutability is impossible. In this way, ANT reveals
the *uncertainty of standards* as both rhetorical positionings and as bases for judgement and governance of educational activity (Fenwick 2010a).

A persisting issue in educational policy research concerns the gap between
official and local enactments of policy, and the proliferation of unintended
consequences. In studies focused on the actual local activities and articulations
stimulated by educational policy, ANT slows down the analysis to attend to the
particulars at play in policy enactment. One is Koyama's (2009) study of the
appropriation of the US policy 'No Child Left Behind' (NCLB) in the New
York City District. She traces the conflicting and diffused material linkages
and disjunctures prompted by NCLB among the district administrators, public
schools, city government, and a for-profit 'supplemental educational services'
(SES) provider legitimated by NCLB's provisions. In one example, Koyama
shows how the enrolment forms through which qualified students could obtain
additional tutoring assistance became important mediators of political action.
These forms allowed some and excluded other students, accounted for billable
service by the for-profit SES provider, and guaranteed sufficient overall student
enrolment numbers to transfer funds from the school district to the SES
provider. Naturally, the forms became a focal point for school administrators'
frustration at the flow of funds from basic school needs to for-profit providers.
The forms were also a symbol for the problematic qualifying process through
which students who received free lunch were eligible for tutoring help, sometimes regardless of their academic need. School administrators began restricting
the number of enrolment forms made available to parent coordinators of the
tutoring programmes, suspecting improper distribution of the forms. The for-
profit provider complained at decreasing enrolments and lost revenue. Individual

parents complained that they were unable to enrol their child in the tutoring services. Some parent coordinators began simply to photocopy more forms to meet the demand. Further parental outcry erupted when the school refused to accept the 'counterfeit' forms, which also worked to prevent qualified students from accessing the programmes that NCLB was intended to provide in the first place. Koyama (2009) calls this a 'vertical' analysis of the particular material linkages through which educational policy actually accomplishes activity across multiple levels – government, schooling and commercial entities. This ANT-inspired analysis reveals how elements come together in shifting networks, how these elements exert power in different ways as local agents take practical action to make sense of their particular shifting circumstances, and how the resulting assemblages and effects produce unintended consequences.

Standards and accountability are also key issues in educational policy that have been tackled through ANT readings. Mulcahy (1999, 2007), for instance, has analysed competency standards prescribed in Australia for teaching practice. In her study of cookery teachers in the classroom, Mulcahy (1999) identifies various forms of standards that are at work simultaneously: national industry standards, local standards of adaptation to available equipment and tastes, teachers' own complex, embodied standards of good cooking and teaching practice, and so forth. She shows that each of these creates a different world, a different ontological form, that practitioners learn to inhabit and juggle. For example, in the world of enacting official teaching standards, policy exists in text circulating through practices of consultation, revision, political consensus-seeking and approvals. In school settings, standards for teaching and learning exist as embodied, messy interactions, where students are significant contributors. The textual representations and the messy embodied interactions coexist in practice as different ontological forms. They jostle in continuous tension in all settings, including classrooms and schools, boardrooms, town halls, parent meetings and so forth.

Another area of jostling and continuous tensions in educational policy involves issues of equity, difference and inclusion: from widening access and participation of learners in educational opportunities, to addressing the inequities and exclusions perpetuated by the very organisation of schooling. Educational researchers have noted the tendency of some ANT studies to focus on 'big' actor-networks such as major policy initiatives, which can blind the analyst to activities and actors relegated to the margins. ANT studies historically have not taken up issues of social justice or of inequities produced through constructions of gender, race, ableism, etc. This is partly because ANT would view such constructions as effects of particular orderings and flows of material rather than as anterior structures. In this way, some educational researchers, such as Waltz (2006), have shown just how human and non-human materials produce these effects, such as gendered forms of play and subjects in the material activities of a school playground. Educators are also starting to work with ANT to trace and name the complex politics, non-coherences, stereotypes, etc. that operate to create oppression. One helpful example is offered by Hunter and Swan (2007). They are interested in what is actually achieved through diversity and equity work in the learning and skills sector in England. They explore the everyday routines of diversity workers, who they refer to as marginalized actors, within networks of contradictory equity policies and agendas, resources, learning materials and educational expectations. Specifically, they follow one worker, Iopia, an African-Caribbean woman who teaches basic skills in an English prison. They focus on Iopia's micro-strategies and achievements in her day-to-day work. What they illuminate is the multiple positionings that Iopia takes up. She is at once marginalized and racialized in the organizational networks, enrolled in a limited network *of* diversity while at the same time being central to a new network *for* diversity. This is a network that is both repressed and made powerful by narrow, decontextualized notions of diversity. The new network is sustained by non-human things that Iopia has enrolled, and that create types of agency and resources that might paradoxically be seen as racist. For Hunter and Swan's (2007) purposes, the study makes visible the complex multiplicities and contradictions of diversity as it is enacted in education, as well as the precarious movements and identity oscillations of educators who struggle to achieve particular agendas within this multiplicity.

These differences and their tensions in educational policy enactments pro-duce dynamic openings, folds and uncharted spaces. To reconcile these different ontological forms, even if possible, would create an undesirable closure. The most generative way forward is to acknowledge the differences, and to hold open the tensions among them.

What constitutes learning and change

ANT is not a theory of learning and does not identify learning as an individual human attribute. Rather, it explores how knowledge is generated and spread through assemblages and enactments. Educational researchers have found that an ANT reading can denaturalize notions of learning as a solely human or mentalist phenomenon. This is because materials, technologies and natural forces are closely woven into development of any form of knowledge, its manifestation in activity and decisions, and its recognition as valuable or not. Learning through an ANT analysis therefore can be viewed as a distributed effect, something that continually emerges through negotiations and struggles at myriad nodes of possible connections between human and non-human elements. In researching learning processes in higher education from an ANT perspective, Fox (2005) writes about learning as struggle. For him, competence or knowledge is not a latent attribute of any one element or individual, but a property of some actions rather than others as a network becomes enacted into being. The process of enactment, this interplay of force relations among technology, things and changes in knowledge at every point in the network, is the continuing struggle of learning. Teaching is implicated in these networks

and struggles, not as independent processes, factors or variables, but as inter-
ruptions and entanglings that help to animate heterogeneous assemblages of
people, knowledge, objects and spaces in motion.

In his by now classic study examining teaching and learning in undergraduate
studies in physics and management in an American university, Nespor (1994)
draws upon ANT to compare how the space–time organization of students
influences knowing and knowledge generation, as well as subjectivity. For
Nespor, these are effects that emerge through the networks and networking
practices in which people enrol and the translations to which they are subject.
The physics students he studied followed a traditional cohort-based, linear,
rigidly sequenced set of courses. For them, space and time were compressed, as
they spent all their time together working in groups long into the night. By
contrast, the management students followed a modular programme with many
electives, and engaged in a diverse set of networks across the business school, as
well as with employers with whom the school was linked. In others words,
'choice' was mobilized as a capacity for management students to develop in a
way in which was not the case for the physics students. Thus, 'instead of having
their spatial and temporal trajectories shaped by programme requirements,
students organized the space–time relations among their courses. Schedules
were composed for reasons unconnected with the substance of the courses'
(Nespor 1994: 89).

Two enactments of universities are at play here. One enacts universities
reproducing themselves through the disciplines. The second enacts universities
within the network of the economy and the forms of knowledge and subjectivity required. It may be no historical accident that the latter has grown in
significance as a greater range of professional education has entered the university, thereby reframing its external relations with professional groups,
employers, etc., and the internal relations with its weakly framed disciplinary
knowledge base. This is suggestive of the different networks that have been
attempting to enrol university education with specific effects. Nespor contrasts
the isolated, almost bunker-like spaces of the physics building with the newer,
lighter, more open spaces of the business school, showing how subjectivities are
influenced through the spaces to be utilized as well as the utilization of those
spaces. 'Unlike the austere physics building, the business school wasn't geared
solely to academic or scholarly activity [. . .] [The] public interior space was
organized in large part to simulate corporate spaces and function as a stage for
the display of sociability' (Nespor 1994: 111).

Nespor shows how a strong disciplinary identity was mobilized for and by
the physics students, but it would seem to be somewhat insular and introverted.
They primarily related to each other in dense, tightly bound networks. By
contrast, the looser organization of space and time associated with the modular,
more broadly networked management programme appeared to mobilize students to be more active and enterprising. The students were more concerned
with management practices in employment than with the academic understand-

ing of management; learning *to be* a manager was more important than learning *about* management. However, the situation may be somewhat more complex, as the overall organization of space and time emphasized the public performance of the management students, their presentational skills and dress, precisely the capabilities they required to mobilize themselves as managers in the employ- ment market. Part of the teaching and learning of management therefore might be said to mobilize and translate an employability or enterprising rather than disciplinary subjectivity.

Another example is provided by Verran (2001), who explored Nigerian students' engagement with concepts of Western science being taught in their classrooms. In her work with these Yoruba children, she shows that while the children were grounded in a Yoruba metaphysical logic, they were expected in the school curricula to reason through Western assumptions about what numbers represent and how they can be manipulated (in terms of measuring volume, quantities, distance, calculating changes in matter and so forth). In contrast, Yoruba understandings begin with the particular sort of matter, and generate a unit appropriate to quantify that matter in the here-and-now. Obviously an important political issue here relates to colonial education and indigenous knowledge. But further, what surprised Verran was finding that Yoruba children not only learned to work within these two non-coherent and profoundly different worlds of working and thinking with the same objects, but that they could work across both accounts of real-ness, choosing one or the other, or juggling both simultaneously. They literally were juggling different ontologies, a form of enactment that Verran (2007: 34–5) calls 'being-ontics':

> Recognizing and being open and explicit about the possibility and nature of interrupting and connecting at a level of cognition that very few people are aware of, we are working at the level of entities' existence or being- ontics. It is about learning to manage knowing along with doubt; weaning oneself from certainty that is allowed by working within just one meta- physical frame. It implies recognizing that reality can be done in this way or that, through this series of gestures, words, and material arrangements, or an alternative set.

This learning to interrupt the very structures of knowledge, to recognize multiple ways of enacting reality, and to even manoeuvre among these different realities is one of the challenges for teaching and learning opened by ANT approaches. The leap away from thinking about entities to understanding that, as Verran (2007: 38) describes it:

> All entities lie suspended between enactments of their possibilities. Entities lurk or loom in the interstices between the repetitions by which they are done. The relationalities through which they exist are external to their being 'clotted' entities. That is how all entities express relationalities; how

entities (actors or actants) are networks; and how networks of relations are entities.

Educators have found ANT also useful in developing critical approaches to teaching and learning that move beyond normative assertions. In one project to articulate a critical sociology of numeracy for the teaching of mathematics, Yasukawa (2003) reveals the ways in which different goals and interests of people, as well as intended purposes of technologies, objects and claims, such as mathematical theorems, penetrate and transform one another. ANT helps trace the practices through which particular mathematical knowledge, such as probability theory, becomes inscribed and mobilized. This provides openings for transgressions to shift existing power relations in numeracy.

> I offer a proposition that if we were to take a radical (or extremist?) view that being numerate means not just having a critical understanding of mathematics, but using that understanding for some form of social action; a framework such as ANT is a resource for numeracy. ANT allows us to focus on how existing interests are translated into something different as a result of interactions across a network of human and non-human actors, including mathematics.
>
> (Yasukawa 2003: 29–30)

In relation to schools and classrooms, Roth (1996: 180) conducted a similar sort of examination to unpack knowledge production and circulation in an elementary science class through the role played by things:

> Science classroom communities are characterized by their knowledge, that is, (a) the material, social, and conceptual resources available to the activities of individual members working alone or collaboratively; and (b) the common, embodied laboratory and discourse practices. By investigating how these different types of knowledge (simple facts, tool-related practices, and intellectual practices) diffuse throughout a classroom and come to be recognized as shared by the students, one can, through this examination of Grade 4–5 children studying an engineering unit, provide empirical evidence for understanding the distributed and situated nature of knowing and learning in school settings.

Roth's study is particularly complex in illustrating at least three levels of knowledge-making that are occurring. There is the ongoing knowledge-in-use of everyday classroom practice, alongside the knowledge generation that each child is being encouraged to develop as an outcome of participation in the pedagogical activities of the classroom network. There is also the researcher's knowledge generation produced from interaction with these networks. Roth discusses the everyday challenges of studying a classroom with a commitment to including all actors and nodes being translated in the various networks, as well as their simultaneous membership within multiple networks.

Roth's team used video to record the children's activities, and directing the focus of those cameras involved a careful consideration made each day of who, what, where, when and how to videotape:

> I wanted to collect data that (a) documented practices (e.g., discourse, tool use, problem solving) and resources (e.g., tools, products of children's work, concepts implemented); (b) showed the same students over longer periods of time; (c) represented a broad range of student abilities, interests, and attitudes; and (d) refuted or supported emerging hypotheses about shared resources and practices in an elementary science classroom.
>
> (Roth 1996: 192)

The class was learning triangle principles of engineering by creating structures. Among the many materials being employed, Roth became interested in how glue guns began to focus the activity. At first there was just one glue gun and one student who knew how to use it. Students used other means to fix joints in their structures, or asked the 'expert' to do some gluing for them. It was four weeks before another student brought a glue gun, despite the evidence that the glued joints were more stable and durable than joints held with pins or tape. Quickly following that, glue guns began to appear as more students brought them, and decided to learn gluing practices. The proliferation of glue guns necessitated reorganizing the classroom space to accommodate new groupings of students, the need for electric plugs, safety measures and containment of glue mess. A range of gluing practices developed as the students solved new problems. Hot glue began to circumscribe the projects as it became ubiquitous, to the point where students were unsuccessfully trying to use it on materials like spaghetti, or solving structural problems by simply using glue on available materials, rather than the triangle formulas that the activity was supposed to teach in the first place.

Overall, Roth's research showed that the knowledge emergence – in this case, technological invention and new cultural norms learned and further developed by the children – occurred through a series of mundane translations with things. The network was created because it could sustain and propagate accomplishments that were desired by all the participants. The glue gun became the dominant technology because it was flexible enough to satisfy students' various needs (for strong joints, faster assembly or more aesthetic product) and could bring together all other necessary entities (glue sticks, power outlets, pedagogy, etc.).

Method and mess in ANT research

> In practice research needs to be messy and heterogeneous. It needs to be messy and heterogeneous because that is the way it – research – actually is.

And also, and more importantly it needs to be messy because that is the way the largest part of the world is: messy, unknowable in a regular and routinized way. Unknowable, therefore, in ways that are definite or coherent.

(Law 2007: 596–7)

Studies like Roth's are useful examples for those who want to know how to 'do' research with an ANT sensibility, especially as it is an arena where researchers are expected to show ANT rather than to write about it. Importantly, ANT does not provide a method. It is more about showing the effects of asking particular kinds of questions. It also cautions against any research approach that attempts to smooth out the mess, to categorize patterns or themes, or to apply predetermined abstractions to complex phenomena such as social structures or big concepts. Some have used an ANT approach to trace minute details through which particular assemblages come into being, or become extended, reconfigured or disjunctured. This approach tries to 'follow the actors' without either becoming lost in endless networks, or 'othering' important rivulets and lumpy messes that may be overlooked or dismissed (Fenwick and Edwards 2010). At the same time, ANT commentators struggle to remain alertly reflexive, to avoid rendering complexities and ambiguities as some sort of networked totality made transparent within the calculating eye of the researcher.

To find a focus for research, ANT-inspired educational studies suggest a number of starting points. One is to choose a site and just sit in it for a while or wander about in it, watching, listening, thinking, perhaps talking with people in the site, until something of interest emerges. Some researchers, such as Roth (1996), wait and watch for a 'tracer' to emerge, an object (tool, idea, text, etc.) that appears to move and organize activity throughout the site. Or one could follow a device across time, as Nespor (2010) does in his study of interactive video and how it was implicated in educational change. Some choose a device or text that appears to be exercising particular force in transforming practices and beliefs, such as Hamilton (2009) in her studies of the work performed by the individual learning plan in literacy education. Others look for a space where various flows appear to converge in a way that orders whole systems, such as Clarke (2002) in her study of the proliferation of new literacy policies, or Fenwick (2010b) in her examination of a province-wide educational reform for school improvement through teacher-directed inquiry projects.

To conduct their research, educational researchers working with ANT concepts gather information in various ways. Most utilize some form of field observation following well known ethnographic and ethnomethodological approaches: immersion in the site, focused observation of particular events or time periods, systematic note-taking in real-time and/or video-recording of action, collection of documents and artefacts, and site conversations with participants, perhaps audio-recorded and transcribed. Interviews with participants may have them narrate exactly how they perform the mundane minutiae of taken-for-granted practices, and their reasons for making small choices. For example, in a 'double' interview, a participant describes moment-by-moment instructions that someone would need in order to act, undetected, as that participant's 'double' in the everyday activities and communities in which the participant moves. These instructions can reveal not only critical sociomaterial connectivities and disjunctures negotiated in everyday practices and learning, but also the normative glue underpinning these practices. Some researchers combine field observation with analysis of relevant policy documents. More rarely, others such as Mulcahy (2007) have worked entirely from interviews, analysing the diverse networks that can be inferred in the discourses and narratives expressed by people. Latour (1999: 20) has emphasized that in talking with human participants, the focus is upon understanding what things and people do, not what they mean: 'actors know what they do and we have to learn from them not only what they do, but how and why they do it'.

The point is to trace complexity and heterogeneity, but also to escape the tendency to homogenize and unify. One way to proceed, suggested by Law (2004a, 2004b), is to 'look down'. Looking down involves focusing on specific material details. It is 'a concern with the sensuous materiality of practice and the scale-destabilizing implications of this materiality' (Law 2004a: 21). For the researcher, 'there is no distinction between the individual and the environment. There are no natural, pre-given boundaries. Instead there is blurring. Everything is connected and contained within everything else. There are, indeed, no limits' (Law 2004a: 23; emphasis in original). Links between things are examined as 'uncertain, contingent, to be explored, and are not given in a general logic of emergence' (Law 2004a: 25). He contrasts this 'baroque' approach with a 'romantic' sensibility, using a distinction proposed by Kwa (2002). A romantic approach 'looks up', trying to achieve an overview and pattern for the whole. It tends to abstraction, treating natural and social entities with the same analytical vocabulary in ways that homogenize and control as it seeks coherence. Law notes that some early ANT studies fell into this tendency to abstraction and looking up. However, a looking-down approach accepts non-coherence and lack of closure. It accepts the problem that complexity cannot possibly be modelled and explicitly represented as a whole without erasing the very contours that enact the complex.

In a looking-up view of context in educational research, for example, we may carefully describe characteristics and various influences (social, economic, cultural, etc.) of a rural or urban region, a school, workplace, community event or college classroom. However, such descriptions abstract the continual contingency and blurrings of people, action, learning and things. In their study of how literacy practices produce and organize space–time, Leander and Lovvorn (2006) set out to interrupt such conceptions of learning contexts. The ANT approach, they argue, helps them focus on what texts *do* in different networks rather than what they *mean* in different contexts, which helps avoid a 'particular myopia in literacy studies of focusing on isolated texts or even textual practices' (Leander and Lovvorn 2006: 292). Their study follows the engagements of one boy, Brian, in what the researchers call three different 'literacy networks'. Two of these literacy networks are at school, and one is a video game that he plays at home. Most of their study traces the moment-to-moment linkages among parts of boy and game. The researchers watch him closely, talking to him about the moves he makes, the objects he uses and the objects that act upon him, and noting what is produced through these interactions. This is what Leander and Lovvorn (2006) call a 'prepositional approach', seeking to spy the relations among actants – beyond, behind, before, between, backward, forward, in, on – as worked out in circulations.

For educational research, this is an important contribution of a looking-down approach to gathering information. It can open conceptual black boxes, such as literacy, access, teaching and learning, to examine how these phenomena actually, and often surprisingly, emerge in real-time among a whole series of heterogeneous relations. Barab *et al*. (2001) complain that learning, for example, is conventionally analysed post-activity, reinforcing received notions about what learning is and how it emerges. They created an ANT-based approach to focus instead upon what they call 'knowing in the making' in classrooms. Their method for gathering information is developed in painstaking detail, complete with suggested templates for researchers' records and technological means for graphically representing the networks that appear. For them, naturalistic observation is central. Human observers provide important insights into the group dynamics, and the many simultaneous interactions among people, resources and environmental elements. In addition, videotaping provides the necessary historical record to supplement this 'real-time, real-place observation' (Barab *et al*. 2001: 73). This is a record that can be engaged with repeatedly by multiple researchers for analysis. They use multiple cameras directed at any one student learning group to capture 'fast-flying' interactions. Further information to support analysis is collected through field notes, student-generated artefacts, and interviews with students and teachers.

Observations are targeted towards documenting episodes of student activities including:

- practices such as tool use;
- problem-solving and use of resources such as tools and concepts;
- discussions among students or students–teacher;
- progress of student projects over time; and
- tracing a particular student, object, action or procedure over time.

An episode contains some information about the object of focus (material, conceptual or social), the initiators of the episode, the participants, the practices in which initiators are engaged, and the resources being used. Like Roth (1996), these researchers select and follow particular tracers to help focus their observations in an episode, where a tracer connects a path of events or network that enacts the development of a particular phenomenon that the researchers wish to understand. The researchers 'chunk', label, code and analyse these episodes. First, they describe the issue, initiator, participants, practice and resources. Then they examine the different links that connect these nodes, asking: What links within a network address the underlying questions? Which links are most productive to represent graphically to understand these questions?

To look more deeply within network links and to represent their often hidden dynamics, Thompson (2010) delineates four methodological 'heuristics' that she found productive in her study exploring online learning practices through ANT approaches. One heuristic was 'following the actors'. The particular actor upon which she chose to focus was the computer's delete button. This is something that Nespor (2010) would term a 'device', an important mediator and coordinator of other actors and actions, which also shifts according to its own enrolments. Thompson interviewed participants to trace the circulations of the delete button, and the ways it mobilized response, information, affect, and even counter-networks. Her second heuristic was to examine breakdowns and accidents, such as password boondoggles for websites and web communities:

> By helping to illuminate objects in action, breakdowns expose the multiplicity—the conglomerates—of networks and more importantly, the work that is being performed continuously to sustain the links between actants in these networks.
>
> (Thompson 2010: 88–9)

Heuristic three was about 'untangling tensions' that emerged in her participants' tales, particularly by attending to 'stabilizations and disruptions' (Thompson 2010: 89). Tensions that she traced included issues such as inclusion and exclusion in online networks, and participants' activities to balance information onslaught online with concerns over control, validation, even deleting. Thompson's fourth heuristic, using an analytical device of co(a)gent, was to identify sites where human and non-human elements coalesced into sociotechnical hybrids that exercise influence in some noteworthy way. These sites can be constructed as co(a)gent by the researcher for the purposes of analysis. Thompson conceptualized a 'deletebutton-being' to represent the confluence of networks at the site of finger, delete button, eye, computer screen, text, assumptions and so forth.

> Using the deletebutton-being as an example, the researcher could pose interview questions such as: how does the delete button mediate what is kept private or made public? Or, what would happen if there was no delete button? Or, when does the deletebutton-being fail or succeed at keeping online work-learning practices manageable? Once I perceived some of the objects in this study as more than objects, and instead, as hybrids of human and non-human actants, I began to see perspectives of relations,

conduits, and circulations that were different than what I observed when just following the actors.

(Thompson 2010: 90)

Much has been learned through experimentation with ANT in empirical research, and through researchers' reflexive attention to the ways they analyse and inscribe what they observe. One important caution that ANT researchers have generated is around the tendency of some early studies to treat the network as itself a static, black-boxed object. As the studies here have emphasized, networks are a dynamic, ever-bubbling series of connections and failed connections. To treat the entities enrolled into the network as unitary identities rather than as fluctuating, partially unknowable and often contradictory, obviously takes research in a different direction. Researchers such as Singleton, Verran and Mol have argued that networks often are performed through ambivalence and ambiguity, marginality and multiple identities.

For example, in their study of organizational learning around implementation of a UK cervical screening programme, Singleton and Michael (1993) show how the general physician acts as both a pivotal enroller and detractor in the network. He translates equipment, women and assistants into the screening practice at the same time as he problematizes and subverts the network. The researchers became interested in the dual insider–outsider role that such participants can play in network assemblages. They concluded that network betrayal and defeat 'can be conceptualized as the congealment of a disparate array of ambivalences into a focused pattern of resistances. And that would be called "building an actor network"' (Singleton and Michael 1993: 259). It is through such insights that ANT researchers have tended to problematize the discourses of constructionism and social constructionism for their implied notions that networks and orders are built (Latour 1999; Mol 2002).

This approach demands a certain willingness of the ANT researcher to not only notice ambivalence, but to dwell within it throughout the analysis process. This means suspending a need for explanation and resisting desires to seek clear patterns, solutions, singularities or other closure in the research. It is about noticing instead the strains, the uncanny, the difficult and the ill-fitting, allowing the messes of difference and tension to emerge alongside each other, rather than smoothing them into some kind of relation. As Mulcahy (1999: 100) explains, 'network analysis is a matter of showing the strain between the symbolic and the material, between representations of the body and embodiment as experience, of rendering the ambivalent character of the network more visible'. An interesting study has been conducted by Sanna Rimpiläinen, investigating precisely this strain between the symbolic and material (Rimpiläinen and Edwards 2009; Rimpiläinen 2010). She is part of a larger multidisciplinary project that examines case-study pedagogy in higher education settings and translates it into semantic web technologies. Rimpiläinen explores the research practices at play in this project. For instance, she analyses the researchers' conversations to examine how a signifier such as ontology mobilizes a conversation that is simultaneously about worldview for some, and about typologies within virtual environment for others, holding in tension the disjunctures of their different disciplinary 'hinterlands'. She examines the ways that living classroom practice becomes framed and then inscribed in the notes made by two observing researchers, which are then circulated among the other team researchers to become translated into something new again, and she compares these inscriptions with the project's research questions. For her, ANT concepts help to see

> how differently researchers working on the same project approach the same problem through the 'same' method, and that this is a way of looking at multiple enactments of reality rather than two separate perspectives on the one underlying 'reality'. It raises questions of how we understand observation in research practices and how a research question acts as an obligatory passage point from which multiple openings are enacted. A research question is therefore an aporia, both pointing towards something specific but also opening up multiplicity.
>
> (Rimpiläinen 2009: 10)

Conclusion

Overall, it is clear that ANT itself is not unified as a field or theory. We referred earlier to ANT as not an 'it', but a cloud – one that emerges through the things with which it is engaged, thought about and spoken of, as well as the words and identities doing the speaking. This still seems appropriate. After-ANT is a troubled and troubling space, always attempting to push at the limits of the attempts to bound it in certain ways, to domesticate it. This is ongoing work, not least as those working in this way respond to its many critics. We have pointed to some of these throughout this text, in particular those who criticize the attempt to treat the human and non-human symmetrically, or the challenges raised about where the limits of analysis lie when working with the concept of network. While attempting to reconfigure the material world as forms of assemblage and agency as effects, the pull to more conventional understandings of the social being about the play of structure and agency remain strong(er). How successfully ANT enrols others in taking up ANT as an orientation is therefore open to question.

ANT progenitors have worried, above all, that ANT can become reified as an immutable research strategy, a fixed and singular standpoint for thinking about the world complete with methodological baggage that would inevitably reduce the phenomena it confronts to conform to its own theoretical content. In the field of educational research, where ANT approaches did not appear until the 1990s, and have enjoyed a surge of attention since 2000, the problem of singularity is not particularly threatening. ANT in education is a lumpy and messy series of uptakes. Educational studies exist that adopt ANT concepts as formulaic models, such as the obligatory point of passage or Callon's four moments of translations, applying them to analyse classroom life, educational policy, curriculum change and so forth in simplistic ways that reduce and contain complexity.

However, there are also a profusion of educational studies that appear deeply committed to the difficulty of ambiguity, non-stability and transgression in fixed methodological approaches. This may be because education, as an impossible practice, is itself located within existential uncertainty and contradiction (Fenwick 2010b). Education as curriculum, as pedagogy, as language and as policy *is* an aporia of (un)becoming. Learning simultaneously enacts both a present activity, a past for un- and re-learning, and a deferred future, a future of imagined ideals as well as fearful anxieties. Learning activity embodies imminent actors (this teacher and this learner with these things and texts) simultaneously with collective dreams and problems imprinted in all of its things. Educational research has hosted rich debates and experimentation about qualitative methods exploring what Lather (2007) has called its margins of intelligibility, working with feminist, post-colonial, narrative, emancipatory, anti-racist, post-structural and complexity analytical approaches. This may be why so many educational researchers working with ANT have combined it with other methodological approaches. With the many critiques of ANT now available, researchers have struggled to avoid applying it as a rigid framework that tames theory, method and the life under observation. As Leander and Lovvorn (2006: 295) explain, voicing what appears to be rather a common orientation in educational research, ANT is drawn upon 'not as a stable body of work, but one that provides some tools and perspectives with which to think and analyze' teaching and learning as sociomaterial practices.

Chapter 8

Spatiality and temporality
Understanding cultural geography

An important emerging line of research in recent years incorporates considerations of space and spatiality into analyses of power and learning in education (e.g. Gulson and Symes 2007), borrowing from cultural geography. This follows what is often referred to as the spatial turn in social sciences in the 1990s, which has found expression in research in a range of domains (e.g. Hearn and Michelson 2006). In such approaches, space is considered not as a static container into which teachers and students are poured, or a backcloth against which they act, but as a dynamic multiplicity that is constantly being produced by simultaneous practices-so-far. Space is not to be considered simply an object of study, as, for instance, in examining how classroom spaces are designed and used. Space is not the equivalent of 'place', which may represent a sedimented region or meaning. Spatiality, the sociomaterial effects and relations of space–time, is, more critically, a tool for analysis. Issues for education and work include how spaces become specifically educational or learning spaces; how they are constituted in ways that enable or inhibit learning, create inequities or exclusions, open or limit possibilities for new practices and knowledge; and how space is represented in the artefacts we use in educational practices, such as maps and pictures. Particularly in new educational arrangements incorporating media and communication technologies, distance and online learning, the ordering of space–time has become a critical influence on learning and working. Spatial theories raise questions about what knowledge counts, where and how it emerges in different time–spaces, how subjectivities are negotiated through movements and locations, and how learning is enmeshed in the making of spaces. They open up new approaches through which to explore educational issues, moving the focus of research from individuals or individual interactions to the ordering of the human and non-human in space–time, where particular spatial practices are enacted as teaching and learning. Thus, in relation to changing spaces of education such as online learning, we can begin to examine both the spatial distancing and distributing that occur, and the new proximities that become possible.

In this chapter, we review those notions of space that have come to be significant for understanding educational phenomena over the past 25 years, emerging in particular from critical, feminist and post-structural geographies. For shorthand, we refer to these diverse practices as forms of cultural geography, although much written in this arena could be referred to more widely as social theory. In examining why 'space is in the midst of a renaissance' (Kaplan 1996: 147), we are inevitably going to be selective. There are different trajectories that have resulted in the increased interest in questions of space, so that it is no longer the concern only of geographers, architects and urban planners. Spatiality has become an issue in many social sciences. Spatial analyses are used to explain the social, and the ordering of spaces is one of the ways in which power is exercised through the social. Thus 'the discourse of geography has become much wider than the discipline' (Gregory 1994: 81), or, as Lefebvre (1996) implied, space is too important to be left to geographers. Similarly, cultural geographers are as likely to draw upon writings from politics, philosophy and history as they are from their own subject discipline.

As Soja and Hooper (1993: 197) pointed out some time ago, there is now a general agreement that 'space makes a difference in theory, culture and politics'. Consequently, we see growing preoccupation with the significance of 'the spatiality of human life' and recognition of the difference that spaces makes. Space is often described as under-theorized and marginalized in relation to the modernist emphasis on time and history. When the latter was emphasized, space was constructed as neutral, fixed and immobile, unrelated to the social, and without impact on the formation of subjectivities. Space was framed as a neutral container or background within or against which activity took place through time. In recent decades, there has been a shift from considering space as universal and abstract in favour of conceptions that make clear the enacted, turbulent, entangled and hybrid nature of space. Thus it can be argued that there has been a movement towards a situation where:

> [S]patial relations are seen to be no less complex and contradictory than historical processes, and space itself refigured as inhabited and hetero-geneous, as a moving cluster of points of intersection for manifold axes of power which cannot be reduced to a unified plane or organized into a single narrative.
>
> (Hebdige 1990: vi–vii)

However, it would be inappropriate to conclude from this that time has now been simply replaced by space. It is more helpful to think of it in the way Massey (1993: 155) does – 'space is not static (i.e. time-less), nor time spaceless [. . .] spatiality and temporality are different from each other but neither can be conceptualized as the absence of the other'. As she goes on to point out, we need to think in terms of 'space–time', of a conception and actuality of time and space as inseparable and interactively relational, as, for example, we witness in school timetables and their organization of spaces, times, bodies and artefacts. Or, as Jones *et al.* (2004) suggest, we may need to consider spacing and timing as actions, verbs rather than nouns, thus pointing to the ways in which they are both performed and performative rather than simply existing. Here, for instance, the school timetable might be said to space and time actions by ordering people and things into particular relations, rather than those relations being ignored and space and time being treated as things.

Educational interest in spatial theory has closely reflected the distinctions and currents more broadly apparent in social theory, where four threads can be identified. None is entirely discrete from the other, and they have emerged from debates within and between the different framings. Each is subject to multiple interpretations. Almost all the threads are in explicit or implicit dialogues with the philosophies of Nietzsche and Heidegger.

First, there is a political economy framing of space. This draws upon Marxist traditions of analysis, in particular those emerging in Western Europe post-Gramsci. It is associated with such writers as Lefebvre (1991) and Harvey (1989). Lefebvre's three aspects, or trialectics, of spatial practices, representations of space and spatial imaginings, has been particularly influential in framing space as materially produced and productive, both manifesting exercises of power and contributing to such exercises. Such analyses focus on the orderings and representations of space as manifestations of changing economic conditions and their effects on everyday life. Industrialization, urbanization and globalization are key themes in such analyses.

Second, there is a feminist framing of space. Emerging from the analysis of the public–private binary as gendered and associated with writers such as Massey (1994, 2005), a key focus is the analysis of the gender inequalities in changing orderings of space–time and, more broadly, the power-geometries of their particular orderings.

Third, there is what we can refer to broadly as the post-structuralist framing of space, emerging from the work of, for instance, Foucault, Deleuze and Guattari, and associated with writers such as Soja (1989). These analyses have been influenced by the linguistic and culturalist turns in social theory from the 1980s and the associated form of 'post-' theorizing – for example, postmodern and post-colonial. Key themes in such approaches are questions of subjectivity, representation and power. Associated with this thread are attempts to examine the spaces of marginalized others, with concern being focused on, for instance, margins (Spivak 1993); interstitial third space (Bhabha 1994); nomadism (Braidotti 1994); and diaspora space (Brah 1996).

Fourth, there is what is referred to as a materialist (re)turn in framings of space (Anderson and Wylie 2009). This turn has attempted to address what are considered to be some of the limitations of the other three threads, but is itself caught up in the debates over how we frame matter and the material (Barad 2007). The materialist turn takes many forms, some of which might be seen as rejections of 'theory' articulated in post-structuralist framings of space. For us, the significant work in this thread is associated with the mobilities paradigm (e.g. Urry 2007), influenced in part by post-humanist and non-representationalist theories such as actor-network theory (ANT), within which particular spaces are network effects (Murdoch 1998). This work has focused on space as material (dis)orderings, as enactments and performances, a view consistent with the positioning of spacing as a verb, mentioned above.

It is important to recognize that material (dis)orderings are not social constructions in the conventional sense, as 'the social' is itself taken to be always, already, a particular ordering of space. Here there is a movement away from framings that assume and reproduce traditional subject-centred epistemologies wherein human intention and action is given an assumed primacy. Spatial orderings are not about human subjects, but are material assemblages of subjects–objects that interrupt and effect, questioning and promising, such as takes place in a kitchen space in the learning of cookery. Thus the material should not be assumed to be a foundational grounding in 'reality' or the 'social' or 'economic', for, as Anderson and Wylie (2009) suggest, materiality can entail an assemblage of any state and element. Following Serres (1995), materiality can be considered a turbulence within which emerge assemblages of (dis)order of various durabilities. Materialities therefore entail a constant process of gathering and distribution and thus their importance for framings of space as (im)mobilities.

It is also important to bear in mind the connections between the four threads. For instance, in different ways, both Harvey and Soja were influenced by Lefebvre's work on urbanization. Lefebvre himself influenced, and was influenced by, situationists such as Debord, who has also influenced strands of 'post' theorizing, and was also more interested in the material than in debates about epistemology. There is much ongoing debate about how to interpret Lefebvre and the diverse uptakes of his work in the English language (Shields 1999; Elden 2001). Massey was initially much influenced in her writing by Marxist feminism, although this shifted somewhat with time. Some of those emphasizing materiality might be described as extending the range of post-structuralist geographies. Many contemporary cultural geographers and social theorists draw upon the different threads in making their own spatial ropes, as is represented in the shift to focus on mobilities rather than place in spatial framings (Sheller and Urry 2006). Spatial theory and analysis is itself, then, a space of turbulence, or (dis)order. Within this turbulence, it is fair to say that, where they have theorized spatiality, educational researchers have mostly drawn upon the works of Lefebvre, Harvey, Soja and Massey rather than the (im)mobilities approach.

While spatial analysis is not new, the major impetus for its increased significance stems from the trends emerging from the recession of the early 1980s, associated with globalizing processes and the accompanying changing material and cultural practices. An increased availability of continental European writings translated into English also added impetus to the spatial study of the social, in addition to the social study of the spatial. Globalizing processes signified changing spatial orderings, which required new forms of spatial analysis. We use some of the writings on this theme as an entry point into questions of space and spatiality. This is followed by outlines of spatial debates about technological spaces, space–time compression, (im)mobilities, and location and politics. In this way, we introduce some of the framings and themes that have been, or could be, taken up in the study of education.

Globalizing spaces

One influential way of theorizing globalization, often referred to as 'world culture' theory, highlights 'the compression of the world and the intensification of consciousness of the world as a whole' (Robertson 1992: 8). Or, as Waters (1995: 3) suggests, globalization is 'a social process in which the constraints of geography on social and cultural arrangements recede and in which people become increasingly aware that they are receding'. As more people experience an apparently shrinking world, certain spatial constraints become less, due to possibilities for the increased mobility of people, goods and services. Spatial analysis emerges, therefore, at the point at which mobilities put into question the notion of space as a closed container, backcloth or constraint. Airline tickets bought in England are processed in India. Workers in the same company can be networked across countries through databases. People migrate globally for work, leisure, and increasingly as refugees. What in the past would have taken months to move around the globe now takes hours or even seconds. Increased mobilities mean that space and time are increasingly compressed. The argument here is that the compression of the world and the intensification of the consciousness of the world produce an interdependence that, in turn, compresses the world even more, with heightened intensification and so on. In this theorization, therefore, globalization is a process that both *connects* and stimulates awareness of connection and interdependence.

Such changes to the spatial orderings do not happen as the result of a natural process, nor are they neutral. Globalizing processes 'can be seen as being a condition resulting from a long history of international exploration, invasion and colonization, fuelled by economic, military, religious and political interests, and enabled through enormous developments in transport and communications technologies' (Evans 1997: 12). Globalizing spaces result from certain actions, as do the continued significance given to territories such as the nation state. Drawing upon Lefebvre's analytical framework of spatial practice, representations of space and representational space, Shields (1997: 194; emphasis in original) therefore argues that:

> [S]ocio-political constructions ideologically coded into cartographic conventions and reified in socio-cognitive mappings of the world [. . .] these serve to exemplify the extent to which we live within the territorializing and boundary-drawing impulse of the *imaginary geography* of the nation-state [. . .] *Representation of space* such as national air space and 200-mile limit inform and delimit our *practical* interventions in these spaces.

The particular representations inscribed in different theorizations of space always need to be borne in mind. Mapping and remapping are powerful practices, and provide a framing for practice and intervening. 'Space' and 'place' are articulated and performed within the spatializing practices of imaginary geographies and political moves (Pile and Keith 1997). Within this are questions of scale and the different scalings of space, for example, as place, as local, regional, national, or international. Here globalization itself can be seen as a form of re-imagining spatial relations in the cause of re-inscribing different practices into and within the world. The scaling of space is not based upon taken-for-granted categories, but is performed.

This is significant if we examine many of the assumptions about spatial orderings and binaries that inform much social theory. For instance, we have the spaces of the nation and the region, and the First, Second and Third worlds, and distinctions between the local and global, and centre and periphery, that tend to be taken for granted. In its many forms, the spatial turn points to these categories and distinctions being enacted or performed. The different threads provide various explanations of how that comes to be. For many contemporary spatial theorists, it is necessary to go beyond the categories of classical sociology and economics, which already tend to assume the nation state and economy as a privileged focus for research, and society as the foremost explanatory concept. In such approaches, the state, economy and society become reified and unquestioned as ways of framing understanding. For writers such as Urry (2000, 2007), it is a question of developing social theory beyond the concept of society. For those within the political economy thread, however, this ignores the powerful relations that remain sedimented in spatial orders such as the nation state. Here one of the arguments is that 'globalization operates as a "necessary myth" through which politicians and governments discipline their citizens to meet the requirements of the global marketplace' (Held and McGrew 2003: 5). However, we feel more sympathy with Massey's (1994: 159) argument that, while most companies have a national origin and with that a clear direction of flows in foreign investment, 'the geography of these flows has been changing and becoming more complex'.

As well as changing spatial relations and orderings of the global economy, it is also suggested that there are different possibilities for globalized forms of sociality, politics and practices, for what some term 'globalization from below' (Falk 1993; Kellner 2000; Singh et al. 2005; Gulson and Symes 2007). This interest in the 'below' can be traced to Lefebvre's critique of strands of deterministic Marxism and his notion that, rather than being a sub-system of the economic system, everyday life is the vital space of social existence. For Lefebvre, the colonization of the everyday by the state and capitalism has made the former a space of alienation, which has enabled the latter to continue, despite wars, recessions, etc. (Goonewardena et al. 2008). It is in state strategies for the production of specific spaces that capitalism reproduces itself. 'Whereas the state and capital attempt to "pulverize" space into a manageable, calculable and abstract grid, diverse social forces simultaneously attempt to create, defend or extend spaces of social reproduction, everyday life and grassroots control' (Brenner and Elden 2009: 367). The inference to be drawn from this was that the ordering of everyday space and time was more significant for analysis than a focus on the state, as it is through change in the former rather than the latter that sustained social changes become possible. In Marxist circles at the time, this was a heresy (Aronowitz 2007).

Globalized spaces are suggestive that the link between nation state and citizenship may be loosened with people acting upon issues of shared concern in and through global networks. This can be understood as a form of cosmopolitanism. National governments become only a partial focus for certain forms of popular intervention, as demonstrated by environmental groups such as Greenpeace, humanitarian groups such as Amnesty, and the anti-globalization movement itself. Globalization therefore provides possibilities as well as threats in the spread of capitalist relations. On the one hand, for instance, there is the feminization of labour where

> global assembly lines are 'manned' by women workers in free trade zones; subcontracted industrial homeworking is performed at kitchen tables by women who 'have time on their hands'; home-based teleworking is carried out by women who can't afford day-care costs and are grateful to have paid work.
>
> (Manicom and Walters 1997: 72)

However, practices also develop which bring together groups affected by economic restructuring in new ways, such as trade unions funding labour and community projects outside their own national base, or landless groups from different nations seeking to support each other's claims for rights (Routledge 2006). This 'globalization from below' is often supported by information and communication technologies (ICTs).

> Affinity groups of 'senior' or retired citizens, feminist scholars, individuals who share knowledge on health afflictions, hobbyists, professionals, political organizations and many others are [. . .] using the Internet to educate, proselytize and organize, cutting across national boundaries with apparent ease.
>
> (Goodenow 1996: 200)

These both expand the possibilities for sociality and politics, but also for some represent a threat to associations, solidarities and actions based upon the local, proximity and place. However, while notions of globalization both from below and from above help to reframe different possibilities, they also present a spatial relationship that seems to be set within binaries of 'above–below', 'power–

resistance' and 'oppression–emancipation', which themselves constrain debate and understanding through the very processes of categorization in play.

Giddens (1990) suggests that, while globalization has resulted in the spread of 'Western' institutions across the globe, this trend also produces a pressure for local autonomy and identity. In other words, globalization is about examining places as simultaneously traversed by the global and local in ways that have been intensified by the compression of space and time. Thus, alongside the global availability of satellite television, McDonald's, Nike and Harry Potter films, there is an affirmation of, for instance, local, regional and ethnic identities. Some transnational companies have explicitly adopted strategies of 'glocalization', extending their influence around the globe, while situating themselves and their products and services within local conditions. Localization can therefore be part of the strategy of companies in seeking a competitive edge in the global marketplace.

What this suggests is that the local is as much a condition for globalization as the global itself; space and place are traversed by the global–local nexus – 'time–space distanciation, disembedding, and reflexivity mean that complex relationships develop between local activities and interaction across distances' (Waters 1995: 50). The integration of the globe *reconfigures* rather than supplants diversity. This is why scalar analysis has become an important part of spatial research (Collinge 2005), as it 'functions by assembling a series of spatial categories into a hierarchical framework that is used to investigate social change' (Robertson 2007: 217). Thus we see attempts to introduce a global policy space, or a European policy state, through which flows of national and local policy can be reconfigured. Attempts to rescale thus become subject to critique and deconstruction.

Globalization 'does not necessarily imply homogenization or integration. Globalization merely implies greater connectedness and de-territorialization' (Waters 1995: 136). Waters draws upon the work of Appadurai (1990) to provide a framework for the assessment of the extent to which a global cultural economy is in the making. Appadurai identified various arenas as 'scapes' within which cultural objects flow. There are 'ethnoscapes, the distribution of mobile individuals (tourists, migrants, refugees, etc.); technoscapes, the distribution of technology; finanscapes, the distribution of capital; mediascapes, the distribution of information; and ideoscapes, the distribution of political ideas and values' (Waters 1995: 126). To these, Waters added sacriscapes and leisurescapes, respectively the distribution of religious ideas, and of tourism. In all these arenas, Waters finds the evidence for cultural globalization well advanced, and, with that, the increased role of the symbolic in the material and political. Massey (1994: 161) writes also that

> each geographical 'place' in the world is being realigned in relation to the new global realities, their roles within the wider whole are being reassigned,

their boundaries dissolve as they are increasingly crossed by everything from investment flows, to cultural influences, to satellite TV networks.

The material and political therefore are to be understood increasingly as mediated by the symbolic and cultural rather than as separate domains.

The assertion of heterogeneity by the locale or by the region may take many forms. For instance, it may involve the protection/assertion of a specific identity as a reaction against the perceived homogeneity introduced by the global. As Turner (1994: 78) argues in relation to contemporary religious fundamentalism, it 'is a two-pronged movement to secure control within the global system and also to maintain regulation of the lifeworld'. Within the global–local nexus, fundamentalism attempts, through the deployment of notions of religious community bounded together by spiritual belief and sentiment, to contain, if not negate, the assertion and spread of difference and secular consumerism. Fundamentalists are opposed to a globalized culture based on secularism, consumerism and modernization, but they themselves have a vision and *modus operandi* which make sense, and are possible, only within a globalized world. Thus, paradoxically, such movements also take their own worldviews to be universal and seek to promote themselves more effectively through the use of new technologies.

What we can say, then, is that spatial analysis of globalization points to the paradoxical and the complex. The integration of the globe reconfigures rather than supplants diversity, in the process introducing forms of economic, social and cultural (im)mobilities and (en)counters. In considering educational issues about, for instance, national policies, online learning or global citizenship in the curriculum, there are many issues that can be explored and framed through spatial theories of globalization.

Technologized spaces

Integral to the discussion of globalizing spaces is the influence of new technologies and forms of connectedness and mobility. ICTs can be framed in a number of ways. They are tools for communicating, ordering goods and services, and organizing lives. They reconfigure the possibilities for relating, supporting the increased forms of mediated sociality of absence–presence beyond the face-to-face through the technoscapes of, for instance, mobile telephones and online social networking (Licoppe 2004). ICTs also enact spaces and ecologies of their own – cyberspaces. For instance, the

> increasingly sophisticated and hyperrealistic graphic representations in video games are able to beckon into being believable environments that possess a genuine sense of spatiality, and often intense sociality, that grips players and pulls them into a compelling ludic realm 'beyond' the screen display.
>
> (Dodge *et al.* 2009: 1288)

There are important affective engagements within such spaces. Computing and software are increasingly pervasive in daily life. ICT is both hardware and software, which combine in the enacting of space in particular ways, what Dodge *et al.* (2009) refers to as 'code/space'. In their study of software in people's homes, Dodge and Kitchen (2009) identify the ways in which coded objects, processes, infrastructures and assemblages embedded in everyday life help to enact socio-spatial life.

In much of the literature there is a shared sense of the centrality of the contributions that media, communication and transport have made to the spatial orderings of globalization (McChesney 2003; Thompson 2003). For some, this signifies a disembedding from the materiality of the local and immediate. Crang *et al.* (2007) argue that much initial discussion of the impact of ICTs and the internet were framed within a set of binaries of, for example, the virtual–real, immaterial–material, cyberspace–physical space, with the former posing a threat to the latter. However, this is a changing form of materiality rather than its loss, as the local cannot be assumed to be the realm of the authentic. This is particularly so when we consider the rise of mobile technologies and their capacity to relate people and places across great distances, and places that are themselves mobile, such as cars, trains and planes. Crang *et al.* (2007: 2406) point to the ways in which technology is part of, and enacted within, the everyday, and that ICTs are not new in that respect: 'online and offline interactions are constituted and constructed together to sustain and transform the complex temporalities and spatialities of everyday urban life'.

For Morley and Robins (1995: 75), new technologies

> are implicated in a complex interplay of deterritorialization and reterritorialization [. . .] Things are no longer defined and distinguished in the ways that they once were, by their boundaries, borders or frontiers [. . .] We can say that the very idea of boundary – the frontier boundary of the nation-state, for example, or the physical boundaries of urban structures – has been rendered problematical.

Dependent upon which part of the globe one lives within and one's position therein, lifestyles, life courses and decision-making are increasingly mediated and re-inscribed through technologically integrated and integrating processes. However, care needs to be taken in framing ICTs as though they are central to spatial orderings, as the result is often a crude form of technological determinism and the complete dematerializing of space. Technological development is necessary, but not sufficient, to these processes, since their development, articulation and deployment is subject to a range of factors and possibilities.

The recognition of ICTs as more than tools for communication is expressed in the notion of cyberspace. For instance, Rheingold (1993) refers to cyberspace as a conceptual space where words, relationships and data are manifested through the use of computer-mediated communication. Kramerae (1995: 38) has another emphasis again: '"cyberspace" refers to the worldwide computer-mediated communication network where words and graphics are shared, and friendships and power relations are manifested'. For Bukatman (1996: 18), cyberspace is 'a completely malleable realm of transitory data structures in which historical time is measured in nanoseconds and spatiality exists somehow both globally and invisibly'.

Featherstone (1995) points out how frequently metaphors of movement and mobility crop up in discussions of cyberspace. Most notably, the metaphor of 'flows' contrasted with those of 'positionalities', originating with Deleuze and Guattari (1988) and their notion of rhizomatic branching networks framed as a critique of fixed boundaries and identities. These flows are held to have a deterritorializing effect – of people, images and information, commodities, money and ideas. This is suggestive, but of course also problematic, for there is the danger of constructing a view of cyberspace, and space more generally, which is transcendental, detached from the practices through which it is formed, the materialities through which it is enacted and the constraints it imposes. Although cyberspace may be malleable, we nonetheless need to be aware of the powerful constraints within it and the forms of regulation to which it is, and can become, subject. For this sort of reason, Urry (2007: 25) prefers to use the notion of flux, as 'flux involves tension, struggle and conflict'. There is a sense in which cyberspace provides metaphorical resources for the reconceptualization of space more generally – emphasizing flows, nodes and networks – even as those notions inform interpretations of cyberspace.

Kaplan (1996) argues that the new relationship between place, space and the social enabled by these new technologies creates new and different networks, communities and subjectivities as more and more people are connected electronically than by conventional geographical proximity. Some of these connectivities are new, some replace the human material face-to-face inter-action, and others facilitate the organization of such interactions. This is a tendency already in place through pre-existing forms of media and communi-cation, such as television and telephone, but it is the possibilities for, and levels of, interactivity that are increasing in relation to more traditional broadcast media. Even desktop computers are becoming staid for those who desire the mobility made possible by smart phones, pocket computers and the like.

The notion that geographical proximity or 'place' is now not so significant is undoubtedly troubled. A common response to this is to question whether cyberspaces are 'real' places. The way such a questioning is expressed is itself interesting. It signifies the difficulty of critiquing, in the language of that which we seek to critique, that which we find difficult to do without – in this case the 'reality' of place. However, as Bukatman (1996: 118) points out, 'whether cyberspace is a "real" place or not, our experience of electronic space is a "real" experience'. Furthermore, cyberspace has to be understood in relation to a techno-social restructuring that is real enough. There is a materiality to people and objects, which is not overcome in the interactive spaces of cyberspace.

Thus, as Crang *et al.* (2007: 2407) suggest, 'ICT-based urban change involves a layering, tangling, and imbrication of new practices and new possibilities alongside old ways and enduring demands'. Based upon their study of a neighbourhood in Newcastle upon Tyne, UK, they (Crang *et al.* 2007: 2411–12) 'see different media technologies offering different affordances and opportunities for ties and actions at different temporal and spatial scales simultaneously'. How such framing of issues influences the study of education and in turn raises new issues is explored in chapter nine.

Space–time compression

Central to the analysis of the reordering of space and time has been its compression, in part, through new and speedier forms of communication and transport, and the general mobilities we witness. This has been the case in aspects of education as well as in culture and society more generally. Soja (1989) suggests that the restructurings of space–time do not simply displace previous conditions, but rather *overlay* and *interweave* them. Compression is basically the notion that the world feels smaller, and in an important sense *is* smaller, as more people, goods, information and services are now able to travel around it and communicate across great distances much more quickly and easily than was previously the case. With compression comes the sense that things have speeded up and possibilities for detached dwelling reduced. Seclusion and detachment from the social order becomes more difficult. However, the process of compression is itself one of uneven development, as there have been periods and places of greater compression than others. Lefebvre's (1991) popular analytical framing of space as lived, perceived and conceived provides a convenient heuristic for exploring this phenomenon, as particular spatial arrangements are argued to emerge from their lived experiences, practices and representations.

Probably the most systematic attempt to chart this process of compression from the Enlightenment is to be found in the work of Harvey (1989), which situates globalization and space–time compression within the current restructurings of capitalism. Here it is the search for increased profits and social discipline on a global scale under conditions of enhanced competition for goods and services that effects change. Drawing on a neo-Marxist framework, Harvey argues that the crises in capital accumulation at various stages in the history of capitalism have resulted in the disruption of established patterns of spatial arrangements and their continual reordering around new centres and forms of production. Harvey is extending the work of Lefebvre, for whom

> spatialization of the state centrally underscores both its intrinsically territorial parameters as an institutional apparatus; and its strategic, if contradictory, role(s) in producing and transforming the territorialized spatial grids that underpin the modern capitalist world order.
>
> (Brenner and Elden 2009: 364)

Here state, space and territory co-emerge as strategies of capital accumulation and governing. Thus the crisis of overaccumulation and revolutionary upsurge in Europe in the 1840s was resolved in part by the expansion of investment and foreign trade through imperialist appropriation. This compression of space–time was made possible by the

> expansion of the railway network, accompanied by the advent of the telegraph, the growth of steam shipping, and the building of the Suez Canal, the beginnings of radio communication and bicycle and automobile travel at the end of the century [. . .]
>
> (Harvey 1989: 264)

As a result of these developments, global processes and change were speeded up. This acceleration was enhanced by the tight ordering of space–time on Fordist production lines, the first of which was built in 1913. For Harvey, the period of the late 1980s was marked by a further intensification of space–time compression, as capitalism was reconfigured with Fordist forms of capital accumulation, giving way to flexible accumulation and what was referred to as post-Fordism. Here the development of new organizational forms made possible by the development of new technology and faster means of communication have resulted in an acceleration in production, also matched by an acceleration in exchange and consumption.

Fordism was deeply paradoxical for capitalism. Industrialization provided the basis for the expansion of capital accumulation. However, the urbanization processes associated with industrialization – bringing together large numbers of people to work in factories – also provided the ground for a sense of solidarity and forms of union organization to oppose capital. In other words, the very processes that created the conditions for the development of capitalism, through the creation of an urban working class, also provided the possibility of a challenge to capitalist organization. In response, as Harvey (1993: 88) suggests, 'spatial dispersal and geographical isolation' have played an important part in capital's attempts to sustain labour market discipline and control, and to displace the challenge potentially posed by an urban working class. Now, this dispersal has been enhanced further by globalized and technologized spaces that compress space–time, allowing new forms of spatial dispersal to develop across the globe, and thus for capital to locate and relocate where returns are highest. This gives place a greater significance for capital as it seeks out the most favourable conditions for its accumulation, a process enhanced by regional competition for inward investment and employment. This echoes the earlier argument that globalization is not in opposition to localization, but rather the latter can be understood as part of the former, and the former as expressing itself through the latter. New patterns of economic inequality are inscribed and re-inscribed in this process, as the current changing economies of China, Brazil and India illustrate.

This geographical dispersal is also taking place within the nation, region and locale. The everyday cannot be scaled as the local, given the changing forms of gathering and distribution. Developments in the organization of work have implications for the reorganization of geographical distances between paid and unpaid work, leisure and other social practices. The need for populations to be concentrated into urban conglomerations is undermined by increasing physical distances, with technology enabling people, goods and services to be brought together by means other than physical proximity. At its most extreme, this provides the possibility for certain groups of people not to have to visit a workplace at all, with an associated blurring of home–work boundaries (Massey 2005). They may live some distance from their employers or even in different countries, but technology and forms of communication enable them to have their activities based within their own homes.

However, the strength of these processes is dependent upon the intensity of the space–time compression and one's place in the global–local nexus. Thus, as Massey (1994: 148–49) argues, in suggesting the need for a power geometry of space–time compression, 'different social groups, and different individuals, are placed in very distinct ways in relation to these flows and interconnections'. This has implications for the relationship between education and the economy, but also for forms and opportunities for workplace learning.

(Im)mobilities

There are also those who pursue de- and re-territorialization and emerging connectivities as pointing to the significance of mobilities, flux and movements in framing understanding of socio-spatial relations (Urry 2007; Watts and Urry 2008). This work seeks to thread a route between sedentary views of space that assume value and authenticity in notions of place and the local, and a post-modern grand narrative of the superiority of mobility or nomadism over other forms of life. In relation to the former,

> sedentarism treats as normal stability, meaning, and place, and treats as abnormal distance, change, and placelessness [. . .] Such sedentarism locates bounded and authentic places or regions or nations as the fundamental basis of human identity and experience and as the basic units of social research.
>
> (Sheller and Urry 2006: 208–9)

What is sometimes termed the mobilities approach can also be seen as contributing to the materialist turn in geography, as 'there are hybrid systems, "materialities and mobilities" that combine objects, technologies, socialities and affects out of which distinct places are produced and reproduced' (Hannam *et al.* 2006: 14). Here place is not bounded or separated from flux and networks, but arises from them.

This work draws from a broad range of influences, including aspects of the work of Harvey, Soja and Massey, and insights from ANT. It also has a relationship to complexity theory (Urry 2003), as it attempts to frame spatially the social as neither fully ordered nor anarchic. Sheller and Urry (2006) identify six threads of theory informing mobilities research: the spatial turn in the social sciences; science and technology studies; the work of Simmel; the recentring of the corporeal body as a matter of concern; the topologies of social networks; and complexity theory. These provide a sophisticated set of resources through which to rework spatial framings.

> Issues of movement, of too little movement or too much or of the wrong sort or at the wrong time, are central to many lives, organizations and governments. Dreams of 'hyper-mobility' and 'instantaneous communication' drive contemporary business strategy, advertising and government policy while also eliciting strong political critiques from those who feel marginalised or harmed by these new developments. Fears of illicit mobilities and their attendant security risks increasingly determine logics of governance and liability protection within both the public and private sectors. From SARS and avian influenza to train crashes, from airport expansion controversies to controlling global warming, from urban congestion charging to networked global terrorism, from emergency management in the onslaught of tsunamis and hurricanes to oil wars in the Middle East, issues of 'mobility' are centre-stage. Many public, private and not-for-profit organizations are seeking to understand, monitor, manage and transform aspects of these multiple mobilities, and of the new 'immobilities', social exclusions and security threats that may be associated with them.
>
> (Hannam *et al.* 2006: 1)

A focus on mobilities points us towards a tracing of the movements, relations and networks of objects, people, information and images, and the ways in which flows are regulated, made possible and constrained. For instance, aircraft require airports and timetables, mobile phones require transmitter masts, rights to travel are restricted for many by laws and borders, and cars require petrol stations. To a large extent, then, mobilities emerge with the development of socio-technical systems or networks, the materialities of which can also produce the immaterialities of the virtual and imagined.

Rather than starting analysis from a space out of which objects move, we are to assume and map mobilities and the ways in which spaces are moored, bounded and stabilized for the moment, and the specific (im)mobilities associated with such moorings. We might take such spaces for granted, as for instance, schools, but a mobilities analysis would examine the ways in which such spaces are enacted and become sedimented across time. These mobilities, immobilities and moorings point to the entanglement and complex patterning of spaces, and the requirement to examine particular empirical tracings of relational and network enactments of space (Murdoch 1998) rather than pro-ducing some overarching spatial explanation. We are therefore interested here in what Massey (1994) referred to as the power geometries of everyday life.

For Hannam *et al.* (2006: 4), the focus on mobilities is not a simple celebration of a privileged mobile existence, but a way to analyse how (im)mobilities are enacted and the power exercised through such enactments: 'the spatialities of social life presuppose, and frequently involve conflict over, both the actual and the imagined movement of people from place to place, event to event'. And not simply people, but also goods, services, news, information and power, which can be exercised at a distance through the use of new technologies, as in the coordination of the transnational production and distribution of goods through the expert systems of computerized databases and communication. In his argument for the deparochialization of the policy research imagination, Lingard (2007: 235) puts it this way: 'the mobilities associated with globalization demand a rethinking of implicit taken-for-granteds in social theory of the relationship between theory and society as a nationally bounded space'. He suggests that this is both difficult but necessary in the context of asymmetrical power relations.

What makes near and far, here or there, is not a static separation between two points that is travelled by some thing, then. Instead, these concepts of distance are created by relations that are always changing, as the introduction of the internet into daily life has made abundantly clear. When multiple points are linked, the concepts of micro- and macro- or local and global thus do not hold as separate spaces or scales. This focus traces the circulations of entities that continue to alter one another and the networks they act within, as well as the empty spaces between networks. For Marxist-informed framings of space, the macro-structures of capitalism are explanatory, whereas for mobilities framings they are to be traced precisely as to how they extend and to what they are connected.

(Dis)location and politics

For some, however, there is a renewed interest in the regional, historical and local in response to the perceived efficiency, functionalism and impersonality of modernism (Robins 1993). This results in a reworked traditional reassertion of the link between place and subjectivity, sometimes associated with what might be referred to as a conservative postmodern stance, although perhaps this should more readily be conceived as anti-modern. Here there is an inversion rather than deconstruction of the modern perspective within which '"time" is equated with movement and progress, "space/place" is equated with stasis and reaction' (Massey 1994: 151). Thus 'it is no coincidence that communities for resistance are termed "movements" in much political struggle' (Pile 1997: 29). Thus 'the ethnic absolutism of "root" metaphors, fixed in place, is replaced by mobile "route" metaphors which can lay down a challenge to the fixed identities of "cultural insiderism"' (Pile and Thrift 1995a: 10).

An important distinction here is between those who assert movement in a radicalized form, which continues to position space as an inert background, and those who emphasize movement as a spatialization of subjectivity and the political (Mohanty 1992). This has been central to much feminist and post-colonial analysis, attempting to theorize new possibilities with which to construct a more equitable dispensation. Here metaphors of movement are deployed to destabilize the centres of power and provide for new power geometries through different mapping practices. Mobility, then, assumes a political as well as a metaphorical role – 'nomadism consists not so much in being homeless, as in being capable of recreating your home everywhere' (Braidotti 1994: 16). Similarly, Chambers (1994: 5) suggests:

> migrancy [. . .] involves movement in which neither the points of departure nor those of arrival are immutable or certain. It calls for a dwelling in language, in histories, in identities that are constantly subject to mutation. Always in transit, the promise of a homecoming – completing the story, domesticating the detour – becomes an impossibility.

However, while such metaphors are productive, engendering as they do a 'landscape of movement and mobility by those for whom movement and mobility are unproblematic' (Pile and Thrift 1995b: 24), the focus on movements and flows can result in place and the local appearing to be annihilated completely or simply dismissed as parochial. There is a danger also of privileging and normalizing the experiences of some as the experiences of all, paradoxically bringing back to centre-stage precisely what the surfacing of difference sought to avoid in the first place. Both roots and routes play a role in subjectivity. However,

> instead of thinking of places as areas with boundaries around, they can be imagined as articulated moments in networks of social relations and understandings, but where a large proportion of those relations, experiences and understandings are constructed on a far larger scale than what we happen to define for that moment as the place itself, whether that be the street, or a region or even a continent.
>
> (Massey 1994: 154)

For some, the de-realization and de-territorialization of place associated with space–time compression results in a loss of social meaning and disruption of established senses of community, culture and identity. This provokes what Robins (1993: 320) refers to as 'feelings of dislocation and disorientation' and homelessness. Here is 'a cultural sense of "postmodern" spatial stress and dislocation can thus be grounded in the material framework of new relationships between spatial regions and localities as well as in the "imaginary geographies" and spatial practices of agents' (Shields 1997: 196). However, feelings such as those of dislocation are not necessarily or inherently negative. Indeed, they can be a springboard for learning and positive forms of change.

For those interested in spatial orderings, politics and their effects on subjectivity, drawing upon 'post-' theories, different possibilities emerge. This is precisely a spatial politics of subjectivity:

> a politics of location as locationality in contradiction – that is a positionality of dispersal; of simultaneous situatedness within gendered spaces of class, racism, ethnicity, sexuality, age; of movement across shifting cultural, religious and linguistic boundaries; of journeys across geographical and psychic borders.
>
> (Brah 1996: 204)

Hybridity rather than homogeneity, and the relational rather than the bounded, characterize the spatial orderings. Within this, 'the significance of new hybrid and syncretic identities shows the potential for crossover identities which destabilize old [. . .] absolutisms' (Rattansi 1995: 280). There are, increasingly, a number of contradictory positionings that foreground the importance of location and locating practices, and with that the metaphor of the *network*. Here 'different social groups, and different individuals belonging to numbers of social groups, are located in many different ways in the new organization of relations over time–space' (Massey 1994: 164).

This identification of a condition that is increasingly one of hybridity, deterritorialization, mobility and disembedding engenders affective and political responses. In what sense, if at all, can this condition be understood as a state of homelessness or dislocation, of insecure boundaries and flux, where a sense of place, meaning and identity become problematic or no longer exist at all? These are themselves complex questions, located in certain traditional assumptions as to the proper relationships among place, meaning and subjectivity, where stability of place is often seen as resulting in stability of meaning and subjectivity. For Massey (1994), the outpouring about homelessness itself signifies a First World/colonizing perspective. For those elsewhere:

> the boundaries of the place one called home must have dissolved long ago, and the coherence of one's local culture must long ago have been under threat, in those parts of the world where the majority of its populations live.
>
> (Massey 1994: 165)

Homelessness and a sense of a loss of place may be a recent experience for those who have been at the centres of power, but a long-standing one for diverse others, and indeed the global majority.

Rather than the loss of home, therefore, it might be more appropriate to reconsider the meaning of home and the possibilities provided when the home is, for instance, networked through telephone, television, mobile phone, the internet, fast jet travel, diverse products and services available on a worldwide basis – and subject to the climatic, environmental and political effects of actions taken elsewhere 'at a distance'. Home therefore becomes an effect of the associations that mark a space as a particular type of place. The stable identities of bounded place – themselves perhaps more nostalgic than actual, for many – may need to be reconfigured as 'diasporic identities [which] are at once local and global [. . .] networks of transnational identifications encompassing "imagined" and "encountered" communities' (Brah 1996: 196). For Brah (1996: 180), this provides a space that takes 'account of a homing desire which is not the same thing as desire for a "homeland"'. It is for these reasons that Brah (1996: 209), like others, has extended the arguments of post-colonialism to suggest that 'the native is as much the diasporan as the diasporan is the native'. In other words, the notion of insiders and outsiders of nation, ethnicity, religion, culture, etc. is unsustainable; the ever-strident attempts to create such bounded spaces and places – through ethnic cleansing – being evidence of the sustained work and exercises of power through which hybridity is fought in the attempt to bound and bind. Here place, rather than being bounded and excluding, is conceived as a meeting place, a point of (en)counter (Massey 1999). Here 'places are not what lies on either side of the boundary, they are constituted through boundary work' (Hetherington 1997: 186). Places do not sit within boundaries, contained, but co-emerge through the enacting of boundaries. Subjectivity may therefore be said to signify (dis)locating practices (Edwards and Usher 2008), enacted by and enacting mobilities *and* moorings.

Conclusion

For us, spatial theory surfaces a number of conceptual metaphors and spaces – (im)mobility, mapping, scale, absence–presence – through which to destabilize the assumed categorizations and binaries which frame much of the thinking about socio-spatial ordering. Spatial framings provide us with the opportunity to enter Bhabha's (1990: 211) interstitial third space, which 'displaces the histories that constitute it, and sets up new structures of authority, new political initiatives, which are inadequately understood through received wisdom'. This is an emergent space of possibilities and constraints, mobilities and moorings, posing interesting questions for education as well as providing theoretical and methodological framings through which those questions can be explored. It is to these explorations we turn in chapter nine.

Chapter 9

Spatial theory in educational research

This chapter describes specific examples of studies of education working with forms of spatial theory. These examples show methodological approaches, as well as the strengths and possibilities of these theories in terms of the questions they ask, what they make visible, and the understandings they can yield. There are two disciplinary strands to this work, which tend to exist in different journal and conference spaces with occasional cross-overs. The first is found among those geographers who pursue educational topics. The second is found among educators who draw upon spatial theories. This work has become more pronounced with both an interest in the learning spaces opened for exploration through the discourses and practices of lifelong learning, what Ferguson and Seddon (2007) refer to as *bubbles*, and the changing educational relationship associated with globalization (Gulson and Syme 2007). We explore some aspects of research by geographers on education in the first section of this chapter. We then go on to examine a number of spatial themes in the educational research literature. These themes recur in the research drawing upon spatial theory. They are curriculum spaces, globalizing educational spaces, technologized educational spaces, gendered spaces, and finally spatializing metaphors in education. This work is itself fragmented and diverse. It draws eclectically, and not always coherently, from the threads of spatial theory identified in chapter eight. Mostly, it attempts to frame education as spatial practices rather than as taking place *in* space or *in* particular contexts (Edwards *et al.* 2009). As with chapter eight, this is an indicative rather than exhaustive exploration.

Geographers on education

Geographers have focused empirical study on many aspects of education. What is perhaps ironic is that some of this work tends to take space for granted in a fairly untheorized way. However, this is not always the case. For instance, feminist scholars such as Buckingham *et al.* (2006: 895) examine the ways in which women's training spaces problematize the public/private distinction: 'in allocating particular *spaces* to particular activities, both activities and spaces tend to be simplified so that they are stripped of their wider resonances'. Spaces, including educational spaces, can be essentialized as being only for certain activities rather than others. In examining the use of training spaces by lone women parents with low educational attainment, Buckingham *et al.* found that, rather than a linear stepping stone from the private (home) into the public (employment) space, their use was far more diverse and multiple, what they term 'liminal'. Liminality is 'ascribed to places which enable users to move beyond their previously circumscribed horizons or ways of behaviour' (Buckingham *et al.* 2006: 898). This is not simply through the acquisition of skills from training, but also through social interactions between the participating women that result in a suspension of their pre-existing identities. While Buckingham *et al.* use the concept of liminality to identify a space that is neither fully private nor public, others have used notions of 'in-betweenness' (Philo *et al.* 2005) and 'third space' (Pahl and Kelly 2005) to identify places and practices that cannot be neatly categorized within existing boundaries and binaries. This starts to raise the question that, if there are so many of these spaces which are not neatly categorizable, then do those binary spaces exist at all? In what sense does the notion of, for instance, separating public and private space continue to make sense if liminality or mobility is pervasive? Study of the practices in which people participate begins to raise questions about any foundational or assumed categorization of spaces as containers. Even prisons have visitors, mail, food deliveries and internet.

Geographers have also researched higher education to analyse, for example, the shifting spatial patterns of recruitment (e.g. Christie 2007); the utilization of educational spaces (Turner and Manderson 2007); and the effects of students becoming a significant part of the population within specified cities and neighbourhoods – 'studentification' (e.g. Hubbard 2008; Munro *et al.* 2009). In respect of the former, for instance, in a study of English higher education, Holdsworth (2009: 1849) argues that:

> While there is an important relationship between widening participation and localized study, observers fear that this will create a two-tier education system, distinguishing between those students who can afford to move away and those 'forced' to stay local. What is apparent in this discourse is the importance placed on the spatial practices of young people's transitions to adulthood, and how the ideal of going away to university offers an opportunity for these to be realized.

Here mobility is associated with privilege, adulthood and independence, although for critics it also represents a loss of community and the growth of individualism. For those who study without moving, there are thus questions raised about the social meanings ascribed to their remaining in their own locale. Holdsworth (2009: 1858) suggests that, rather than a rejection of independence, studying from home can signify an alternative form of adulthood:

Young people who attend a local university in order to care for a relative or because of the close interdependent relationships they have with family members or friends, are constructing a different model of adulthood and intimacy that is centred on obligations rather than distance.

Holdsworth adopts a mobilities framing of the issue to enhance research on educational transitions, such as home-to-school and college-to-work, in particular examining the spatial practices as well as the spatial metaphors within these movements.

Students are constantly on the move: between lecture halls; from place of residence (which may be halls of residence, privately rented accommodation, or parental home) to campus; as well as from 'home' to university. Yet very little attention has been given to these different mobility practices; rather, it is the semi-permanent move associated with leaving home that is most closely associated with student life.

(Holdsworth 2009: 1852)

In relation to studentification in the UK, the movement of large number of students into a locale has evoked crisis narratives of student ghettos, communities ripped apart, urban and environmental decay, and an overload on services such as healthcare. Seasonal student populations are held to undermine community cohesions in local areas. 'Much of the mediated opposition to studentification thus focuses on the antisocial behaviour perpetrated by (some) students, marking them out as an "other" population whose values and lifestyles do not accord with those ascribed to by the majority' (Hubbard 2008: 332). Here the effects of mobility are positioned as far from advantageous by the receiving community. Alternative tropes of gentrification and spatial marginalization have also been used to characterize the effects of studentification, alongside claims of the economic and social benefits generally that middle-class students bring to an area.

While not widespread and having differential impacting upon different areas within different urban spaces, studentification is identified as a growing phenomenon associated with the overall growth in post-secondary school education in the UK. In later work, Hubbard (2009) identifies a growing trend of purpose-built accommodation in urban areas for students in England as part of an extended gentrification process, given that many graduates continue to live and work in the towns and cities in which they studied. Here,

whilst lacking the economic capital associated with the 'new middle class' that is centrally implicated in processes of gentrification [. . .] it appears that students are increasingly involved in a form of urban gentrification underpinned by the same logics of social withdrawal and search for cultural exclusivity that help to explain the rise of middle-class gated communities.

(Hubbard 2009: 1920)

While these writers focus on the studentification of neighbourhoods, researchers have also studied the neighbourhood effects on student attainment, particularly mapping relationships between socio-economic status, neighbourhood and attainment (Sykes and Kuyper 2009). Disruption emerges as an important theme here, and in higher education spatiality more generally. For instance, in their study of a higher education labour dispute in the USA, Wilton and Cranford (2002) draw upon Lefebvre, Harvey and Soja to examine how a movement was mobilized, and the spatial disruptions that were enacted to support its goals. Drawing upon an ethnographic case study, they conclude that

> attention to the spatiality of social life suggests that disruption, as a movement tactic, works not only by upsetting the operations of institutions, but also through its power to disturb taken-for-granted routines and meanings inscribed into and reproduced by social space. This is not to suggest that all forms of disruption are inherently spatial.
>
> (Wilton and Cranford 2002: 389)

Spatial disruption as a progressive practice is obviously different from the safe or protected spaces that educators sometimes seek to occasion to support students and learning. It points to the ways in which spaces can be inscribed with particular meanings and different values for particular purposes.

Finally, as part of the emergence of interdisciplinary social studies of childhood, geographers have also sought to explore the spatial practices of children and the ways in which space helps to shape those practices (e.g Holloway and Valentine 2000). The use of ICTs and technological toys by children, and the spatial disciplining of the school in constructing childhood and children's identities, have become particular foci of attention. Holloway and Valentine (2000) point to the ways in which schools are not bounded but interconnected with society in ways that both reproduce unequal gender relations, and also provide possibilities for the expression of active subjectivity and resistance from children. There is also work on the othering, exclusions and agencies of children within the socio-spatial practices of disabilities, focusing on schools, playgrounds and homes (e.g. Holt 2007); and research on the specific conditions of traveller children (Vanderbeck 2005). The study of childhood is therefore one of the areas where geographers and educators, alongside researchers from other disciplines, may engage in shared dialogue and research. Methodologically, this usually entails the use of ethnographic methods of observation and interview, and increasingly the use of visual methods such as participants taking photos.

What is interesting is that the research on education conducted by geographers is often not referred to by educational researchers. Nor is it always strongly located in the literature of educational research. The scope for more trans-disciplinary research is obvious, especially given their shared social scientific methods. Having outlined some of the spatial research in education conducted by geographers, we now turn to the work conducted by educational researchers drawing upon spatial theory.

Curriculum spaces

Given the decentring of education to which Ferguson and Seddon (2007) refer, it is perhaps unsurprising that the most significant uptake of spatial theory in educational research is in relation to comprehending learning spaces and the spatio-temporal orderings of practices (e.g. Nespor 1994, 1997; Edwards and Usher 2003). In such work,

> the physical school is more than a context; it is an aspect in the shaping of these practices and processes producing differentiation. Decisions about the use of space involve decisions about location and movement of bodies in specific areas of the school.
>
> (Gordon and Lahelma 1996: 303)

And not simply bodies – educative spaces also have material components integral to them. Thus in her study of school departments as workplaces and spaces, and drawing upon the work of Massey and actor-network theory, McGregor (2003) suggests the need to adopt what she refers to as a topo-graphical approach to research based upon observation, interviews and photography. Here the physical and built environments can be considered as part of the hidden curriculum of education, enabling and constraining the practices possible within particular settings – schools, colleges, the home, workplaces, etc. For instance, an elite university system can rely on room spaces that comfortably house groups of 10–15 students. A mass university system requires rooms that many more students can occupy together. Similarly, drawing upon visual methods, Edwards and Clarke (2002) point to the different spatial orderings of educational practices associated with attempts to introduce greater flexibility into the curriculum.

In such spatial approaches, conceptions of inside (classroom, school) and outside (home, community) are problematized. In a sense, there is no inside and outside, but rather a relational set of practices and mobilities. We see this in the increased research on playground spaces and environmental learning beyond the walls of schools (e.g. Mannion 2003). We also see it in the study of institutions as spaces of flux and flows rather than simple bounded spaces. Students and teachers do not drop their everyday knowledge and experiences at the entrance of the institution. Both will do school work at home, and bring objects and aspects of home into school. Similarly, the activities of work, study and leisure can all take place in the home. Aligning particular spaces with educational practices as taken for granted would therefore miss the spatial spread of such activities and their complex patterns, relations and mobilities. Particular places such as classrooms can be considered therefore as *knots* of things, practices and mobilities, and not simply as isolated islands. Thus, in his study of the work of the field trip in US schools, Nespor (2000: 28, emphasis in original) argues that

> schools are *vehicles*. Field trips, along with sports events and daily bus rides to and from school, physically and symbolically transport young people through and across social and material landscapes. In the process, they help *produce* what people think of as 'public' spaces – indeed, they are of singular importance in the performance of public space to the degree that they serve as the means by which children are introduced to the downtowns, museums, national parks, monuments and historical sites that symbolize the public sphere.

In this case, the students are both introduced to, and participate in, practices that prefigure certain dispositions towards the public sphere as a space of individual consumption.

Such spatial studies are usually based upon detailed ethnographies, including observation, detailed field notes and interviews. They often draw upon visual methodologies to map interactions and the spatial organization of the settings studied through floor maps and the use of photographs as interview prompts. McGregor (2003, 2004) studied two schools in England, while Nespor (1994, 1997) has focused a series of studies on a small number of educational settings. Overall, McGregor found that teachers viewed their workplace as primarily *their* classroom, and secondarily the department to which they belonged. The staffrooms were the places where personal/social interaction and discourse was greatest. This was signified through the actual use of space by teachers, and points to the way in which, within education, educators' affiliation to students and subjects may be stronger than institutional affiliation. In McGregor's study, the spatial ordering of buildings, objects and people provide possibilities for *knowing locations* wherein knowledge production can be achieved. The potential for examining pedagogy as the enactment of knowing locations, rather than simply focusing on individual cognitive gain or collective participation, has yet to be fully explored, not least because a knowing location is not necessarily human alone.

Perhaps the most important, if not necessarily the most influential, spatial study of education in the past 20 years is provided by Nespor (1994). In his exploration of teaching, learning and curriculum in undergraduate studies in physics and management in an American university, Nespor draws upon early actor-network theory to examine the ways in which students are organized in space and time, and the implications of this for both knowledge and knowledge-building practices, and also for subjectivity (see chapter seven). He illustrates that the different practices associated with the two subject areas result in different subjectivities, networks and representational practices. In other words, learning entails ways of being, ways of acting, ways of feeling, ways of interacting, ways of representing, as well as ways of knowing. For Nespor, these emerge through the networks and networking practices in which people are enrolled and the translations to which they are subject. These are network effects, arising from the specific orderings of humans and things in space–time, which he traces ethnographically in great detail.

Curriculum and pedagogy cannot therefore be identified as taking place in enclosed or contained spaces, for they are themselves assemblages of the human and non-human and multiple in their enactments. Here, Paechter (2004) provides a helpful typology of different spaces at play in education:

- area space – concerned with the drawing of boundaries, e.g. field of study;
- movement through space – concerned with how learners move in, through and around the curriculum, e.g. learning as a journey;
- structural space – concerned with how learning is constructed, e.g. on foundations;
- hierarchical space – concerned with assessment and attainment, e.g. top of the class;
- distance space – concerned with teacher/student interactions, e.g. distance learning.

Paechter rightly points to the spatialization in different discourses of teaching, learning and the curriculum, and the conflicting ideologies they represent. This provides a useful heuristic through which to explore how many of the struggles in education are played out discursively through contrasting spatial metaphors.

Globalizing educational spaces

While there has been much discussion of globalization in education, less attention has been paid specifically to the changing spatial relationships and their significance. Most of the discussion has focused on policy critiques of globalization as an outcome of the spread of neoliberal capitalist relations and on the global reach of certain forms of policy (Gulson and Symes 2007; Ferrare and Apple 2010). Lefebvre's work has been particularly influential here. There have also been discussions of the impact of globalization on curriculum and pedagogy, on those matters that need to be covered where the aim is to enable students to engage as global citizens or consumers – covering, for example, issues such as global values, social justice, sustainable development and environmental education (Gough 1998). A further explicit study of globalization and education drawing upon post-structuralist spatial theory is provided by Edwards and Usher (2008). This is largely conceptual, drawing evidence from pre-existing studies. Inevitably, as with the wider spatial literature on globalization, it is closely linked to discussions of technologized spaces and the relationships and mobilities associated with them, including the ways in which workplaces are linked by databases across continents and the learning associated with this (Farrell and Holkner 2004).

A question that is constantly asked is: does the spread of certain forms of Western curricula and pedagogy around the globe, accelerated through the use of ICTs, constitute a form of new and more subtle cultural colonization that replaces the more complete forms of economic and political colonization from which arguably so many parts of the globe have only so recently emerged? For, as Evans (1997: 18) puts it, nation-states are now presented with a dilemma wherein 'they access the world but the world invades them'. The very connectedness of globalization creates the conditions for possible new forms of colonization. Here we see the concern that the national or local is the space of the authentic, of bounded indigenous cultures. For instance, in relation to the spread of distance learning across the South Pacific from Australia:

> Recent and future advances in their electronic media would mean that in our region [the South Pacific] multiculturality, people's sense of situational geography will become disorientated and it is possible that where people are physically will no longer determine who and where they are socially [. . .] This trend may have serious implications for Pacific people's sense of identity.
>
> (Thamen 1997: 31)

Disorientation, dislocation and loss of identity are the consequences of the spatial distribution of Western education. On the face of it, this seems a reasonable argument and it raises the larger issue of cultural imperialism through globalized education, particularly in an era of the greater international commercialisation of education. As Cunningham *et al.* (1997: 163) point out, 'there appears to be a rising level of concern in Asia that both exporting students and importing courses presents a very real threat of students' loss of identity, culture and family values'. Educational researchers are able to draw upon the work of both Lefebvre and Harvey to explore the annihilation of everyday culture and the spread of urbanization around the globe based upon the search for profit, with the associated educational policies and strategies, supported by bodies such as the OECD (Organisation for Economic Co-operation and Development).

However, it is also not unreasonable to question whether it is always desirable for place, the local and particular, to determine who and where people are socially. Clearly, place is an important factor, but it now makes more sense to look at place as globally mediated space, where difference is an effect of (en)counters rather than an expression of an essentialized bounded identity. Furthermore, the developments being pointed to here occur where there is a demand for such learning. As Mason (1998: 45) suggests, what is involved perhaps is 'not so much an exporting as a re-engineering of the educational paradigm'. Should it be assumed that those in the West who oppose colonization are always in the best position to prescribe what is best for those elsewhere – an invasion of good intentions – and is it colonization in the way suggested? And, as with other goods and services, is there not the potential for what some call the glocalization of education? As one of the respondents from Malaysia in the survey carried out by Cunningham *et al.* argues, globalization can be welcomed if it means 'we build bridges together' and is 'only a threat if it is used for a one-sided victory' (Cunningham *et al.* 1997: 163). And, as Rizvi (2000: 221) argues, based upon his study of Malaysian students in Australia, 'the suggestion that international education represents an accelerating trend towards Westernization is unfounded'. He and his colleagues (Singh *et al.* 2007) argue that the mobility of students engenders more cosmopolitan identities, which displace what might be seen as the more parochial dispositions developed within place-based identities.

Thus the colonization–anti-colonization binary can work to produce an essentialism that can be challenged from more detailed spatial analysis of globalization. Edwards and Usher (2008) use the latter to suggest an active production of different forms of hybridity. The consciousness of the globe as one place is the very consciousness that heightens a sense of the relativity and value of particular location(s). They suggest therefore that pedagogy can be explored spatially through the mapping of (dis)locating practices, both dis-locating and locating, where no *a priori* status is given to specific spaces and places. This is in tune with the mobilities thread of spatial theory introduced in chapter eight.

Technologized educational spaces

The impact of information and communication technologies (ICTs), of space–time compression, of physical absence and virtual presence, and of emerging forms of global education enabled by these developments has become a signifi-cant focus for educational researchers (Mason 1998). Lankshear *et al.* (1996) argue that education as a modernist institution is characterized by the 'spaces of enclosure' of the book, the classroom and the curriculum that work to enclose meaning and experience. Here the learner's task becomes one of extracting and re-presenting a singular canonical meaning, and the teacher's that of being the authority in terms of interpretation and accuracy. The implication of this is that there is a single definitive meaning waiting to be found.

Lankshear *et al.* maintain that developments made possible by the use of ICTs in education work in ways that call these spaces of enclosure into question. There is a questioning of underlying assumptions about the fixity and stability of the word, the linear text and the teacher as authoritative bearer of meaning. This opens up possibilities for learning to be more diverse, purpose-driven, self-imposed and self-monitored than that normally found in current mainstream educational practices. The claim is that cyberspaces create environments where the distinction between readers and writers becomes blurred and where, consequently, textual production and interpretation become less bounded. In cyberspace practices, there are no authoritative meanings waiting to be found by the suitably trained mind. By contrast, meanings are negotiated by participants. Image and text, multimodality and semiotics come to the fore in this respect (Snyder 2002; Kress 2003; Jewitt 2006). The possibility is that students do not simply interpret meanings, but actively collaborate in creating meanings. The emphasis shifts from meaning-taking to meaning-making, from canonical knowledge to transferable skills. Relationality and connectivity become more significant than dwelling and reflecting.

This, of course, is overgeneralized. However, cyberspaces and the increasing availability of a wide and diverse range of mobile technologies both to source information and to communicate do allow students more scope to construct knowledge in multimodal ways, and to interact more continuously. Practices based on multilinearity, nodes, links, flows and networks seem more appropriate to understand educating practices in such situations. Furthermore, by undermining the stability and coherence of the book, cyberspaces contribute to a questioning of the modernist subject with its assumption of a core, fixed identity. Lankshear *et al.* (1996) argue that new forms of textuality, intertextuality and hypertextuality necessarily imply a reconfiguration of the subject – in both knowledge and subjectivity. With this comes the need to rethink pedagogy in terms of multiple paths and non-linear forms of learning and teacher–student transactions. Cyberspaces are therefore not merely a new educational tool, but can spatially reconfigure the forms of knowing, sociality and subjectivity enacted through educational (en)counters. It is fair to say that this has yet to be examined empirically to the extent it has been explored theoretically.

Words of caution are necessary here, however, since there are binaries at play in this scenario which it is necessary to question. First, there is the binary of enclosure–openness, which confers an emancipatory and democratic value to learning in cyberspace. It may well be that in both historical and contemporary classroom practices a pedagogy of transmission remains to the fore, but the learning within those spaces has always been configured by resources, discourses and experiences beyond the walls of the institution. Cyberspaces may intensify and highlight the ways in which learning is not confined either to the classroom or to educational institutions. However, whether such spaces and the practices associated with them are necessarily more open and egalitarian is another matter. The panoptic surveillance of online learning and online learners, the largely text-based modes of transaction, and the rules governing online participation, often informal and difficult to ascertain, may actually close possibilities. Second, the binary logic of code/space in ICTs needs itself to be taken into account. Although the possibilities for communication may grow, interactions with software work within the logic of either/or; the resulting logorhythms inevitably restrict the range of meanings that can be generated. This is a tension at the heart of many pedagogical practices, ones that are not resolved at a stroke through the mere existence of cyberspaces. The work of Bayne (2004) is careful in this respect. She has drawn from Deleuze and Guattari the contrast between smooth and striated space to analyse digital learning spaces. Smooth spaces are open and nomadic, while striated spaces are closed and bounded. Each pervades the other, and Bayne argues that cyberspaces are often more striated than smooth. The important point here is that smooth and striated spaces are not either/or, but both/and. Mobility through cyberspaces is neither inherently emancipatory nor positive and relies upon its own immobilities and moorings. This is a point made by Edwards (2010) in an argument for a spatial analysis of the use of semantic technologies in case-based learning. He argues that educational researchers could formulate cyberspace as engendering practices of (im)mobility rather than those of learning. This entails examining education as a spatio-temporal ordering of mobilizing, mooring and boundary-making in the valuing and enacting of certain forms of subjectivities and practices, rather than focusing on a psychological or sociological framing of learning *per se*.

The non-linearity of technologized educational spaces is a significant strand to research. For Tabbi (1997: 239), 'the digital medium encourages a branching discussion in which students link up to a network – the pedagogical dynamic is more provisional, not question–answer but comment–elaboration with cues coming from a number of centres besides that of the teacher'. Lankshear *et al.* (1996: 172) emphasize the greater possibilities for teachers and students in developing understanding or meta-level awareness through 'communicative practices [that] presuppose openness, self-monitoring and constant reflexivity on the part of participants'. Any critical understanding of the effects of ICTs therefore requires an evaluation of the type of subject it encourages. When information can be taken up and used freely, the subjectivities of learners (and their identities as learners) are shaped without the policing of a traditional external epistemological authority. In cyberspaces, the disciplinary boundaries and legitimations of knowledge and information, undermined already with the widespread use of computers, becomes even more difficult to maintain. Legitimate or worthwhile knowledge becomes anything generated and used in the self-directing and self-monitored practices of cyberspace's virtual communities.

One set of questions is hotly debated in the discussion of technologized educational spaces. Can cyberspaces ever be universally accessible, and can they replace face-to-face interaction; can cyberspace ever be a true public sphere, and thus both educational and educative, in the way that the enthusiastic proponents of virtual communities argue? The fact is, of course, that cyberspaces are not universally accessible and perhaps never will be. Tabbi (1997) argues also that it is precisely the disembodiment, disembeddedness and decontextualization (no bodies, no history, no place) of electronic interchange that will always limit the democratic and educational potential of cyberspaces. In addition to the pedagogical question, there is also the wider question as to whether, given their characteristics of disembodiedness and disembeddedness, cyberspaces can ever be a site of culture, although, as Porter (1997) argues, being able to construct and exhibit mobile, multiple and made-up identities, which now can be made manifest through avatars, may not necessarily be a bad thing. Perhaps what this implies is that we need to rethink any sense of culture as a homogeneous social sphere and as a means of realizing a core identity; instead, we might imagine culture as 'the collective response to this experience of ambiguity, the gradual process of adaptation to the semiotic universe of free-floating electronic alibis' (Porter 1997: xii). Here what is being suggested is the possibility of different post-Enlightenment conceptions of subjectivity, identity formation and what it means to be educated, certain aspects of which are manifested in the burgeoning phenomenon of blogging. As Burbules (2000: 352) argues, 'the traditional associations of community with proximity, homogeneity, and familiarity can be an impediment for forming *actual* communities – including online communities.'

At this stage, all that can be said with any degree of certainty is that the globalizing effects of ICTs and their associated modes of communication bring to the fore the need for thinking anew about what constitutes community, interaction and learning in virtual times. Examining the spatial orderings and knowing locations within different forms of technologized space provides an alternative to overgeneralized views on the implications of technology for education, reframing the debate from the universal to the specific and material.

Gendered educational space

The spatial framings of inequality and exclusion are important parts of critical educational research (e.g. Lipman 2007; Thomson 2007). In particular, feminist researchers have examined the gendered enactments of space. McGregor (2003) and Paechter (2003, 2007), whose works are described above, both demonstrate the spatialization of unequal gender relations within the schools they studied in the UK. This is something the latter has studied in relation to attempts to develop cross-subject curriculum in schools and in relation to playground interactions and orderings of space.

Quinn (2003) has adopted a spatial form of analysis to examine women's participation in universities in England and question some of the conventional understandings in the research literature. She notes that, while the massification of higher education has resulted in more women than men participating, universities nonetheless remain spaces marked as masculine, although with some internal differentiations dependent upon the history of the institution and subject area. Quinn used focus groups, interviews, diaries, observations and discourse analysis with women students in two contrasting institutions in England to examine their active constructions of these spaces and what they represent for them:

> The students make close connections between studying and selfhood, and the notion of protected space is integral to these accounts. In analysing how the students construct belonging, in the face of events and processes that

seem to point to marginalisation, the university is revealed not as a trans-
parently understandable space, but a space constructed from their own
desires. However, this is also a space with material limits and always under
threat from the encroachments of others.

(Quinn 2003: 450)

There is a question about how different actors enact educational spaces here.
For Quinn's participants, universities are transitory protected spaces under
threat – 'havens from the outside world and from various forms of threat'
(Quinn 2003: 451). They are a bounded space away from other spaces and places
for these students. Here boundaries are not simply or inherently a sign of
exclusion, but can mark a protected space within which some things are
allowable which would not otherwise be the case. For the women students,
therefore, the boundedness of the space of the university was a positive aspect,
which troubles any universal association of boundaries with enclosure, and the
associated negative connotations. Quinn's spatial analysis raises questions for
alternative spatial formulations, such as Hughes' (2002) argument that women
'returners' can be conceptualized as nomads and exiles.

There is sometimes a tendency to position educational settings as needing to
provide safe spaces, especially those associated with children, and particularly in
relation to children and youth who are excluded or marginalized by formal
educational structures. Safety imperatives in policies affecting school spaces can
be argued to discourage creativity, challenge and experimentation when the
ideal of 'safe space' becomes a preoccupation. The dynamics of both safety and
risk, and their relationship in education, are rich issues to explore in spatial
terms. Preoccupations with educational 'safety' can reflect conflicting desires and
fears projected into educational spaces, which configure particular constellations
of circumstances for students and teachers. Perhaps we could examine education as enactments of specific and diverse forms of precarious space and the
(in)equalities they effect.

Spatializing metaphors

A key rationale for educational practices is that they produce change and
development – that we are all engaged in learning journeys of one sort or
another. However, with increased interest in the spatial framings of practices in
recent years, educators have also given more attention to the spatial metaphors
in the enacting of such practices (e.g. Gordon and Lahelma 1996; Sfard 1998;
Edwards et al. 2004). Thus, for instance, Gordon and Lahelma (1996: 305) use
the metaphor of the ants' nest to make sense of the complex interactions and
practices that go on in schools.

When we approach an ants' nest we see a great deal of hustle and bustle, we
see a living, undifferentiated mass moving to and fro. When we look closer,
we begin to see more organised activity; we see paths that are followed, and

we see movement with more direction. We see ant soldiers looking after order. We see corridors and corners. We look for peace and quiet and see guarded nooks. We also see co-operation and caring for others. We see closeness and overlapping of spaces. We notice neutral embodiment; where are the differences – where is gender? We know that somewhere in the depths of the nest lies the queen.

They use this metaphor to illuminate the production of difference in schools. However, they also point to the limits of the metaphor, as they are unable to identify a queen at the heart of the school. We do need to bear in mind Lefebvre's (1991) warning that metaphors conceal as much as they reveal.

Lakoff and Johnson (1980) are influential in the specific moves to examine spatial metaphors. They argue that

> most of our fundamental concepts are organized in terms of one or more spatialization metaphors [. . .] In some cases spatialization is so essential a part of a concept that it is difficult for us to imagine any alternative metaphor that might structure the concept.
>
> (Lakoff and Johnson 1980: 17–18)

It therefore becomes possible to examine the spatialization metaphors at play and, indeed, the metaphorical contestations which attempt to be persuasive in constituting educational practices. In their rhetorical analysis of educational discourses, Edwards *et al.* (2004) point to spatial metaphors of teacher-centredness, student-centredness, subject-centredness, ladders of learning, distance learning, open learning, flexible learning, situated learning, distributed learning, distributed cognition, mobile learning, networked learning, deep and surface learning, legitimate peripheral participation, communities of practice, work-based learning, border crossing and (dis)location. In each of these there is a spatial orientation, drawing upon and supporting a particular spatialization of pedagogy, teachers and students, as well as often locating pedagogy in particular places. Education is being put in its place in these different spatial framings (Ferguson and Seddon 2007), yet how often do educators explore such issues and their effects?

Some of the metaphors of pedagogy are more explicitly spatial than others in their orientation. Either implicitly or explicitly, there is a temporal ordering here as well. A spatial ordering of pedagogy is also a temporal ordering, a dynamic embedded, for example, in the texts of school timetables, which distribute people and artefacts to both times *and* places, ostensibly to learn and to teach. Each such ordering has effects on what is taught, learned, by whom, where, what subjectivity work is being attempted, and how power is exercised in these particular orders of sociality. As Paechter (2004) points out, this is not trivial. To achieve their discursive goals, these spatializing metaphors have to be rhetorically powerful.

What rhetorical work is being done in adopting particular spatial metaphors as figures of speech? Let us take some examples. For instance, in certain contexts student-centred learning has been prominent as an approach among progressive educators for many years. These ideas, derived from and supported by the humanist psychology of Rogers (1983), position the student at the centre of the learning process. In responding to their full range of needs – intellectual, practical and emotional – it is argued that teachers will enable students to learn more effectively and realize their full potential. Learning is 'facilitated' rather than poured into the empty heads of students, as is argued to be the case with teacher-centred approaches. This points to the embodied as well as the spatial work of metaphor. The argument is, in itself, an attempt to persuade by constructing a polarized choice of either student- or teacher-centred approaches and projecting a simplified caricature of the latter. At one level, this positioning of the student as central in the learning process seems like common sense, as does the notion that learning is about the whole person and not simply about the mind and the acquisition of abstract bodies of knowledge. Student-centredness seems to be about student autonomy and responsibility, which are obviously worthwhile.

Student-centred learning is powerful as a rhetorical apparatus, generating warm feelings among many educators in providing a discourse through which to manage and legitimize their practices. It is persuasive as a discourse of learning, even if it cannot be taken literally. One reason for this is that the spatializing of the student at the centre of the learning process cannot be matched in pedagogical practices founded on the mass processing of students through educational institutions. Nor should we ignore the performative aspects of such discourses. To promote a student-centred approach puts every aspect of the student under the spotlight and thereby more subject to surveillance. Normalizing processes of learning relate not merely to the mind, but extend to the person's values and feelings, evidenced in the growth of use of portfolios, reflective diaries and learning logs. Students are both worked on and encouraged to work on themselves, to become a liberally educated subjectivity. The spatialization in student-centredness has been related to Foucault's (1979) panopticon, wherein the student is constantly subject to the real and imagined gaze of the educator, a gaze that is internalized to produce self-disciplining subjects caring for themselves.

A second example is that of communities of practice, and associated concepts of legitimate peripheral participation and situated learning. Despite a great deal of critique (e.g. Hughes *et al.* 2007), the notion of communities of practice has exercised widespread influence. Based on ethnographic studies of learning in diverse settings, Lave and Wenger (1991) provide descriptions of the practices though which people move from a community's periphery to its centre, from apprenticeship to mastery, in specific areas. They learn to participate by participating; they become part of the community of practice. Learning in these contexts is located in the specific day-to-day practices of groups; it is situated.

Wenger (1998) later went on to develop a pedagogy from this description and explanation of learning, which has almost become a technology, mobilized to support the development of communities of practice in many settings.

An interesting aspect of this particular discourse is the spatial tension within it. On one hand, it could be said to decentre learning, which is constructed as taking place in the enacting of particular spaces and relations. As Lave and Wenger (1991: 94) put it, learning

> depends upon *decentring* common notions of mastery and pedagogy [. . .] To take a decentred view of master–apprentice relations leads to an understanding that mastery resides not in the master but in the organisation of the community of practice of which the master is part: the master as the locus of authority (in several senses) is after all as much a product of the conventional centred theory of learning as is the individual learner. Similarly a decentred view of the master as pedagogue moves the focus of analysis away from teaching and onto the intricate structuring of a community's learning resources.

However, as well as this decentring, there is also a centring at play, as each community has a boundary, however fuzzy, which one crosses – legitimate peripheral participation – and then moves within as one gains mastery of the particular practice. This centring does not focus on the individual student, but is inherent in the practices of the community. Thus, rather than the student being the centre, the focus here is on centring as such as the metaphor for learning, while that for teaching is decentring.

The persuasiveness of this as a discourse of learning is interesting, as there is evidence for it, based on empirical studies. However, to adopt it is not simply a matter of rational choice, as there is an emotional and values-based appeal as well. Lave and Wenger (1991) refer to 'communities', and the positive value of the notion of community is apparent. It evokes feelings of belonging, proximity, and certain shared collective values. There is a rhetorical warmth in the notion of community, even though many communities are far from inclusive or warm. This is why it is important to consider the significance and effect of terms rather than simply taking them literally. The spatial ordering of a community of practice to which one belongs or could belong rhetorically evokes powerful feelings of identification. This is so, even when to be part of a community of practice means to exclude others, when communities can be oppressive to those who do not accept their explicit and implicit rules, and when they are riven by tensions and conflicts. And what happens to those who belong or aspire to belong to numerous communities of practice? The community may be centred, but the individual learner is in pieces, torn and stretched between the various communities and situations to which they belong, for example workplace, family, pub, political party, prenatal group.

Such analysis, as Davis and Sumara (2004) suggest, points to a notion of the curriculum based less on Euclidian geometrical metaphors of linearity, norms and right angles, and more towards one based on fractal geometry and chaos. 'People are not fumbling along a more-or-less straight road towards a totalizing and self-contained knowledge of the universe. Rather, they are all taking part in structuring knowledge [. . .] and this requires a completely different image' (Davis and Sumara 2000: 821). However, how persuasive the notion of a chaotic or non-normal school might be is open to question.

Conclusion

The changing spaces of education and the framing of education as spatializing practices are clearly developing, both theoretically and as a focus for empirical studies. Ferguson and Seddon (2007: 127) suggest this points to a decentred education, and that this

> begins to open up a landscape where the centre has not held, where the established institutions that consolidated that centre have been reconfigured as particularistic learning bubbles, where flows flow in all directions and accentuated diversity and proliferating movement serve the nation as sites of social production and localized control.

While we might not accept this completely, it is suggestive of a spatial socio-material agenda for educational research.

Chapter 10

Sociomaterial approaches

Contributions and issues for educational research

This book explores a potential 'break' or palpable 'turn' in emerging arenas of educational research. We refer to these arenas as sociomaterial. Constituting this sociomaterial turn, a particular set of boundaries has been opened for debate, research and conceptual development. Boundaries that were at one time invisible, imperceptible and assumed by educators have come more clearly into view through changes in research practices associated with sociomaterialism. Our view is that the contemporary state of these arenas, taken together, says something important about the nature of these boundaries, and that engagement with them has reached a critical mass.

More specifically, the foregoing chapters have offered a brief overview of four analytical arenas that are proliferating rapidly in contemporary educational research and in the social sciences more generally. All four can help us trace the materiality, and with that the temporal and historical sociality, of everyday practices. These are certainly not the only approaches available for those interested in understanding sociomateriality and education, as we discussed at the beginning of this book. However, these four in particular are becoming increasingly evident in educational research in their contributions to the theoretical framing of practices and issues, if less so in relation to how we do research. At present, and with some notable exceptions, they perhaps contribute more to educational theories than to the methodologies of educational studies.

As these arenas appear to show overlaps in terms of discourses, themes and preoccupations – not least the focus on materiality and its co-emergence with activity, practices and things, and appear to be so unique, as a group, in their emphasis on analysing material processes – it is tempting to try and compare their premises and approaches. Certainly, we can discern in the preceding chapters complementarities and possibilities where these orientations come together, as well as clear discontinuities and incommensurabilities where they do not. Following all of these comparative tributaries might be an interesting, if protracted, task. However, given the immense diversity and debate within these four arenas, we risk collapsing their colourful internal differences into a very misleading representation of flat, singular lines of exploration. And such a comparison may not yield the most useful information for educational researchers.

Instead, this chapter begins by highlighting what appear to us to be particularly prominent understandings and questions that are shared across these four arenas to varying degrees: things that we believe may be pertinent in considering educational practices and issues. We then turn to methodologies, drawing together certain similar approaches to research and questions for educational researchers that are offered from within these diverse arenas.

Sociomaterial questions in education

At the most general level, we can state that all four arenas we have explored in this book *focus on the relations among entities through which actions occur, rather than entities themselves as the source of actions*. Objects and things are enacted in relations and practices. What attracting forces bring some things together, but make other things resist and separate from each other? What dynamics cause some things to move, and in what directions? What flows cause other things to extend themselves and wield force? When and how do things hold together despite, or perhaps even because of, the disjunctures or contradictions between them? Things themselves are not stable, identifiable objects and subjects, but teeming masses of particles or waves, energies, ideas, signs and boundaries, that are interesting in terms of the relations that hold them together, pull them apart, reorganize and change them. This means that educational processes are not simply about forming particular subjects as learners, or using particular objects, such as texts, or understanding objects such as a policy. Sociomaterial approaches trace the shifting webs of dynamics that hold these processes together and shape their properties and interactions. Rather than simply asserting that practices are complex or messy, sociomateriality provides us with ways of engaging that complexity in detail to understand better its implications for learning, education and change.

All four arenas *decentre the individualized human as the strict focal point for education*, the human brain as the primary centre of consciousness, and human development as the primary trajectory of learning and change. All four turn from the individual subject to the educational assemblage in one formulation or another, to focus on action as a dimension of assemblage: not only on the relationships between physical and mental action, but on the myriad interactions among countless entities that are continually bringing forth what we observe in any moment to be particular educational environments, subjectivities and objects.

All four approaches *challenge the binaries through which many of our understandings of practices are framed*. For instance, binaries between subject and object, nature and society, matter and meaning, meaning and sense are taken to be the effects of (re)assembled practices. They are the basis upon which other things can be explained, rather than anterior or *a priori* categorizations. Boundary making and marking are recognized as ways in which the world is divided and actively produced, reproduced and transformed rather than as naturally occurring phenomena. Similarly, all four arenas *challenge notions of context-as-container* or backcloth against which action takes place. There is thus an implicit, and sometimes explicit, focus on the spatiality and temporality of entities and practices as well as shifting relations. Education, then, does not sit within a context, but is traversed by visible, opaque and invisible relation, dependent upon how it is practised.

All four arenas attend to dynamic (social and material) relations to *produce an anti-reductionist and specifically anti-Cartesian position on education, learning and human development*. Reflecting the materialist aspect of learning in their sociomaterialism, in distinctive ways each articulates a role for non-human actors, things, their relations to each other and to people, in space and time. None of the four stops there however. They each suggest that people in concert with other entities produce changes or transformations, and it is this constant series of transformation that constitute the learning as well as specifically educational processes. Without entities, there would be no actions enacted as learning among humans.

Each *embraces the notion of categorical complexity or mess* in one form or other. For some readers, the recognition of complicated systems, overlapping activities, overdeterminations – in sum, the weight of social, material, cultural and spatial patterns of and within practices – may suggest a shared (over-)emphasis on what could be called structures. In other words, such arenas are sometimes felt to project and position a highly mechanistic view of reality that effectively marginalizes consideration of people. These concerns are understandable in some instances and applications, and particularly where a practice offers descriptive analysis that begins – and unfortunately too often ends – with simply a new, complex mapping or modelling of practices. However, our readings suggest something quite different. They suggest that, in distinct ways, each arena (albeit not all those who seek to apply them) expresses the view that the more deeply conceptual practices assist us in recognizing and accounting for the complexity (of systems, assemblages, activities and spatial relations), the more meaningful is our appreciation of the potential openness of human practice. Sociomaterial arenas contain the potential to bring into view the multiple instances and opportunities for the exercise of individual and collective agency, but not as we have conventionally understood it.

It is in these and other ways that we argue, finally, that *sociomaterial arenas accept the fundamental uncertainty of practices and activity, such as those involved in educational processes.* They suggest practical approaches for both understanding and experimenting productively with and inside education's radical contingency, without resorting simply to either complicated mechanisms of control, or to passive surrender to impossible undecidability. This does not mean that these arenas fail to generate a political project, educative purpose, or practical strategies for more democratic, more just and imaginative education. What their proponents argue, in fact, is that to actually reconfigure, even transform, the complexities of systems holding current practices firmly in place, we need educational analyses and alternatives that take account of all the materialities in play. These are often difficult to discern and understand as they engage with much more than the human social, cultural and psychological elements that are so central in much educational research.

In sum, what these arenas tend to share is a focus on tracing materiality in the enactment of social processes. They are concerned with how human/non-human vitalities and entities assemble, and are held together, in ways that exert force and orderings on the one hand, and the pressure for change and trans-formations on the other. They appreciate the productive ambivalences, inco-herences and contradictions that are opened within and around these assemblages and systems. And they all help both to delineate and to engage productively with multiplicity and difference, including the possibility of multiple coexisting worlds in everyday processes.

Of course, such general-level comparisons are terribly abstract. They can obscure important analytical distinctions between and within the different arenas we are exploring. Let us turn to more specific questions raised for educational research and educational practice by sociomaterial practices.

Materiality in education

> The world is an ongoing open process of mattering through which 'matter-ing' itself acquires meaning and form in the realization of different agential possibilities.
>
> (Barad 2003: 817)

Barad's work with complexity theory is discussed in chapter two. However, this is a powerful statement that bears repeating. The emphasis on materiality as intricately linked with the social is not simply about acknowledging things. It is about recognizing the vital energies at work that are continuously bringing forth or 'mattering' a world. And in this process of mattering, possibilities for intervening and agents of intervention are far more prevalent than we often realize when we focus only on human intention and practices alone. Everyday educational activity and knowing are critically shaped through material ele-ments and material forces. Things matter, not as discrete and reified objects with properties, but as effects of dynamic materializing practices that cause them to emerge and act in entanglements of both patterned, yet open, local everyday practice. In any given thing, whether a list of educational objectives, a child's sandwich lunch, a human being, a policy, a learning activity or a website, various matters are mingling. These include inorganic physical materials, forms of energy such as electricity or those used in our bodies, barely visible organic matter such as bacteria, semiotic materials such as inscriptions, and what Bennett (2010) calls human intensities woven throughout materialities, such as values and desires, ideas, fears, habits and addictions. When these entities – each itself bound with the heterogeneous flow of matter – come together and connect in an assemblage, they change one another. Possibilities and constraints emerge in different configurations of connections.

In examining any educational process or practice – whether a group of students meeting online, teachers finalizing an instructional module, a supervisor assessing a trainee's performance, or a school board implementing a change initiative – locating them within a sociomaterial arena enables us to ask a specific series of questions. These include questions about the relations across people, objects, tools, signs, texts, conventions, values, cognitive or affective schema and memories, as well as questions about the spatiality that they produce together in particular configurations, what mediates this process, and about the changes that are set in motion.

- What objects, texts, bodies and human intensities, including objects of knowledge, and including CHAT's conception of object-relatedness and contradictions across activity that drive a system, are actually enacted in educational processes? Which are afforded the most power and possibility?
- Through what sociomaterial connections, negotiations and mediations do these things emerge and come to be assembled in the ways that they are? What other assemblages or networks or activities overlap with and inter-penetrate them, and, with what implications for learning, education and change? What important histories of their production have been forgotten?
- What optional possibilities for education exist in these connections? What re-assemblages or reconfigurations in these networks and systems are possible? What alternative mediations are probable, unlikely or seemingly unimaginable? How are domination, accommodation, contestation, resistance and transformation sustained through assemblages in educational practices?
- What constitutes 'context' in education, when everything that exists is a sociomaterial assemblage, network, activity linked with other systems across both space and time? If everything that we are used to treating as contextual 'background' in education is in fact a teeming and continually emerging set of interrelated assemblages flowing into and through the educational occasion or object, how (and why) do we distinguish foreground from background, text from context, the given from the problematic and changeable?

In these four arenas, change is configured as emergence, occurring through both disordering as well as ordering processes. In this sense, fluidity requires stabilization, and education can be viewed as spaces of uncertainty within, and escaping from, spaces of control. Complexity, for example, views all things as emerging in a dynamic conversation among order and disorder: particular ordering rules and relations are iterated recursively, while amidst them disordering perturbations, novel encounters and continuous improvisation upon these rules contribute to the emergence of new patterns. The dialectical materialism underlying CHAT, likewise, is oriented to the study of social relations in motion, historically *vis-à-vis* the myriad (both grand and mundane) contradictions: thesis, anti-thesis, synthesis, and over again.

While ANT does not use these terms, it also treats all things, and the relations holding them together, as effects that emerge through a continuing series of complex interactions. As we saw in chapter seven, the teacher, then, is not an originator of knowledge but is a knowing location; standards of teaching practice are effects performed through multiple contradictory networks, always in flux and held in productive tension. To view educational practices as effects of emerging networks and the mobilities and immobilities sustained is to recognize the many unpredictable negotiations that lead to the translations and resistances of entities at each node of the enactment: specific terms of language, materials, coalitions of people, existing documents, disciplinary bodies of knowledge, and so on. ANT helps locate the exclusions that occur in assembling these emergent networks, exclusions that can easily be obscured in references to objects with properties that appear to exist as inevitable and immutable. Thus, like complexity theory, ANT suggests a way to understand educational activity as radically contingent. And, not unlike ANT, dialectical applications of CHAT forefront the relations of people and things that constitute the contingent transformations that constitute learning.

In these four arenas, learning is taken to be an effect of the relational activities, systems or networks of material, humans and non-humans, which enact certain practices *as* learned. In what ways is human learning itself material? To what extent is learning produced by activity, and where is human meaning and change in activity? How can the individual learning process be best understood as part of an assemblage? For education, questions for study hover around finding the points for potential intervention and transformation. For example, rather than asking how teachers might better motivate or deliver instruction to learners, these orientations might ask: where are the weak links in the networks that entrench particular behavioural patterns; where are the ambivalences that open spaces for new possibilities; or where are the perturbations that can be amplified in the complex adaptive systems of a classroom, community or human mind? Or, where are the contradictions in an activity system that can be intervened upon, clarified or exacerbated to bring about the forms of externalizations we register as social change? Or, where are the particular moorings and mobilities through which a curriculum is enacted? Inescapably, such accomplishments entail a value judgement – in fact, a constant production, reproduction and transformation of value. This constitutes particular visions of what is thought to be worthwhile learning, which in turn plays a dominant role in that learning. Teaching is not simply about the relationships between humans, but it is about the networks of entities – always expressing, addressing and contesting values, or mediated by values – through which teaching and learning are translated and enacted with humans located as learning subjects. Teaching and learning do not exist, and cannot be identified, as separate from the networks through which they are themselves enacted. They are not independent transcendental entities or processes, but immanent assemblages. Educators have found important opportunities for re-envisioning learning in terms of sociomaterial processes, such as expansion, emergence, translation, (dis)location. Likewise, they have found important opportunities in recognizing how new artefacts induce new zones of proximal development and broader patterns of mediation that transform activity, participation in it, memory, meaning, sense and communication.

Agency and subjectivity

Inherent in the foregoing chapters is a position on the matter of agency and human subjectivity. To different degrees, sociomaterial orientations refuse to attribute agency and intention solely to individual human beings, and to ascribe the energy and power that unfolds in a system to human agency and will alone. Certain ANT proponents would dismiss the concept of agency altogether as human-centric and misleading. But how, ask educators concerned about empowerment and development, is agency manifested and enacted in these sociomaterial approaches? Or, if we are to avoid a simplistic reduction of all phenomena, organic and inorganic, to ongoing relations among quirks, quarks and other bits, how is the unique human contribution to activity understood? How is human subjectivity understood within the webs of relations with material and non-human elements?

The idea of human agency has become, and has probably always been, a source of conceptual strain and confusion. A partial reflection of this is the barrage of terms that have become linked to explanations of it, typically with their own disciplinary lineage. It has been associated with terms such as self-hood, motivation, will, purposiveness, intentionality, choice, initiative, imagination, freedom, empowerment and creativity, for example. Over the course of several centuries, the issue has likewise been partially explained, interwoven with, and/or further obfuscated by distinctions between instrumental, rational, non-rational, moral and/or norm-oriented forms of action. Recent literature points to issues such as the importance of dynamic relations, time and meaning in enacting agency. Sociomaterial orientations describe and analyse forms of dynamic relations in very specific and detailed ways. They have had to partially invent a conceptual language to enact a commitment to concrete analysis. In fact, they regularly centre on real, living people, tracing the power that flows and accumulates through their ongoing everyday use of, and relationships with, specific material and symbolic things, in particular assemblages, in particular places, responding to and creating concrete situations. There is little reliance on the idea of the general or abstract agentic human subject within these situations. Human agency is practised as a location and effect, or locational effect within a network, assemblage, activity system. Agency is made, remade, contested and transformed, as well as experienced by people or subjects in these terms. However, humans alone are not the source of agency.

Here it is important to distinguish different types of human agency, beginning with notions of adaption and transformation, given that a minimal feature of any form of agency includes active attention and effort. In this context, even something that can be referred to as recursive, pre-conscious or rather *adaptive human agency* requires forms of active effort and attention. As ethnometho-dologists and conversation analysts have shown so well, all human interaction involves a level of active attention and effortful intervention, even if it typically occurs below the level of self-conscious thought. Principally, these form an element of either adaptive or transformational agency. In terms of the former, such instances of human agency could be seen in the case that a person or people seek to maintain or perpetuate a particular assemblage, network or system of activity. Due to the types of complex interplay of social and material relations we have discussed throughout this text, the changing conditions that this interplay of relations produces demand that people, individually and collectively, must actively engage, attend to and modify their roles and relations, even when such practice is reproductive of an existing order. Our point is that this, too, requires active attention and effort. In such instances, the exercise of something identifiable as human agency is therefore very much an effect of location in the sense we have described.

There is also the matter of transformative human agency, which necessarily opens up additional matters for discussion. Here human agency as *simply* a location and effect of an assemblage seems to us to be notably underwhelming. Thus, in relation to this second form of human agency, located through a consideration of the arenas of the sociomaterial theory outlined, we suggest attention to something more than active adaptation and locational effects. This is because within an assemblage, individual and collective human actors are, lest we forget (and so fall ever more deeply down the rabbit hole of structuralist accounts), disproportionately capable of *volitionally altering relationships to other actants within assemblages*.

However, it is the degree of this flexibility that is particularly noticeable in some humans in some relations. This may partially reflect a particular orientation to time. The capacity to orient to time is always also mediated by relational and locational effect. Nevertheless, we find within individual and collective human actors the capacity to orient to time in ways that non-human actors within assemblages simply do not share. An issue of importance in some non-materialist traditions of research as well (e.g. social phenomenology), this orientation to time highlights the uniquely *projective* capacities of human beings; or, in other words, the imagining of possible future trajectories of action, implicating the array of what we referred to earlier as human intensities such as fear, desire, pleasure, hope and so on. It is a capacity for (re)orienting to time, recomposing one's relationship with time, that necessarily implicates the past, present and future, but which becomes clearest, perhaps, when we think of the processes – again, always mediated by locational effects – which produce different, alternative futures. While all (human and non-human) actors within assemblages have a relation to time, it is only humans who have the capacity to recompose these orientations of past, present and future. A book, for example, has a clear orientation to the past (it embodies a long history of relations within assemblages of content, form, publication and marketing). Of course, a book has a relationship to the present (as commodity, classic or doorstopper, say, invoked anew through each interpretation and response) and even the future (when what is read mediates practices that project beyond it in time). A book embodies the past, present and future all at once. However, a book does not have any capacity to recompose its orientation to these constitutive dimensions of time, nor does it have the capacity to get together with other books to create a grievance and remedy the situation: selections from available orientations to the time, and with them the possibility of generating alternative futures, elude the book. However, as sociomateriality tells us, people do not have an autonomous capacity to re-orient to time. Their capacities are always and forever mediated by the affordances of the artefact, the system, the network, the assemblages, the activities; that is, the social and material relations.

Stemming from, and contributing to, this disproportionately greater flexibility of human actors to recompose their orientation to time, in particular the future, is what could be called interpretational flexibility (practical evaluation, meaning- or sense-making). The recomposition of time gives, and depends on, meaning/ sense-making, itself encompassing another recompositional affordance: symbolic recompositions that can be extended all the way to the capacity to recompose roles and personal identities. These affordances – meaning/sense-making and time recomposition – are the likeliest routes to understanding human agency generally. In adaptive human agency, these types of process may or may not be as clear. In transformational human agency, similarly and always, there are also the effects of location, but nevertheless these unique affordances become accentuated. In either case, our point is that here we see the type of interplay and mutual constitutions of thinking, communication as dimensions of the myriad mediations that make up learning and human development, in particular the sociomaterial enactments of reflection, imagination and creativity in human beings.

Taken as a whole, this notion of human agency is better described as a matter of *manoeuvrability*. Locations in space–time and in relational assemblages are fundamental to defining the possibilities or degrees of manoeuvrability. Clearly, non-human actors are not devoid of the affordance for change. Our discussions of ANT, complexity and CHAT are particularly rich in explanations of how this is the case. However, capacity for change or plasticity is not synonymous with the types of time-recomposition process we have described above that account for manoeuvrability. This term, in our view, simultaneously expresses the thoroughly relational, active, transformational, material and spatialized ontological principles outlined in various ways across the individual chapters.

Each sociomaterial arena we have outlined makes a distinctive contribution to engaging with the practices and possibilities, as well as the limits, of human agency. They all position structures as not external or anterior to practice, but rather as inherent to it in the form of mutualistic relational mediations (people acting on and with things; things acting on and with people, and so on). To suggest that such arenas are not interested in questions of agency is therefore to miss the point. They actually expand the possibilities for the practice of agency by refusing to generalize, and abstract it from the materialities within which it is enacted.

Power relations and politics

Power flows and accumulates in all systems. The four arenas all address power relations and individual differences at play in educational processes. ANT, for instance, critically traces the ordering practices through which power is exercised. The post-structuralist antecedents of ANT become apparent in its approach to power, as power is viewed as circulating through regimes of know-ledge and discursive practices. Power is not possessed by particular people or institutions, but is constantly created and readjusted through relations among people, practices and things. Actor-network studies bring a new focus to the complex negotiations of power among human and non-human elements in these processes. They enrich, but also identify, limitations in certain existing readings of power in education, and point to some new possibilities in research-ing education. ANT sensibilities ask: How do powerful networks in education (particular stabilized knowledges, accountability systems, evaluative practices) emerge? How do people and objects become part of the network? What individual subjectivities and behaviours does the network mobilize? What knowledge circulates, and what does not? What and who become included and excluded? What negotiations occur as individual elements take up, resist, or compete with the attempts to enrol and mobilize them into particular patterns of action and knowledge? ANT approaches power relations by questioning the very connections that build and hold together those black-boxed, taken-for-granted networks that entrench oppressive or just plain unproductive practices and block new possibilities. ANT analyses unpick what appears to be stable; highlight ambivalences; and locate weak connections where intervention can transfigure, dissolve or initiate new networks of activity and imagination. They also trace what Latour (2005) refers to as the 'hidden geography' of the political, the spaces through which we are gathered by the objects that affect us.

CHAT seems to vary widely in its orientation to issues of power relations across a continuum of Marxist and other critical analyses of domination and resistance, to an almost organizational development/consultant usage that, from the perspective of the former, may further entrench unequal relations of power. Here, respectively, contradictions can focus on those of capitalism, exploita-tion, domination and the division of labour, or conversely upon pragmatic contradictions in organizational routines, barriers to the efficient achievement of organizational goals, and so on. In either instance, issues of human needs (material, social, emotional, developmental, etc.) and their satisfaction are at stake. Clearly, some participants find their needs met disproportionately more than others. The view of power relations echoes what might be identified as a radical position: organizations are viewed as sites of central contradictions, material as well as ideological struggle between those who exercise control and those who disproportionately experience their lives as the object of control. However, the seeming clarity offered by these types of description is hardly definitive – on its own – of the way the contradictions of capitalism can and do play out in the lives of each and every participant, whether they are professional, blue- or pink-collar workers, students, parents, administrators or teachers. CHAT studies have oriented to conceptions of hierarchical class struggle as well as engaged in analyses, where learning is conceived as either reproducing and adapting to given power relations, or transforming them, often through formal or informal, collective contestation and resistance, across the full range of multi-voiced standpoints. In CHAT, an emphasis may be placed on a full range of contradictions, such as the common tension between an emphasis on competency and control, and injunctions for innovation involving risk and experimentation. Individual perspectives and interests are constantly at play in negotiating these contradictions; and it is the identification of contradictions in CHAT research that allows the identification of power relations. When people themselves undergo change, either to confront the challenges of the contradiction or to adapt to them, or when new forms of practice seep into, for example, the organizational life of a workplace, home or school, 'learning' occurs. People, things and the relations between them, including their social and material organization, both adapt and are transformed. That, and how these changes involve the transformation of individuals, groups and/or the relations of a broader activity (or even networks of activity systems), is a matter of empirical investigation.

Questions of power that CHAT raises in the field of educational practice are vast. They have included, for instance, how relations of gender, race, disability, sexuality and social class are reproduced through forms of activity, differential uses of artefacts, or the effects that the structure of an activity has on conscious goal generation in students. Can seemingly specific artefactual interventions (such as the introduction of new software, or student report cards) have broader, radiating effects on power differentials and/or learning outcomes? How does the analysis of activity systems explain the ongoing performance of students from linguistic minority groups? Why does concept formation seem to function differently among different social groups in a school setting? And what role might overlapping activity systems (such as the effects of an emergent parental or community organization, or a newly legislated occupational association) have in shaping new patterns of mediated regulation of teachers' or educational administrator's work? In responding to these types of question, CHAT analysis explores how power relates to the differential satisfaction of human need as expressed in the many forms of object–relatedness of activity.

Complexity treats systems as fundamentally configured by flows of power, as we saw in chapters two and three. The dynamic, non–linear interactions that lead to novel patterns of emergence are the traces of power in a system. Bennett's (2010) notion of vitalities that propel complex assemblages reflects this. Prigogine's (1997) insistence that emergence – the dynamic state of a system far from equilibrium – depends upon external sources of energy, or at least internal amplification, also reflects this. When experiencing the condition of emergence, a system endlessly throws up new possibilities for action, and with each (irreversible) choice from among these, the system is slightly reconfigured, and even further possibilities of choice unfold for all elements of the system. Here we see complexity's position on power: a complex adaptive system presents a continual radical undecidability of possibilities as it continues to expand pro-ductively. For Barad (2007), this offers a new configuration of agency and politics. For Osberg (2010), this suggests a reconceptualization of justice. For Davis and Sumara (2008), it reveals how all complex systems are learning systems: ever improvising and experimenting. For Bennett (2010: 107), as described in chapter one, it suggests a new materialist theory of democracy as we encounter the world 'as a swarm of vibrant materials entering and leaving agentic assemblages'. Bennett shows that the power to disrupt public arrange-ments, in ways that change the boundaries that distribute bodies to recognize some and dismiss others, is wielded through non–human as well as human energies. However, in terms of equity issues, complexity dynamics do not favour any element of the system just because it experiences disadvantage. Nor is emergence governed by any normative criteria for good or bad emergence – this must be imposed by elements outside complexity theory. But complexity does emphasize the critical need for internal diversity if emergence (of new possibilities, innovations, practices) is to occur. Diversity cannot be managed towards producing greater homogeneity, but a system's diverse elements must become interconnected in some way. In elaborating this with respect to human systems of learning, Davis (2004) explains that difference in a system needs to be recognized, which it often is not. Different entities or parts of the system also must be substantively connected to one another: through redundancy or overlap of activities and tools shared among them, through decentralized organizational processes, through environments and projects that encourage continuous interaction, and through multiple feedback loops across parts of the system. Educators have extrapolated from these principles to show how complexity offers an expansive approach to encouraging learners' positive recognition of, and engagement with, difference in social markers, unfamiliar practices and disquieting new ideas.

Spatial arenas position power as reflected in the ways in which space is ordered into particular places and the mooring and mobilities associated with them, and the ways in which such orderings enable and constrain particular mobilities and moorings. Opening up the spaces of enclosure through which the institutions of education and their practices have been subject to more relational and material positionings points to both the ways in which particular practices of teaching, learning and assessment are put and held in place, and the multiple possibilities that exist for reconfiguring those spaces. Thus, for instance, the power given to parents and their 'choices' for their children reconfigure the possibilities for schools as spaces of enclosure and the forms of professional accountability to which teachers become subject. The growth of e-learning was at first critiqued as a way of keeping people in their place by excluding them from the necessity of moving across space and time to occupy spaces other than the home. With the growth of mobile e-learning, and with the expansion of the possibilities for online mobility and relatedness, we now have a far more complex educational picture within which power is enacted in particular ways as both constraint and possibility.

It is sometimes claimed that issues of power and politics are marginal to sociomaterial research. However, this is clearly not the case. Political questions may take different forms through these approaches, and relations of power and difference may be analysed in surprising ways, but they are certainly not absent.

Sociomaterial methods and educational research

Sociomaterial approaches to research to date more often appear to suggest a sensibility, rather than a specified set of methods for conducting research. As Law (2004b: 195) writes of ANT, the question is of 'method assemblage', which is not quite a method but a 'resonance': 'a continual process of crafting and enacting necessary boundaries between presence, manifest absence, and Otherness'. Nonetheless, ANT, CHAT, and spatiality and complexity theory have stimulated, contributed to and drawn upon a rich expansion of empirical approaches in education. These tend to begin from the local and the singular, following details of everyday interactions to understand practice *in situ*. They usually attempt to avoid a humanist bias and anterior abstract categories that homogenize and control. They include fine-grained ethnographic tracings, sometimes liaise with ethnomethodological studies, and have engaged groups in dialogue to analyse their own practices. Spatial research in education has also drawn widely upon cartographic methods (physically mapping institutional arrangements, social groupings, community resources, flows of movement and talk, etc.) and visual narrative (digital photography and film, for instance) to compare diverse meanings of space. Complexity theory has perhaps been most active in educational research as an analytical tool rather than a series of particular methods. In chapter three, we saw much application of complexity concepts in philosophical inquiry examining knowledge, curriculum, subjectivity and responsibility. Researchers have focused particularly on understanding the unfolding dimensions in motion of complex adaptive systems, with some struggling to account adequately for the researcher's own entanglements in the system or dimension under study. In education, complexity researchers tend to understand systems as learning systems. Therefore, among some there is particular interest in tracing processes of learning and how these are produced through dynamics commonly understood to be required for emergence: such as diversity, redundancy, recursive reiterations, distributed organization, feedback and constraints. What is important is following the relations between things, not the things themselves, and the ways in which changes over time produce emergence in systems held together by these relations. The problem is not only the researcher's entanglements in apprehending and representing systems, but also the principle that the elements of a system exceed attempts to demonstrate it.

In ANT, researchers have debated ways to trace material assemblages that neither over-privilege the human actors and their meanings, nor ascribe human capability to non-human elements. In chapter seven, we saw various experiments with methods undertaken by educational researchers adopting ANT sensibilities to maintain some sense of human/non-human symmetry. In certain recent ANT-related traditions that are exploring multiple ontologies, researchers have been working through methods that can help to appreciate, without colonizing, the multiple worlds that are often at play in everyday encounters. A major concern described below is how to represent these multiple orientations, and their political negotiations for recognition, in ways that avoid collapsing them into one language and one logic – that of the researcher.

In CHAT research, there has been wide experimentation with methods that allow the gathering of information about detailed uses, meanings and relations across people and specific mediating artefacts. Most contemporary CHAT research draws on case-study techniques and ethnographic accounts, alongside a tradition of using fine-grained socio-linguistic, conversational analysis or ethnomethodological techniques. We see examples of all these in CHAT-based educational research, as well as some examples of survey methods and quasi-experimental design methods (in psychology-oriented studies). Uniquely, CHAT has a long and recently reinvigorated tradition of interventionist research, particularly in organizational settings such as Developmental Work Research (Daniels *et al.* 2009), described in chapter five, itself based on the innovations developed at the Center for Research on Activity, Development and Learning (CRADLE) at the University of Helsinki. Several contemporary researchers, such as Stetsenko, have however offered detailed arguments regarding the ontological basis of CHAT, as discussed in chapter four. However, CHAT researchers have not tended to discuss multiple ontologies, the representation of multiple worlds and so on in depth, beyond the treatment of multi-voiced-ness discussed in chapter four [cf. Mietinnin's (1999) concern for the practical work-ability of research in the face of multiple ontologies]. Nevertheless, there is strong interest in understanding the multiplicity of participants' own, distinctive standpoints and worldviews in practice, and even to intervene to help participants understand and engage these differences themselves. Despite this, and informed (mostly implicitly) by a type of ontology that can perhaps best be affiliated with the critical realist tradition, there is a relative paucity of CHAT studies offering sustained treatments of the potentially distinctive researcher worldview.

Clearly, there are important distinctions in the methodological foci and commitments across these sociomaterial approaches. Respecting this caveat, we turn now to highlight themes of interest that are shared across at least some of the educational studies outlined in previous chapters. Some of these themes are not particularly new or unique, as researchers accustomed to neo-Marxist, feminist, post-structuralist, or postmodern research approaches might attest. However, there is power in highlighting the material as well as the social dynamics to press these issues in research.

The inclusion and exclusion of actors and objects in delineating a line of inquiry is an ongoing struggle. All researchers must make decisions in disentangling a particular focus of study or unit of analysis from networks or webs of complexity. Perhaps these problems of selection and focus are especially difficult when the point of the research is to highlight the myriad overlapping relations producing these entities. Which are the most interesting, worthwhile, or important from an educational standpoint? Moreover, we can ask what is being ignored or banished from the study gaze, and how such omissions distort the visible. Here the implications are well documented by Law (2004b). The corollary problem is that of presumption, as though any research conducted by ubiquitously fallible researchers, who can only ever see partially, can or should try to capture the totality of a system with all its human and non-human interconnective tissues. And, of course, researchers need to be cognizant of how, within any particular sociomaterial arena, some phenomena will be immediately rendered more visible and valuable than others by virtue of particular theoretical flashlights and microphones.

Further, in sociomaterial orientations, educational researchers confront significant difficulties in shifting from intersubjectivity to interobjectivity, excluding for a moment the use of the latter term in a different way in CHAT research. This can be a question of how to conduct research working with artefacts without subordinating them entirely to human intentions and meanings: asking, as Thompson (2010) did in chapter seven, for example, how does one interview an object? It is also a question about the nature of privileging and status in shifting to an orientation of interobjectivity. Who is speaking for the materializing forces that cannot provide a direct account on their own? How are these objects and forces constituted in particular ways, with selected conceptual apparatus that delineate relations and connections to 'cut' material webs into particular things, patterns and concepts? How are researchers to shift beyond a sense of themselves as subjects to understand themselves as apart, but not distinct, from the objects of their inquiry?

Representation, always a struggle for researchers sensitive to the ways in which they construct and participate in their own worlds of inquiry, also raises particular problems in the non-representationalist commitments of much sociomaterial inquiry. There is a fundamental tension between the material-embodied mode of enaction and imminence, and the symbolic mode of declaration and displacement when one thing represents another. Yet the researcher's act of representation itself involves both modes. All of these issues circle back to researchers' awareness and accounting of their entanglements in producing the assemblages of research. Researchers must be especially reflexive about what categories they have adopted from the beginning, what is banished from view and for what reasons, what is conjured into view, and what is flattened into a pattern. They need continually to interrupt their own apparatus and categories of knowledge-making, and to interrupt the drift to identify the human actor as self-evident. Such a process, where it works well, is partially reflected in the interventionist methods of CHAT researchers, who embrace a co-construction model, working closely with, and regularly being guided and directed by, those who in conventional research would be reduced simply to the researched.

The challenge to researchers in working with these approaches is to produce accounts that are sufficiently robust to avoid charges of both 'symmetrical absence and symmetrical absurdity' (McLean and Hassard 2004: 494). Some balance must be struck. Educational researchers may need to experiment with ways actually to examine and invoke the materiality of educational processes as ongoing materializing dynamics, which is much more than adding a discussion of objects to accounts that are fundamentally concerned with the human and intersubjective. And researchers need to do this without romanticizing materiality, occluding humanity, or failing to distinguish the unique energies, limitations, and types of connections among diverse entities as they assemble and reassemble. Researchers must also acknowledge the sociomaterial relations in which they themselves are meshed, and on which they are dependent.

Finally, and perhaps most interesting for future educational research, these sociomaterial approaches throw forward the question of difference with new challenges for methodology. Elements that are fundamentally different – such as electrical particles, medication, a hot classroom, a peer's taunt, a heavy portfolio, a longing for recognition, a popular label of illness – are treated as uniquely important: each holding important histories, each mediating action, connecting and reconnecting in ways that produce particular assemblages of identity, values, purpose and knowledge. Fundamental difference is assumed to be a central focus in research – difference not just among worldviews and webs or networks holding together different systems, but also, for some orientations, difference between simultaneously existing and overlapping *worlds*. The practical problem of such assumptions is, first, somehow to communicate across these different worlds. The language we use to discuss a phenomenon is deeply embedded in the ontology we inhabit. From within the methods, desires and instruments available to us in this ontology, and through our participation in the method assemblages of this ontology, particular phenomena materialize that we come to recognize and name as learning. Our tendency when we communicate with others who talk about learning from within a different but coexisting ontology is to fold these others into our own world. Perhaps we recognize different meanings at play, or different purposes, for the same word. But this is folding, so long as we continue to insist upon one ontology (ours) where different subjective perspectives (theirs) move about. However, to what extent can we permit that others are enacting fundamentally different phenomena, *different objects* that are also learning, and that are held together in material assemblages that are more-than-human? As long as we explain away such difference as subjective constructions, or perhaps as rhetorical flexibility, we are sustaining a singular and universal material ontology. Here is where the notion of multiple ontologies becomes tricky. Henare *et al.* (2007) point to the obvious issue that it is partly through our subjective construction that we engage our world and try to appreciate others' worlds. It is through our conceptual capacity that we attempt to understand these worlds using the conceptual categories, theoretical resources and other apparatus emerging from our own ontology. Ultimately, Henare *et al.* (2007) worry that it may be impossible to communicate across ontologies without dissolving the other's world. Can we ever break sufficiently from our own subjective perspectives to engage in the 'method assemblages' of utterly different ontologies? Some, such as Verran (2001), have argued not only that this is possible, but that people like the Yoruba children she taught in Nigeria have impressive capacities to move between ontologies – a phenomenon she calls 'being-ontics'. Researchers like Verran have found sociomaterial and socio-technical approaches useful in apprehending multiple ontologies. These sociomaterial approaches decentre human agency and perspectives, and try to trace materiality in ways not possible with traditional resources of phenomenology, sociology, anthropology, even pragmatism.

Even if we can identify multiple ontologies without folding them into our own, what do we do with this multiplicity? Law (2009b) suggests four possible approaches. One way is to trace different 'reals', examining the intersections and interactions between these worlds. This approach, suggests Law, can counter tendencies to view different realities as simply a question of perspective. It opens possible alternatives, by highlighting the complexity of objects and underscoring ontological incoherence. A second approach is to explore the different 'goods' embedded in each real. For instance, in democratic citizenship education, as Westheimer and Kahn (2004) point out, learning can be oriented to at least three different enactments: (1) personally responsible citizens (focusing on character building, doing good deeds, etc.); (2) participatory citizens (focusing on skills for collective action, such as participating in community or national affairs); or (3) justice-oriented citizens (focusing on promoting social justice and addressing social injustice through political analysis and change of structural issues). Comparing these helps bring to the surface hidden normativities woven into the very fabric of different worlds and steps aside from ideological deadlock over ethics and purpose. Law's third methodological option is to explore what he calls collateral realities, performing a sort of ontological archaeology to examine the qualities of different objects in different spatialities. This approach, he suggests, can expose hidden enacted realities, their collusions and their limits. A fourth option is juxtaposition, placing non-coherent objects against one another, then moving them around, to explore the tensions and fluidities that emerge among them in different configurations.

The continuing dilemma in this work, taking up any of Law's suggested methodological approaches to study education, is the researcher's implication in the enactment of the different reals. What is being enacted and represented as multiple ontologies still emanates from a knowledge-making authority, a certain knowing location. The demands are high in such work for reflexivity, for tracing the researcher's complicity in the webs of action, and for accounts explicitly acknowledging their fragility and their presumptions.

Conclusion

Many of the sociomaterial approaches within and across the four orientations discussed in this volume raise significant challenges to educational researchers. In fact, most offer questions rather than solutions. In considering their demands in educational research, Alhadeff-Jones (2010) writes, from a complexity orientation, of the difficulties as well as the productive possibilities that are opened. These resonate well with other perspectives described in this book. Educational researchers interested in sociomaterial approaches likely will find themselves

> tolerating continuous negotiation between order and disorder, [. . .] rethinking constantly the organization legitimizing one's own assertions, [. . .] embracing a radical uncertainty [. . .] [and] engaging a permanent process of self-reflection whereby researchers continuously question their doubts, their ignorance and their confusion.
>
> (Alhadeff-Jones 2010: 480)

These may not sound like conventional starting points for research, but they can be an impetus for innovation and creativity in researching education. This, in part, is the potential offered by sociomaterial practices.

The arenas we have explored each theorize, in very different and very precise ways, the interactions and interconnections between different movements: between the particular and general in learning; between what appear to be system structures and individual actions; between planned and emergent processes; and between continuity and discontinuity. Most of all, they help us to delineate and accept difference in a wildly complex world, rather than always seeking relations, singularity and seamless continuity. Taken together, they demonstrate the very rich and multi-dimensional relations among human and non-human participants in learning processes. They also demonstrate the impossibility of conventional certainty in explaining these relations. No one model of connections can account for the complexities afoot totally and for all time.

No single orientation attempts to speak for all phenomena, nor should any be treated as inherently superior. Each offers particular conceptual resources and questions that accentuate relations in ways that are more useful for some educational questions than for others. In our summaries of these orientations, we hope to have indicated what may be considered to be their strengths and limitations. Assigning limitations is a very limited way to view what are in fact vibrant debates and issues being pushed ever forward within and between these arenas. Our discussion of these does not mean to imply essential limitations, but rather currently existing ones, as we see them. Likewise, the notion of strengths implies normative judgments that we are not prepared to make across these four complex arenas of research. Throughout this volume, which in fairness can be considered only an introduction to sociomateriality in education, we have tried to address each arena of theory and research mostly by demonstrating its creative use and critical considerations by educational researchers. Their studies focus upon different issues and are propelled by different purposes. However, most are interested primarily in understanding how *matter* matters in education, and how this understanding can open more generative practices, inquiries, policies and engagements that can be called educative as well as emergent, and even trans-formative.

That said, there are yet many gaps and opportunities in the unfolding work being conducted with complexity theory, cultural-historical activity theory, actor-network theory and spatiality theories, as they beckon to education. Our hope is that ever more educational researchers will consider entering these arenas, to experiment with new theoretical contributions and the issues arising in seeking to address the questions and commitments we have as educators. Education matters in every sense of the word and, borrowing from Latour (2005), things bind us in educational spaces that are quite different from those we associate with the term 'education'. The task of educational researchers is to trace those spaces, as well as the human and non-human practices and relations through which they are enacted. Sociomaterial approaches provide certain ways in which this can be done, but they are never final or finalized. And, lest we forget, matter is never entirely inert.

Bibliography

van der Aalsvoort, G. and Ghesquiere, P. (2004) 'The realities of learners with special educational needs and their contexts: a methodological challenge', *International Journal of Disability, Development, and Education*, 51(2): 131–222.

Alhadeff-Jones, M. (2008) 'Three generations of complexity theories: nuances and ambiguities', *Educational Philosophy and Theory* 40(1): 66–82.

——(2010) 'Challenging the limits of critique in education through Morin's paradigm of complexity', *Studies in Philosophy and Education*, 29(5): 477–90.

Anderson, B. and Wylie, J. (2009) 'On geography and materiality', *Environment and Planning A*, 41: 318–35.

Angus, T., Cook, I. and Evans, J. (2001) 'A manifesto for cyborg pedagogy?', *International Research in Geographical and Environmental Education*, 10(2): 195–201.

Appadurai, A. (1990) 'Disjuncture and difference in the global cultural economy', in M. Featherstone (ed.), *Global Culture: Nationalism, Globalisation and Modernity*, London: Sage.

Archer, M. (1995) *Realist Social Theory: The Morphogenetic Approach*, Cambridge: Cambridge University Press.

Arievitch, I. (2003) 'A potential for an integrated view of development and learning: Galperin's contribution to sociocultural psychology', *Mind, Culture, and Activity*, 10: 278–88.

Aronowitz, S. (2007) 'The ignored philosopher and social theorist: the work of Henri Lefebvre', *Situations*, 2(1): 133–55.

Au, W. (2007) 'Vygotsky and Lenin on learning: the parallel structures of individual and social development', *Science and Society*, 71(3): 273–98.

Avis, J. (2007) 'Engeström's version of activity theory: a conservative praxis?', *Journal of Education and Work*, 20(3): 161–77.

——(2009) 'Transformation or transformism: Engestrom's version of activity theory?' *Educational Review*, 61(2): 151–65.

Bai, H. (2001) 'Beyond the educated mind: towards a pedagogy of mindfulness, body and mind', in B. Hocking, A. Haskell and W. Linds (eds), *Body and Mind: Exploring Possibility Through Education*, Vermont, NH: Foundation for Educational Renewal, pp. 86–99.

——(2003) 'On the edge of chaos: complexity and ethics', in *Proceedings of the First Conference on Complexity Science and Educational Research*, Edmonton, Alberta: University of Alberta, pp. 19–30. www.complexityandeducation.ualberta.ca/conferences/2003/proceedings.htm

Bakhurst, D. (1991) *Consciousness and Revolution in Soviet Philosophy: From the Bolsheviks to Evald Ilyenkov*, New York: Cambridge University Press.

——(2009) 'Reflections on activity theory', *Educational Review*, 61(2): 197–210.

Barab, S.A., Hay, K.E. and Yamagata-Lynch, L.C. (2001) 'Constructing networks of action-relevant episodes: an *in situ* research methodology', *Journal of the Learning Sciences*, 10(1): 63–112.

Barab, S., Thomas, M., Dodge, T., Carteaux, R. and Tuzun, H. (2005) 'Making learning fun: Quest Atlantis, a game without guns', *Educational Technology Research and Development*, 53(1): 86–107.

Barad, K. (2003) 'Posthumanist performativity: toward an understanding of how matter comes to matter', *Signs: Journal of Women in Culture and Society*, 28(3): 801–31.

——(2007) *Meeting the Universe Halfway*, Durham, NC: Duke University Press.

Barowy, W. and Smith, J. (2008) 'Ecology and development in classroom communication', *Linguistics & Education*, 19(2): 149–65.

Bauman, Z. (1993) *Postmodern Ethics*, Oxford: Blackwell.

Bayne, S. (2004) 'Smoothness and striation in digital learning spaces', *E-Learning*, 1(2): 302–16.

Beach, K. (1999) 'Consequential transitions: a socio-cultural expedition beyond transfer in education', *Review of Research in Education*, 28: 46–69.

Beauchamp, C., Jazvac-Martek, M. and McAlpine, L. (2009) 'Studying doctoral education: using activity theory to shape methodological tools', *Innovations in Education and Teaching International*, 46(3): 265–77.

Bennett, J. (2010) *Vibrant Matter: A Political Ecology of Things*, Durham, NC: Duke University Press.

Bhabha, H. (1990) 'The third space: interview with Homi Bhabha', in J. Rutherford (ed.), *Identity: Community, Culture, Difference*, London: Lawrence & Wishart.

——(1994) *The Location of Culture*, London: Routledge.

Bhaskar, R. (1998) 'Societies' (pp. 206–57) and 'Critical realism and dialectics' (pp. 575–640), in M. Archer, R. Bhaskar, T. Lawson and A. Norrie (eds), *Critical Realism: Essential readings*, London: Routledge.

Biesta, G.J.J. (2006a) 'Pedagogy with empty hands: Levinas, education and the question of being human', in D. Egéa-Kuehne (ed.), *Levinas and Education: At the Intersection of Faith and Reason*, London: Routledge.

——(2006b) *Beyond Learning: Democratic Education for a Human Future*, Boulder, CO: Paradigm.

Blackler, F. and McDonald, S. (2000) 'Power, mastery and organizational learning', *Journal of Management Studies*, 37: 833–52.

Blanchot, M. (1995) *The Writing of the Disaster*, trans. Ann Smock, Lincoln, NE: University of Nebraska Press.

Blanton, W.E., Moorman, G.B. and Hayes, B.A. (1997) 'Effects of participation in the fifth dimension on far transfer', *Journal of Educational Computing Research*, 16(4): 371–96.

Blanton, W., Simmons, E. and Warner, M. (2001) 'The fifth dimension: application of cultural–historical activity theory, inquiry-based learning, computers and telecommunications to change prospective teachers' preconceptions', *Journal of Educational Computing Research*, 24: 435–63.

Blanton, W., Menendez, R., Moorman, G.B. and Pacifici, L. (2003) 'Learning to comprehend written directions through participation in a mixed activity system', *Early Education and Development*, 14(3): 313–34.

Blunden, A. (2010) *An Interdisciplinary Theory of Activity*, Leiden, the Netherlands: Brill.

Bogg, J. and Geyer, R. (2007) *Complexity, Science and Society*, Oxford: Radcliffe.

Bosco, F. (2006) 'Actor-network theory, networks, and relational approaches in human geography', in S. Aitken and G. Valentine (eds), *Approaches to Human Geography*, London: Sage, pp. 136–46.

Brah, A. (1996) *Cartographies of Diaspora: Contesting Identities*, London: Routledge.

Braidotti, R. (1994) *Nomadic Subjects: Embodiment and Sexual Difference in Contemporary Feminist Theory*, New York: Columbia University Press.

Brenner, N. and Elden, S. (2009) 'Henri Lefebvre on state, space and territory', *International Political Sociology*, 3(4): 353–77.

Brian, A.W. (1994) *Increasing Returns and Path Dependence in the Economy*, Ann Arbor, MI: University of Michigan Press.

Bruner, J. (1987) 'Prologue to the English edition', in R. Rieber and A. Carton (eds), *The Collected works of L. S. Vygotsky. Volume 1*, London: Plenum, pp. 1–17.

Buckingham, S., Marandet, E., Smith, F., Wainwright, E. and Diosi, M. (2006) 'The liminality of training spaces: places of private/public transitions', *Geoforum*, 37: 895–905.

Bukatman, S. (1996) *Terminal Identity*, Durham, NC: Duke University Press.

Burbules, N. (2000) 'Does the internet constitute a global educational community?', in N. Burbules and C. Torres (eds), *Globalisation and Education: Critical Perspectives*, New York: Routledge.

Byrne, D. (2005) 'Complexity, configurations and cases', *Theory, Culture & Society*, 22(5): 95–111.

Byrne, D.S. (1998) *Complexity Theory and the Social Sciences*, London: Routledge.

Callon, M. (1986) 'Some elements of a sociology of translation: domestication of the scallops and the fishermen of Saint Brieuc Bay', in J. Law (ed.), *Power, Action and Belief: A New Sociology of Knowledge?* London: Routledge & Kegan Paul, pp. 196–233.

——(1998) *The Laws of the Market*, Oxford: Blackwell.

Capra, F. (1996) *The Web of Life: A New Scientific Understanding of Living Systems*, New York: Anchor Books.

——(2002) *The Hidden Connections: Integrating the Biological, Cognitive, and Social Dimensions of Life into a Science of Sustainability*, New York: Doubleday.

Carter, K. (2010) 'Re-thinking learning–work transitions in the context of community training for racialized youth', in P. Sawchuk and A. Taylor (eds), *Challenging Transitions in Learning and Work: Reflections on Policy and Practice*, Rotterdam, the Netherlands: Sense Publishing.

Chaiklin, S. (ed.), (2001) *The Theory and Practice of Cultural–Historical Psychology*, Aarhus, Denmark: Aarhus University Press.

Chaiklin, S. and Lave, Jean (eds) (1996) *Understanding Practice – Perspectives on Activity and Context*, New York: Cambridge University Press.

Chaiklin, S., Hedegaard, M. and Jensen, U.J. (eds) (1999) *Activity Theory and Social Practice*, Aarhus, Denmark: Aarhus University Press.

Chambers, I. (1994) *Migrancy, Culture, Identity*, London: Routledge.

Christie, H. (2007) 'Higher education and spatial (im)mobility: nontraditional students and living at home', *Environment and Planning A*, 39: 2445–63.

Clarke, J. (2002) 'A new kind of symmetry: actor-network theories and the new literacy studies', *Studies in the Education of Adults*, 34(2): 107–22.

Clegg, S. (2005) 'Evidence-based practice in educational research: a critical realist critique of systematic review', *British Journal of Sociology of Education*, 26(3): 415–28.

Cole, M. (1995) 'The supra-individual envelope of development: activity and practice: situation and context', in J. Goodnow, P. Miller and F. Kessel (eds), *Cultural Practices as Contexts for Development*, San Francisco, CA: Jossey-Bass.

——(1996) *Cultural Psychology: A Once and Future Discipline*, Cambridge: Cambridge University Press.

Cole, M. and Engeström, Y. (2007) 'Cultural–historical approaches to designing for development', in J. Valsiner and A. Rosa (eds), *The Cambridge Handbook of Sociocultural Psychology*, New York: Cambridge University Press.

Cole, M., Engeström, Y. and Vasquez, O. (eds) (1997) *Mind, Culture, and Activity*, New York: Cambridge University Press.

Collinge, C. (2005) 'The difference between society and space: nested scales and the returns of spatial fetishism', *Environment and Planning D*, 23: 189–206.

Collins, C. (1999) *Language, Ideology and Social Consciousness: Developing a Sociohistorical Approach*, Aldershot: Ashgate.

——(2008) 'Discourse in cultural–historical perspective: critical discourse analysis, CHAT and the study of social change', in B. Van Oers, E. Elbers, W. Wardekker and R. van der Veer (eds), *The Transformation of Learning: Advances in Cultural–Historical Activity Theory*, Cambridge: Cambridge University Press, pp. 242–72.

Cooper, H. and Spencer-Dawe, E. (2006) 'Involving service users in interprofessional education narrowing the gap between theory and practice', *Journal of Interprofessional Care*, 20(6): 603–17.

Coughenour, C.M. (2003) 'Innovating conservation agriculture: the case of no-till cropping', *Rural Sociology*, 68(2): 278–304.

Crang, M., Crosbie, T. and Graham, S. (2007) 'Technology, time–space, and the remediation of neighbourhood life', *Environment and Planning A*, 39: 2405–22.

Crick, F. (1994) *The Astonishing Hypothesis: The Scientific Search for the Soul*, New York: Simon & Schuster.

Cunningham, S., Tapsall, S., Ryan, Y., Stedman, L., Bagdon, K. and Flew, T. (1997) *New Media and Borderless Education: A Review of the Convergence between Global Media Networks and Higher Education Provision*, Canberra, Australia: Department of Employment, Education, Training and Youth Affairs.

Cutright, M. (ed.) (2001) *Chaos Theory and Higher Education: Leadership, Planning and Policy*, New York: Peter Lang.

Daniels, H. (ed.) (1996) *An Introduction to Vygotsky*, London: Routledge.

——(2001) *Vygotsky and Pedagogy*, London: Routledge.

——(2004) 'Cultural historical activity theory and professional learning', *International Journal of Disability Development and Education*, 51(2): 185–200.

——(2009) 'Mediation in the development of interagency work', in H. Daniels, A. Edwards, Y. Engeström, T. Gallagher and S. Ludvigsen (eds), *Activity Theory in Practice: Promoting Learning across Boundaries and Agencies*, London: Routledge, pp. 105–25.

Daniels, H. and Edwards, A. (eds) (2004) 'Sociocultural and activity theory in educational research' (special issue), *Educational Review*, 56(2): 107–205.

Daniels, H. and Warmington, P. (2007) 'Analysing third generation activity systems: power, contradictions and personal transformation', *Journal of Workplace Learning*, 19(6): 377–91.

Daniels, H., Cole, T. and Visser, J. (2000) 'Values and behaviour in education: an activity theory approach to research', in K. Ruoho (ed.), *Emotional and Behavioural Difficulties*, Joensuun Yliopisto, Finland: University of Joensuu.

Daniels, H., Leadbetter, J., Warmington, P., Edwards, A., Martin, D., Popova, A., Apostolov, A., Middleton, D. and Brown, S. (2007) 'Learning in and for multi-agency working', *Oxford Review of Education*, 33(4): 521–38.

Daniels, H., Edwards, A., Engeström, Y., Gallagher, T. and Ludvigsen, S. (eds) (2009) *Activity Theory in Practice: Promoting Learning across Boundaries and Agencies*, London: Routledge.

Davis, B. (2004) *Inventions of Teaching: A Genealogy*, Mahwah, NJ: Lawrence Erlbaum.

Davis, B. and Sumara, D.J. (1997) 'Cognition, complexity, and teacher education', *Harvard Educational Review*, 67(1): 105–25.

——(2000) 'Curriculum forms: on the assumed shapes of knowing and knowledge', *Journal of Curriculum Studies*, 32(6): 821–45.

——(2004) 'The hidden geometry of curriculum', in R. Edwards and R. Usher (eds), *Space, Curriculum and Learning*, Greenwich, CT: Information Age Publishing.

——(2005) 'Challenging images of knowing: complexity science and educational research', *International Journal of Qualitative Studies in Education*, 18(3): 305–21.

——(2006) *Complexity and Education: Inquiries into Learning, Teaching and Research*, Mahwah, NJ: Lawrence Erlbaum.

——(2008) 'The death and life of great educational ideas: why we might want to avoid a critical complexity theory', *Journal of the Canadian Association for Curriculum Studies*, 6(1): 163–76.

Davis, B., Sumara, D.J. and Luce-Kapler, R. (2000) *Engaging Minds: Learning and Teaching in a Complex World*, Mahwah, NJ: Lawrence Erlbaum.

Davis, P. (2007) 'How cultural models about reading mediate classroom (pedagogic) practice', *International Journal of Educational Research*, 46(1): 31–42.

Davydov, V. (1988) 'Problems of developmental teaching: the experience of theoretical and experimental psychological research', *Soviet Education*, 30(9): 3–83.

——(1990) *Types of Generalization in Instruction: Logical and psychological problems in the structuring of school curricula*, Reston, VA: National Council of Teachers of Mathematics.

Deleuze, G. and Guattari, F. (1987) *A Thousand Plateaus: Capitalism and Schizophrenia*, trans. B. Massumi, Minneapolis, MN: University of Minnesota Press.

Demiraslan, Y. and Usluel, Y. (2008) 'ICT integration processes in Turkish schools: using activity theory to study issues and contradictions', *Australasian Journal of Educational Technology*, 24(4): 458–74.

Dewey, J. (1938) *Experience and Education*, New York: Macmillan.

DeWitt, J. and Osborne, J. (2007) 'Supporting teachers on science-focused school trips: towards an integrated framework of theory and practice', *International Journal of Science Education*, 29(6): 685–710.

Dodge, M. and Kitchen, R. (2009) 'Software, objects and home space', *Environment and Planning A*, 41: 1344–65.

Dodge, M., Kitchen, R. and Zook, M. (2009) 'How does software make space? Exploring some geographical dimensions of pervasive computing and software studies', *Environment and Planning A*, 41: 1283–93.

Doll Jr, W.E. (1989) 'Foundations for a post-modern curriculum', *Journal of Curriculum Studies*, 21(3): 243–253.

——(1993) *A Post-Modern Perspective on Curriculum*, New York: Teachers College Press.

——(2005) 'The culture of method', in W.E. Doll, J.M. Fleener, D. Trueit and J. St Julien (eds), *Chaos, Complexity, Curriculum, and Culture: A Conversation*, New York: Peter Lang.

Doll Jr, W.E., Fleener, M.J., Trueit, D., St Julien, J. (eds) (2005) *Chaos, Complexity, Curriculum, and Culture: A Conversation*, New York: Peter Lang.

EASST (2010) European Association for the Study of Science and Technology: Conference 2010, University of Trento, Italy. www.easst.net

Edwards, A. (2004) 'The new multi-agency working: collaborating to prevent the social exclusion of children and families', *Journal of Integrated Care*, 12(5): 3–10.

——(2005) 'Let's get beyond community and practice: the many meanings of learning by participating', *Curriculum Journal*, 16(1): 49–65.

Edwards, A. and Fox, C. (2005) 'Using activity theory to evaluate a complex response to social exclusion', *Educational and Child Psychology*, 22(1): 51–61.

Edwards, A. and Kinti, I. (2009) 'Working relationally at organisational boundaries: negotiating expertise and identity', in H. Daniels, A. Edwards, Y. Engeström, T. Gallagher and S. Ludvigsen (eds), *Activity Theory in Practice: Promoting Learning across Boundaries and Agencies*, London: Routledge, pp. 126–39.

Edwards, A., Daniels, H., Gallagher, T., Leadbetter, J. and Warmington, P. (2009) *Improving Inter-professional Collaborations: Multi-Agency Working for Children's Wellbeing*, London: Routledge.

Edwards, R. (2010) '(Im)mobilities and (dis)locating practices in cybereducation', paper presented at Economic and Social Research Council (ESRC) seminar, University of Southampton.

Edwards, R. and Clarke, J. (2002) 'Flexible learning, spatiality and identity', *Studies in the Continuing Education*, 24(2): 153–65.

Edwards, R. and Usher, R. (2003) (eds), *Space, Curriculum and Learning*, Greenwich, CT: Information Age Publishing.

——(2008) *Globalisation and Pedagogy: Space, Place, Identity*, London: Routledge.

Edwards, R., Nicoll, K., Solomon, N. and Usher, R. (2004) *Rhetoric and Educational Discourse*, London: Routledge.

Edwards, R., Biesta, G. and Thorpe, M. (2009) (eds), *Rethinking Contexts of Learning and Teaching*, London: Routledge.

van Eijck, M. and Roth, W. (2007) 'Rethinking the role of information technology-based research tools in students' development of scientific literacy', *Journal of Science Education and Technology*, 16(3): 225–38.

Elden, S. (2001) 'Politics, philosophy, geography: Henri Lefebvre in recent Anglo-American scholarship', *Antipode*, 33: 809–25.

Elhammoumi, M. (2006) 'Is there a Marxist Psychology?', in P. Sawchuk, N. Duarte and M. Elhammoumi (eds), *Critical Perspectives on Activity: Explorations across Education, Work and Everyday Life*, New York: Cambridge University Press, pp. 23–34.

Engeström, Y. (1987) *Learning by Expanding: An Activity-Theoretical Approach to Developmental Research*, Helsinki: Orienta-Konsultit.

——(1992) *Interactive Expertise: Studies in Distributed Working Intelligence*, Research Bulletin 83, Helsinki: Department of Education, Helsinki University.

——(1996a) 'Developmental work research as educational research: looking ten years back and into the zone of proximal development', *Nordisk Pedagogik: Journal of Nordic Educational Research*, 16: 131–43.

Engeström, Y. (1996b) 'Interobjectivity, ideality, and dialectics', *Mind, Culture, and Activity*, 3(4): 259–65.

——(1999a) 'Innovative learning in work teams', in Y. Engeström, R. Miettinen and R.-L. Punamäki (eds), *Perspectives on Activity Theory*, Cambridge: Cambridge University Press, pp. 377–406.

——(1999b) 'Activity theory and individual and social transformation', in Y. Engeström, R. Miettinen and R.-L. Punamäki (eds) *Perspectives on Activity Theory*, New York: Cambridge University Press, pp. 19–38.

——(2001) 'Expansive learning at work: toward an activity theoretical reconceptualization', *Journal of Education and Work*, 14(1): 133–46.

——(2004) 'The new generation of expertise: seven theses', in H. Rainbird, A. Fuller and A. Munro (eds), *Workplace Learning in Context*, London: Routledge, pp. 145–65.

——(2007) 'Putting Vygotsky to work: the Change Laboratory as an application of double stimulation', in H. Daniels, M. Cole and J. Wertsch (eds), *Cambridge Companion to Vygotsky*, New York: Cambridge University Press.

——(2009) 'The future of activity theory: a rough draft', in A. Sannino, H. Daniels and K.D. Gutierrez (eds), *Learning and Expanding with Activity Theory*, Cambridge: Cambridge University Press, pp. 303–28.

Engeström, Y. and Kerosuo, H. (2007) 'From workplace learning to interorganizational learning and back: the contribution of activity theory', *Journal of Workplace Learning*, 19(6): 336–42.

Engeström, Y., Engeström, R. and Kärkkäinen, M. (1995) 'Polycontextuality and boundary crossing in expert cognition: learning and problem solving in complex work activities', *Learning and Instruction*, 5: 319–36.

Engeström, Y., Miettinen, R. and Punamäki, R.-L. (eds) (1999) *Perspectives on Activity Theory*, New York: Cambridge University Press.

Eoyang, G (2004) 'The practitioner's landscape', *E:Co* 6(1–2): 55–60.

Evans, T. (1997) '(En)countering globalisation: issues for open and distance education', in L. Rowan, L. Bartlett and T. Evans (eds), *Shifting Borders: Globalisation, Localisation and Open and Distance Education*, Geelong, Australia: Deakin University Press.

Falk, R. (1993) 'The making of global citizenship', in J. Brecher, J. Brown Childs and J. Cutler (eds), *Global Visions: Beyond the New World Order*, Montreal: Black Rose Books.

Farrell, L. and Holkner, B. (2004) 'Points of vulnerability and presence: knowing and learning in globally networked communities', *Discourse*, 25(2): 133–44.

Fazio, X. and Gallagher, T.L. (2009) 'Supporting learning: an examination of two teacher development collectives', *Complicity: An International Journal of Complexity and Education* 6(1): 1–19.

Featherstone, M. (1995) *Undoing Culture: Globalisation, Postmodernism and Identity*, London: Sage.

Fenwick, T. (2001) 'Questioning the concept of the learning organization', in C. Paechter, M. Preedy, D. Scott and J. Soler (eds), *Knowledge, Power and Learning*, London: Paul Chapman/Sage, pp. 74–88.

——(2006a) 'The audacity of hope: towards poorer pedagogies', *Studies in the Education of Adults*, 38(1): 9–24.

——(2006b) 'Toward enriched conceptions of work learning: participation, expansion, and translation among individuals with/in activity', *Human Resource Development Review*, 5(3): 285–302.

Fenwick, T. (2009a) 'Responsibility, complexity science and education: dilemmas and uncertain responses', *Studies in Philosophy and Education*, 28(2): 101–18.

——(2009b) 'Making to measure? Reconsidering assessment in professional continuing education', *Studies in Continuing Education*, 31(3): 229–44.

——(2010a) '(Un)doing standards in education with actor-network theory', *Journal of Education Policy*, 25(2): 117–33.

——(2010b) 'Reading educational reform with actor network theory: fluid spaces, otherings, and ambivalences', *Educational Philosophy and Theory*, DOI: 10.1111/j.1469–5812.2009.00609.x

——(2010c) 'Rethinking the thing: sociomaterial approaches to understanding and researching learning in work', *Journal of Workplace Learning*, 22(1): 104–16.

——(2010d) 'Accountability practices in adult education: insights from actor-network theory', *Studies in the Education of Adults*, 42(2): 170–85.

Fenwick, T. and Edwards, R. (2010) *Actor-Network Theory and Education*, London: Routledge.

Ferguson, K. and Seddon, T. (2007) 'Decentred education: suggestions for framing a socio-spatial research agenda', *Critical Studies in Education*, 48(1): 111–29.

Ferrare, J. and Apple, M. (2010) 'Spatializing critical education: progress and cautions', *Critical Studies in Education*, 51(2): 209–21.

Feryok, A. (2009) 'Activity theory, imitation and their role in teacher development', *Language Teaching Research*, 13(3): 279–99.

Flint, K. (2009) 'A Derridaean reading of the zone of proximal development (ZPD): the monster in the play of différance', *Educational Review*, 61(2): 211–27.

Foucault, M. (1979) *Discipline and Punish: The Birth of the Prison*, Harmondsworth: Penguin.

Fountain, R.M. (1999) 'Socio-scientific issues via actor network theory', *Journal of Curriculum Studies*, 31(3): 339–58.

Fox, S. (2005) 'An actor-network critique of community in higher education: implications for networked learning', *Studies in Higher Education*, 30(1): 95–110.

Frankham, J. (2006) 'Network utopias and alternative entanglements for educational research and practice', *Journal of Education Policy*, 21(6): 661–77.

Fukuyama, F. (2002) *Our Post Human Future: Consequences of the Biotechnology*, New York: Farrar Straus & Giroux.

Fullan, M. (2003) *Change Forces with a Vengeance*, New York: Routledge.

——(2007) *Leading in a Culture of Change*, San Francisco, CA: Jossey-Bass.

Galperin, P. (1989) 'Organization of mental activity and the effectiveness of learning', *Soviet Psychology*, 27: 65–82.

——(1992) 'The problem of activity in Soviet psychology', *Journal of Russian and East European Psychology*, 30(4): 37–59.

Garrison, J. (2001) 'An introduction to Dewey's theory of functional "trans-action": an alternative paradigm for activity theory', *Mind, Culture, and Activity*, 8: 275–96.

Gherardi, S. and Nicolini, D. (2000) 'To transfer is to transform: the circulation of safety knowledge', *Organization*, 7(2): 329–48.

Gibbs, R. (2000) *Why Ethics? Signs of Responsibilities*, Princeton, NJ: Princeton University Press.

Giddens, A. (1990) *The Consequences of Modernity*, Cambridge: Polity Press.

Gilstrap, D. (2008) 'Dialogic and the emergence of criticality in complex group processes', *Journal of the Canadian Association for Curriculum Studies*, 6(1): 91–112.

Gindis, B. (1999) 'Vygotsky's vision: reshaping the practice of special education for the 21st century', *Remedial & Special Education*, 20(6): 32–64.

Gladwell, M. (2002) *Tipping Points: How Little Things Can Make a Big Difference*. Boston, MA: Little, Brown.

Glassman, M. (2001) 'Dewey and Vygotsky: society, experience, and inquiry in educational practice', *Educational Researcher*, 30(4): 3–14.

Goodenow, R. (1996) 'The cyberspace challenge: modernity, post-modernity and reflections on international networking policy', *Comparative Education*, 32(2): 197–216.

Goonewardena, K., Kipfer, S., Milgrom, R. and Schmid, C. (eds) (2008) *Space, Difference, Everyday Life: Reading Henri Lefebvre*, New York: Routledge.

Gordon, T. and Lahelma, E. (1996) '"School is like an ant's nest": spatiality and embodiment in schools', *Gender and Education*, 8(3): 301–10.

Gough, N. (1998) 'Globalisation and curriculum: theorising a transnational imaginary', paper presented at the Conference of the American Educational Research Association, San Diego, CA, USA.

——(2004) 'RhizomANTically becoming-cyborg: performing posthuman pedagogies', *Educational Philosophy & Theory*, 36(3): 253–65.

Greenhill, A. and Fletcher, G. (2009) 'Tacos, clothes and spimes', paper presented to the conference, Objects – What Matters? Technology, Values and Social Change, University of Manchester, 3 September. www.slideshare.net/salfordbizsch/tacos-3078289

Gregory, D. (1994) 'Social theory and human geography', in D. Gregory, R. Martin and G. Smith (eds), *Human Geography*, Minneapolis, MN: University of Minneapolis Press.

Griffiths, T. and Guile, D. (2003) 'A connective model of learning: the implications for work process knowledge', *European Educational Research Journal*, 2(1): 56–73.

Grosz, E. (1994) *Volatile Bodies: Toward a Corporeal Feminism (Theories of Representation and Difference)*, Bloomington, IN: Indiana Press.

Guile, D. and Griffiths, T. (2001) 'Learning through work experience', *Journal of Education and Work*, 14(1): 113–31.

Guile, D. and Young, M. (2003) 'Transfer and transition in vocational education: some theoretical considerations', in Y. Engeström and T. Gronin (eds), *Between Work and School: New Perspectives on Transfer and Boundary-crossing*, London: Pergamon, pp. 63–81.

Gulson, K. and Symes, C. (eds) (2007) *Spatial Theories of Education: Policy and Geography Matters*, New York: Routledge.

Gutiérrez, K. (2002) 'Studying cultural practices in urban learning communities', *Human Development*, 45(4): 312–21.

Gutiérrez, K., Asato, J., Santos, M. and Gotanda, N. (2002) 'Backlash pedagogy: language and culture and the politics of reform', *Review of Education, Pedagogy, & Cultural Studies*, 24(4): 335–51.

Habib, L. and Wittek, L. (2007) 'The portfolio as artifact and actor', *Mind, Culture, and Activity*, 14(4): 266–82.

Hager, P., Lee, A. and Reich, A. (eds) (2011) *Learning Practice*, New York: Springer.

Haggis T. (2004) 'Meaning, identity and "motivation": expanding what matters in understanding learning in higher education?', *Studies in Higher Education*, 29(3): 335–52.

Haggis T. (2007) 'Conceptualising the case in adult and higher education research: a dynamic systems view', in J. Bogg and R. Geyer (eds), *Complexity, Science and Society*, Oxford: Radcliffe.

——(2008) 'Knowledge must be contextual: exploring some possible implications of complexity and dynamic systems theories for educational research', *Educational Philosophy and Theory*, 40(1): 159–76.

——(2009) 'Beyond "mutual constitution": looking at learning and context from the perspective of complexity theory', in R. Edwards, G. Biesta and M. Thorpe (eds), *Rethinking Contexts for Learning and Teaching: Communities, Activities and Networks*, London: Routledge.

Hall, P. (2008) 'Critical visualization', in P. Antonelli (ed.), *Design and the Elastic Mind*, New York: Museum of Modern Art.

Hamilton, M. (2009) 'Putting words in their mouths: the alignment of identities with system goals through the use of individual learning plans', *British Educational Research Journal*, 35(2): 221–42.

Hannam, K., Sheller, M. and Urry, J. (2006) 'Editorial: Mobilities, immobilities and moorings', *Mobilities*, 1(1): 1–22.

Haraway, D. (1991) 'Cyborg manifesto: science, technology, and socialist-feminism in the late twentieth century', in *Simians, Cyborgs and Women: The Reinvention of Nature*. New York: Routledge.

Hardman, J. (2005) 'An exploratory case study of computer use in a primary school mathematics classroom: new technology, new pedagogy?' *Perspectives in Education*, 23(4): 99–111.

Harman, G. (2007) 'The importance of Bruno Latour for philosophy', *Cultural Studies Review*, 13(1): 31–49.

——(2009) *Prince of Networks: Bruno Latour and Metaphysics*, Melbourne: re.press books.

Hartley, D. (2009) 'Education policy, distributed leadership and socio-cultural theory', *Educational Review*, 61(2): 139–50.

Harvey, D. (1989) *The Condition of Postmodernity: An Enquiry into the Origins of Social Change*, Oxford: Basil Blackwell.

——(1993) 'Class relations, social justice and the politics of difference', in J. Squires (ed.), *Principled Positions: Postmodernism and the Rediscovery of Value*, London: Lawrence & Wishart.

Hassard, J., Law, J. and Lee, N. (1999) 'Introduction: actor-network theory and managerialism', *Organization*, 6(3): 387–91.

Hayles, K. (1999) *How We Became Posthuman: Virtual Bodies in Cybernetics, Literature and Informatics*, Chicago, IL: University of Chicago Press.

Hearn, M. and Michelson, G. (2006) (eds) *Rethinking Work: Time, Space and Discourse*, Cambridge: Cambridge University Press.

Hebdige, D. (1990) 'Introduction – subjects in space', *New Formations*, 11: vi–vii.

Hedegaard, M. and Lompscher, J. (eds)(1999) *Learning Activity and Development*, Aarhus, Denmark: Aarhus University Press.

Held, D. and McGrew, A. (eds) (2003) *The Global Transformations Reader*, Cambridge: Polity Press.

Henare, A., Holbraad, M. and Wastell, S. (eds) (2007) *Thinking Through Things: Theorising Artefacts Ethnographically*, London: Routledge.

Hennessey, R. (1993) *Materialist Feminism and the Politics of Discourse (Thinking Gender)*, London: Routledge.

Hetherington, K. (1997) 'In place of geometry: the materiality of place', in K. Hetherington and R. Munro (eds), *Ideas of Difference: Social Spaces and the Labour of Division*, Oxford: Blackwell.

Hetherington, K. and Law, J. (2000) 'After networks', *Environment and Planning D: Space and Society* 18: 127–32.

Holdsworth, C. (2009) '"Going away to uni": mobility, modernity, and independence of English higher education students', *Environment and Planning A*, 41: 1849–64.

Holland, D., Lachicotte, W., Skinner, D. and Cain, C. (1998) *Identity and Agency in Cultural Worlds*, Cambridge, MA: Harvard University Press.

Holland, J. (1995) *Hidden Order: How Adaptation Builds Complexity*, Reading, MA: Perseus Books.

Holloway, S. and Valentine, G. (2000) 'Spatiality and the new social studies of childhood', *Sociology*, 34(4): 763–83.

Holt, L. (2007) 'Children's sociospatial (re)production of disability within primary school playgrounds', *Environment and Planning D: Society and Space*, 25: 783–802.

Holzman, L. (1990) 'Lev and let Lev: an interview on the life and works of Lev Vygotsky', *Practice: The Magazine of Psychology and Political Economy*, 7(3): 11–23.

——(1997) *Schools for Growth: Radical Alternatives to Current Educational Models*, Mahwah, NJ: Lawrence Erlbaum.

——(2006a) 'What kind of theory is activity theory: introduction', *Theory & Psychology*, 16(1): 5–11.

——(2006b) 'Activating postmodernism', *Theory & Psychology*, 16(1): 109–23.

Hopwood, N. and Stocks, C. (2008) 'Teaching development for doctoral students: what can we learn from activity theory?' *International Journal for Academic Development*, 13(3): 187–98.

Houchin, K. and MacLean, D. (2005) 'Complexity theory and strategic change: an empirically informed critique', *British Journal of Management*, 16: 149–66.

Hubbard, P. (2008) 'Regulating the social impacts of studentification: a Loughborough case study', *Environment and Planning A*, 40: 323–41.

——(2009) 'Geographies of studentification and purpose-built student accommodation: leading separate lives?', *Environment and Planning A*, 41: 1903–23.

Hughes, C. (2002) 'Beyond the poststructuralist–modern impasse: the women returner as "exile" and "nomad"', *Gender and Education*, 14(4): 411–24.

Hughes, J., Jewson, N. and Unwin, L. (eds) (2007) *Communities of Practice: Critical Perspectives*, Abingdon and New York: Routledge.

Hunter, S. and Swan, E. (2007) 'Oscillating politics and shifting agencies: equalities and diversity work and actor network theory', *Equal Opportunities International*, 26(5): 402–19.

Hutchins, E. (1995) *Cognition in the Wild*, Cambridge, MA: MIT Press.

Ilyenkov, C. (2009) *The Ideal in Human Activity: A Selection of Essays by Evald Vasilyevich Ilyenkov*, Pacifica, CA: Marxist Internet Archive.

Ilyenkov, E.V. (1982) *The Dialectics of the Abstract and the Concrete in Marx's Capital*, Moscow: Progress Publishers.

Jacobs, G. (2006) 'Fast times and digital literacy: participation roles and portfolio construction within instant messaging', *Journal of Literacy Research*, 38(2): 171–96.

Jantzen, W. (2002) 'The Spinozist programme for psychology: an attempt to reconstruct Vygotsky's methodology of psychological materialism in view of his theories of emotions', in D. Robbins and A. Stetsenko (eds), *Voices within Vygotsky's Non-Classical Psychology: Past, Present, Future*, New York: Nova Science, pp. 101–12.

Jaworski, B. and Potari, D. (2009) 'Bridging the macro- and micro-divide: using an activity theory model to capture sociocultural complexity in mathematics teaching and its development', *Educational Studies in Mathematics*, 72(2): 219–36.

Jensen, C.B. (2010) *Ontologies for Developing Things: Making Health Care Futures Through Technology*, Rotterdam: Sense.

Jensen, K. (2007) 'The desire to learn: an analysis of knowledge-seeking practices among professionals', *Oxford Review of Education*, 33(4): 489–502.

Jewitt, C. (2006) *Technology, Literacy and Learning: A Multimodal Approach*, London: RoutledgeFalmer.

Johnson, S. (2001) *Emergence: The Connected Lives of Ants, Brains, Cities, and Software*, New York: Scribner.

Jones, G., McLean, C. and Quattrone, P. (2004) 'Spacing and timing', *Organisation*, 11(6): 723–41.

Jones, P. (2001) 'The ideal in cultural–historical activity theory: issues and perspectives', in S. Chaiklin (ed.), *The Theory and Practice of Cultural–Historical Psychology*, Aarhus, Denmark: Aarhus University, pp. 283–315.

——(2002) '"The word becoming a deed": the dialectic of "free action" in Vygotsky's *Tool and Sign in the Development of the Child*', in D. Robbins and A. Stetsenko (eds), *Voices within Vygotsky's Non-classical Psychology: Past, Present, Future*, New York: Nova Science, pp. 143–59.

——(2009) 'Breaking away from *Capital*? Theorising activity in the shadow of Marx', *Critical Social Studies – Outlines*, 11(1): 45–58.

Joung, Y.J. (2008) 'A 5-year-old's initiation into scientific ways of knowing', in Y.-J. Lee and A.-L. Tan (eds), *Science Education at the Nexus of Theory and Practice*, Rotterdam: Sense, pp. 317–32.

Kahveci, A., Gilmer, P. and Southerland, S. (2008) 'Understanding chemistry professors' use of educational technologies: an activity theoretical approach', *International Journal of Science Education*, 30: 323–51.

Kang, H. and Gyorke, A. (2008) 'Rethinking distance learning activities: a comparison of transactional distance theory and activity theory', *Open Learning*, 2(3): 203–14.

Kaplan, C. (1996) *Questions of Travel*, London: Duke University Press.

Kaptelinin, V. (2005) 'The object of activity: making sense of the sense-maker', *Mind, Culture, and Activity*, 12(1): 4–18.

Kaptelinin, V. and Nardi, B. (2006) *Acting with Technology: Activity Theory and Interaction Design*, Cambridge, MA: MIT Press.

Karpiak, I. (2000) 'Evolutionary theory and the new sciences', *Studies in Continuing Education*, 22(1): 29–44.

Kauffman, S. (1995) *At Home in the Universe: The Search for Laws of Complexity*, London: Penguin.

Keith, M. and Pile, S. (eds) (1993) *Place and the Politics of Identity*, London: Routledge.

Kellner, D. (2000) 'Globalisation and new social movements: lessons from critical theory and pedagogy', in N. Burbules and C. Torres (eds), *Globalisation and Education: Critical Perspectives*, New York: Routledge.

Kelly, G. (2008) 'Inquiry, activity, and epistemic practice', in R. Duschl and R. Grandy (eds), *Establishing a Consensus Agenda for K-12 Science Inquiry*, Rotterdam: Sense, pp. 99–117.

Knorr Cetina, K. (1997) 'Sociality with objects: social relations in post-social knowledge societies', *Theory, Culture & Society*, 14(4): 1–25.

Knorr Cetina, K. (2001) 'Objectual practice', in T.R. Schatzki, K. Knorr Cetina and E. von Savigny (eds), *The Practice Turn in Contemporary Theory*, London: Routledge, pp. 175–88.

Koszalka, T. and Wu, C. (2004) *A Cultural Historical Activity Theory [CHAT] Analysis of Technology Integration: Case Study of Two Teachers*, Chicago, IL: Association for Educational Communications and Technology.

Koyama, J.P. (2009) 'Localizing No Child Left Behind: supplemental educational services (SES) in New York City', in F. Vavrus and L. Bartlett (eds), *Critical Approaches to Comparative Education: Vertical Case Studies from Africa, Europe, the Middle East, and the Americas*, New York: Palgrave Macmillan, pp. 21–37.

Kozulin, A. (1986) 'The concept of activity in Soviet psychology', *American Psychologist*, 41(3): 264–74.

——(1990) *Vygotsky's Psychology: A Biography of Ideas*, New York: Harvester Wheatsheaf.

Kramerae, C. (1995) 'A backstage critique of virtual reality', in S. Jones (ed.), *Cybersociety*, London: Sage.

Krange, I. (2008) *Computer-based 3D models in Science Education: Studying Artefacts and Students' Knowledge Constructions*, Oslo: University of Oslo.

Kress, G. (2003) *Literacy in the New Media Age*, London: Routledge.

Kwa, C. (2002) 'Romantic and baroque conceptions of complex wholes in the sciences', in J. Law and A. Mol (eds), *Complexities: Social Studies of Knowledge Practices*, Durham, NC: Duke University Press, pp. 23–52.

Laidlaw, L. (2005) *Reinventing Curriculum: A Complexity Perspective on Literacy and Writing*, Mahwah, NJ: Lawrence Erlbaum.

Lakoff, G. and Johnston, M. (1980) *Metaphors We Live By*, Chicago, IL: University of Chicago Press.

Landri, P. (2007) 'The pragmatics of passion: a sociology of attachment to mathematics', *Organization*, 14(3): 407–29.

Langemeyer, I. and Roth, W.-M. (2006) 'Is Cultural–Historical Activity Theory threatened to fall short of its own principles and possibilities as a dialectical social science?', *Critical Social Studies – Outlines*, 8(2): 20–42.

Lankshear, C., Peters, M. and Knobel, M. (1996) 'Critical pedagogy and cyberspace', in H.A. Giroux, C. Lankshear, P. McLaren and M. Peters (eds), *Counternarratives*, London: Routledge.

Lather, P. (2007) *Getting Lost: Feminist Practices toward a Double(d) Science*, Albany, NY: SUNY Press.

Latour, B. (1987) *Science in Action: How to Follow Scientists and Engineers through Society*, Cambridge, MA: Harvard University Press.

——(1996) 'On interobjectivity', *Mind, Culture, and Activity*, 3(4): 228–45.

——(1999) 'On recalling ANT', in J. Law and J. Hassard (eds), *Actor Network and After*, Oxford: Blackwell/*The Sociological Review*, pp. 15–25.

——(2005) *Reassembling the Social: An Introduction to Actor-Network Theory*, Oxford: Oxford University Press.

Latour, B. and Woolgar, S. (1979) *Laboratory Life: The Social Construction of Scientific Facts*, London: Sage.

Lave, J. (1988) *Cognition in Practice: Mind, Mathematics and Culture in Everyday Life*, New York: Cambridge University Press.

Lave, J. and Wenger, E. (1991) *Situated Learning: Legitimate Peripheral Participation*, Cambridge: Cambridge University Press.

Law, J. (1999) 'After ANT: topology, naming and complexity', in J. Law and J. Hassard (eds), *Actor Network Theory and After*, Oxford: Blackwell/*The Sociological Review*, pp. 1–14.

——(2004a) 'And if the global were small and noncoherent? Method, complexity, and the baroque', *Environment and Planning D: Society and Space*, 22(1): 13–26.

——(2004b) *After Method: Mess in Social Science Research*, London: Routledge.

——(2007) 'Making a mess with method', in W. Outhwaite and S.P. Turner (eds), *The Sage Handbook of Social Science Methodology*, London and Beverly Hills: Sage, pp. 595–606.

——(2009a) 'Actor network theory and material semiotics', in B.S. Turner (ed.), *The New Blackwell Companion to Social Theory*, Chichester: Wiley-Blackwell, pp. 141–58.

——(2009b) 'Multiplicity, mess, and modes of enacting', paper presented to Objects – What Matters? Technology, Value and Social Change Conference, University of Manchester, 3 September.

Law, J. and Hassard, J. (eds) (1999) *Actor Network Theory and After*, Oxford: Blackwell/*The Sociological Review*.

Law, J. and Hetherington, K. (2003) 'Materialities, spatialities, globalities', in M. Dear and S. Flusty (eds), *The Spaces of Postmodernism: Readings in Human Geography*, Oxford: Blackwell, pp. 390–401.

Law, J. and Singleton, V. (2005) 'Object lessons', *Organization*, 12(3): 331–55.

Lawn, M. and Grosvenor, I. (eds) (2005) *Materialities of Schooling*, Oxford: Symposium Books.

Leadbetter, J. (2004) 'The role of mediating artefacts in the work of educational psychologists during consultative conversations in schools', *Educational Review*, 56(2): 133–45.

——(2005) 'Activity theory as a conceptual framework and analytical tool within the practice of educational psychology', *Educational and Child Psychology*, 22(1): 18–28.

——(2006) 'New ways of working and new ways of being: multi-agency working and professional identity', *Educational and Child Psychology*, 23(4): 47–59.

Leadbetter, J., Daniels, H., Edwards, A., Martin, D., Middleton, D., Popova, A., Warmington, P., Apostolov, A. and Brown, S. (2007) 'Professional learning within multi-agency children's services: researching into practice', *Educational Research*, 49(1): 83–98.

Leander, K.M. and Lovvorn, J.F. (2006) 'Literacy networks: following the circulation of texts, bodies, and objects in the schooling and online gaming of one youth', *Cognition & Instruction*, 24(3): 291–340.

Lecusay, R., Rossen, L. and Cole, M. (2008) 'Cultural–historical activity theory and the zone of proximal development in the study of idioculture design and implementation', *Cognitive Systems Research*, 9(1–2): 92–103.

Lee, S. and Roth, W.-M. (2003) 'Of traversals and hybrid spaces: science in the community', *Mind, Culture, and Activity*, 10: 120–42.

Lefebvre, H. (1991) *The Production of Space*, Oxford: Blackwell.

——(1996) *Writings on Cities*, Oxford: Blackwell.

Lektorsky, V. (1999) 'Activity theory in a new era', in Y. Engeström, R. Miettinen and R.-L. Punamäki (eds), *Perspectives on Activity Theory*, Cambridge: Cambridge University Press.

Lemke, J.L. and Sabelli, N.H. (2008) 'Complex systems and educational change: towards a new research agenda', *Educational Philosophy and Theory*, 40(1): 118–29.

Leontiev, A.N. (1978) *Activity, Consciousness, and Personality*, Englewood Cliffs, NJ: Prentice Hall.

——(1981) *Problems of the Development of the Mind*, Moscow: Progress.

Licoppe, C. (2004) '"Connected" presence: the emergence of a new repertoire for managing social relationships in a changing communication technoscape', *Environment and Planning D: Society and Space*, 22: 135–56.

Lim, C.P. and Hang, D. (2003) 'An activity theory approach to research of ICT integration in Singapore schools', *Computers & Education* 4(1): 49–63.

Lingard, B. (2007) 'Deparochializing the study of education: globalization and the research imagination?', in K. Gulson and C. Symes (eds), *Spatial Theories of Education*, London: Routledge.

Lipman, P. (2007) 'Education and the spatialization of urban inequality: a case study of Chicago's Renaissance 2010', in K. Gulson and C. Symes (eds), *Spatial Theories of Education*, London: Routledge.

Luhmann, N. (1995) *Social Systems*, Stanford, CA: Stanford University Press.

Luria, A. R. (1976) *Cognitive Development: Its Cultural and Social Foundations.* Cambridge, MA: Harvard University Press.

Maasen, S. and Weingart, P. (2000) *Metaphors and the Dynamics of Knowledge*, London: Routledge.

Manicom, L. and Walters, S. (1997) 'Feminist popular education in the light of globalisation', in S. Walters (ed.), *Globalisation, Adult Education and Training: Impacts and Issues*, London: Zed Books.

Mannion, G. (2003) 'Learning, participation and identification through school grounds development', in R. Edwards and R. Usher (eds), *Space, Curriculum and Learning*, Greenwich, CT: Information Age Publishing.

Martin, D. (2008). 'A new paradigm to inform inter-professional learning for integrating speech and language provision into secondary schools: a socio-cultural activity theory approach', *Child Language Teaching and Therapy*, 24(2): 173–92.

Martin, D. and Peim, N. (2009) 'Critical perspectives on activity theory', *Educational Review*, 61(2): 131–38.

Martin, I (2003) 'Adult education, lifelong learning and citizenship: some ifs and buts', *International Journal of Lifelong Education*, 22(6): 566–79.

Marx, K. (1971) *A Contribution to the Critique of Political Economy*, London: Lawrence & Wishart.

Mason, M. (ed.) (2008a) *Complexity Theory and the Philosophy of Education*, Bognor Regis: Wiley-Blackwell.

——(2008b) 'Complexity theory and the philosophy of education', *Educational Philosophy and Theory*, 40(1): 4–18.

——(2008c) 'What is complexity theory and what are its implications for educational change?' *Educational Philosophy and Theory*, 40(1): 35–49.

——(2009) 'Making educational development and change sustainable: Insights from complexity theory', *International Journal of Educational Development*, 29(2): 117–24.

Mason, R. (1998) *Globalising Education: Trends and Challenges*, London: Routledge.

Massey, D. (1991) 'A global sense of place', *Marxism Today*, June: 24–29.

Massey, D. (1993) 'Politics and space/time', in M. Keith and S. Pile (eds), *Place and the Politics of Identity*, London: Routledge.

——(1994) *Space, Place and Gender*, Cambridge: Polity Press.

——(1999) 'Imagining globalisation: power-geometries of time–space', in A. Brah, M. Hickman and M. Mac an Ghail (eds), *Global Futures: Migration, Environment and Globalisation*, Basingstoke: Macmillan.

——(2005) *For Space*, London: Sage.

Maturana, H. and Varela, F. (1987) *The Tree of Knowledge: The Biological Roots of Human Understanding*, Boston, MA: Shambhala.

McChesney, R. (2003) 'The new global media', in D. Held and A. McGrew (eds), *The Global Transformations Reader*, Cambridge: Polity Press.

McGregor, J. (2003) 'Making space: teachers' workplace topologies', *Pedagogy, Culture & Society*, 11(3): 353–77.

——(2004) 'Spatiality and the place of the material in schools', *Pedagogy, Culture & Society*, 12(3): 347–72.

McLean, C. and Hassard, J. (2004) 'Symmetrical absence/symmetrical absurdity: critical notes on the production of actor-network accounts', *Journal of Management Studies*, 41(3): 493–519.

McMurtry, A. (2007) 'Complexity science and the education of interdisciplinary health teams', PhD thesis, Edmonton, Canada: University of Alberta.

——(2010) 'Complexity, collective learning and the education of interdisciplinary health teams: insights from a university-level course', *Journal of Interprofessional Care*, 24(3): 220–29.

Miettinen, R. (1999) 'The riddle of things: activity theory and actor-network theory as approaches to studying innovations', *Mind, Culture, and Activity*, 6(3): 170–95.

——(2005) 'Object of activity and individual motivation', *Mind, Culture, and Activity*, 12(1): 52–69.

Miettinen, R. and Peisa, S. (2002) 'Integrating school-based learning with the study of change in working life: the alternative enterprise method', *Journal of Education and Work*, 15(3): 303–19.

Miettinen, R., Lehenkari, J. and Tuunainen, J. (2008) 'Learning and network collaboration in product development: how things work for human use', *Management Learning*, 39(2): 203–19.

Minick, N. (1987) 'The development of Vygotsky's thought', in R.W. Reiber and A.S. Carton (eds), *The Collected Works of L.S. Vygotsky*, Vol. 1, New York: Plenum.

Miranda, H., Beisigel, M., Simmt, E., Davis, B. and Sumara, D. (2006) 'Consciousness, collectivity and culture: experiences of intimacy in mathematics learning', *Journal of the Canadian Association for Curriculum Studies*, 4(2): 123–37.

Mohanty, C. (1992) 'Feminist encounters: locating the politics of experience', in M. Barrett and A. Phillips (eds), *Destabilising Theory: Contemporary Feminist Debates*, Cambridge: Polity Press.

Mojab, S. and Gorman, R. (2003) 'Women and consciousness in the "learning organization": emancipation or exploitation?' *Adult Education Quarterly*, 53(4): 228–41.

Mol, A. (2002) *The Body Multiple: Ontology in Medical Practice*, Durham, NC: Duke University Press.

Mol, A. and Law, J. (1994) 'Regions, networks and fluids: anaemia and social topology', *Social Studies of Science*, 24(4): 641–71.

Morin, E. (1990/2008) *On Complexity*, Cresskill, NJ: Hampton Press.

——(2007) 'Restricted complexity, general complexity', in C. Gershenson, D. Aerts and B. Edmonds (eds), *Worldviews, Science and Us: Philosophy and Complexity*, Singapore: World Scientific, pp. 5–29.

Morley, D. and Robins, K. (1995) *Spaces of Identity: Global Media, Electronic Landscapes and Cultural Boundaries*, London: Routledge.

Morrison, K. (2008) 'Educational philosophy and the challenge of complexity theory', *Educational Philosophy and Theory*, 40(1): 19–34.

Moscovici, S. (1996) 'Who is the most Marxist of the two?', *Swiss Journal of Psychology*, 55(2/3): 70–73.

Mulcahy, D. (1999) '(Actor-net) working bodies and representations: tales from a training field', *Science, Technology & Human Values*, 24(1): 80–104.

——(2006) 'The salience of space for pedagogy and identity: problem based learning as a case in point', *Pedagogy, Culture & Society*, 14(1): 55–69.

——(2007) 'Managing spaces: (re)working relations of strategy and spatiality in vocational education and training', *Studies in Continuing Education*, 29(2): 143–62.

——(2010) 'Assembling the accomplished teacher: the performativity and politics of professional teaching standards', *Educational Philosophy and Theory*, DOI: 10.1111/j.1469-5812.2009.00617.x

Munro, M., Turok, I. and Livingstone, M. (2009) 'Students in cities: a preliminary analysis of their patterns and effects', *Environment and Planning A*, 41: 1805–25.

Murdoch, J. (1998) 'The spaces of actor-network theory', *Geoforum*, 29(4): 357–74.

——(2006) *Post-Structural Geography*, London: Sage.

Murphy, C. and Carlisle, K. (2008) 'Situating relational ontology and transformative activist stance within the "everyday" practice of co-teaching and co-generative dialogue', *Cultural Studies of Science Education*, 3(2): 493–506.

Murphy, E. and Manzanares, M.R. (2008) 'Contradictions between the virtual and physical high school classroom: a third-generation Activity Theory perspective', *British Journal of Educational Technology*, 39(6): 1061–72.

Nerland, M. (2010) 'Transnational discourses of knowledge and learning in professional work: examples from computer engineering', *Studies in Philosophy and Education*, 29(2): 183–95.

Nespor, J. (1994) *Knowledge in Motion: Space, Time and Curriculum in Undergraduate Physics and Management*, Philadelphia, PA: Falmer Press.

——(1997) *Tangled up in School: Politics, Space, Bodies, and Signs in the Educational Process*, Mahwah, NJ: Lawrence Erlbaum.

——(2000) 'School field trips and the curriculum of public spaces', *Journal of Curriculum Studies*, 32(1): 25–43.

——(2002) 'Networks and contexts of reform', *Journal of Educational Change*, 3(3–4): 365–82.

——(2003) 'Undergraduate curricula as networks and trajectories', in R. Edwards and R. Usher (eds), *Space, Curriculum and Learning*, Greenwich, CT: Information Age Publishing.

——(2010) 'Devices and educational change', *Educational Philosophy and Theory*, DOI: 10.1111/j.1469–5812.2009.00611.x.

New, R. (2007) 'Reggio Emilia as cultural activity theory in practice', *Theory into Practice*, 46(1): 5–13.

Newman, F. and Holzman, L. (1993) *Lev Vygotsky: Revolutionary Scientist*, London: Routledge.

Neyland, D. (2006) 'Dismissed content and discontent: an analysis of the strategic aspects of actor-network theory', *Science, Technology & Human Values*, 31(1): 29–51.

Niewolny, K. and Wilson, A. (2009) 'What happened to the promise? A critical (re)orientation of two sociocultural learning traditions', *Adult Education Quarterly* 60(1): 26–45.

Ollman, B. (1991) *Dialectical Investigations*, New York: Routledge.

Olson, E. and Eoyang, G. (2001) *Facilitating Organizational Change: Lessons From Complexity Science*, San Francisco, CA: Jossey-Bass.

Osberg, D. (2005) 'Redescribing "education", in complex terms', *Complicity: An International Journal of Complexity and Education*, 2(1): 81–83.

——(2008) 'The logic of emergence: an alternative conceptual space for theorizing critical education', *Journal of the Canadian Association for Curriculum Studies*, 6(1): 133–61.

——(2010) 'Taking care of the future? the complex responsibility of education and politics', in D.C. Osberg and G.J.J. Biesta (eds), *Complexity Theory and the Politics of Education*, Rotterdam: Sense, pp. 157–70.

Osberg, D.C. and Biesta, G.J.J. (2003) 'Complexity, representation and the epistemology of schooling', in *Conference Proceedings of the First Conference of Complexity Science and Educational Research*, Edmonton, Canada: University of Alberta. www.complexity andeducation.ualberta.ca/conferences/2003/proceedings.htm

——(2007) 'Beyond presence: epistemological and pedagogical implications of strong emergence', *Interchange*, 38(1): 31–51.

——(2008) 'The emergent curriculum: navigating a complex course between unguided learning and planned enculturation', *Journal of Curriculum Studies*, 40(3): 313–28.

——(eds) (2010) Complexity Theory and the Politics of Education, Rotterdam: Sense.

Osberg, D.C., Biesta, G.J.J. and Cilliers, P. (2008a) 'From representation to emergence: complexity's challenge to the epistemology of schooling', *Educational Philosophy and Theory*, 40(1): 213–27.

Osberg, D.C., Doll Jr, W.E. and Trueit, D. (2008b) 'Gatekeepers of a complex field?' *Complicity*, 5(1): iii–ix.

Owen, H. (1997/2008) *Open Space Technology: A User's Guide* (3rd edn), San Francisco, CA: Berrett-Koehler.

Paechter, C. (2003) 'Territoriality, inter-disciplinarity and school space', in R. Edwards and R. Usher (eds), *Space, Curriculum and Learning*, Greenwich, CT: Information Age Publishing.

——(2004) 'Metaphors of space in educational theory and practice', *Pedagogy, Culture & Society* 12(3): 449–64.

——(2007) *Being Boys, Being Girls: Learning Masculinities and Femininities*, Buckingham: Open University Press.

Pahl, K. and Kelly, S. (2005) 'Family literacy as a third space between home and school: some case studies of practice', *Literacy*, 39(2): 91–96.

Paley, J. (2007) 'Complex adaptive systems and nursing', *Nursing Inquiry*, 14(3): 233–42.

Panofsky, C. (2003) 'The relations of learning and student social class: toward re-'socializing' sociocultural learning theory', in A. Kozulin, B. Gindis, V. Ageyev and S. Miller (eds), *Vygotsky's Educational Theory in Cultural Context*, New York: Cambridge University Press, pp. 411–31.

Peim, N. (2009) 'Activity theory and ontology', *Educational Review*, 61(2): 167–80.

Philo, C., Parr, H. and Burns, N. (2005) '"An oasis for us": "in-between" spaces of training for people with mental health problems in the Scottish Highlands', *Geoforum*, 36(6): 778–91.

Pile, S. (1997) 'Introduction: opposition, political identities and the spaces of resistance', in S. Pile and M. Keith (eds), *Geographies of Resistance*, London: Routledge.

Pile, S. and Keith, M. (eds) (1997) *Geographies of Resistance*, London: Routledge.

Pile, S. and Thrift, N. (1995a) 'Introduction', in S. Pile and N. Thrift (eds), *Mapping the Subject: Geographies of Cultural Transformation*, London: Routledge.

——(1995b) 'Mapping the subject', in S. Pile and N. Thrift (eds), *Mapping the Subject: Geographies of Cultural Transformation*, London: Routledge.

Pinar, W.F. and Grumet, M.R. (1976) *Toward a Poor Curriculum*, Dubuque, IA: Kendall/Hunt.

Pinch, T. (2010) 'On making infrastructure visible: putting the non-humans to rights', *Cambridge Journal of Economics*, 34: 77–89.

Plessis, A. and Webb, P. (2008) 'Generative use of computers: promoting critical outcomes of the South African curriculum', *Education as Change*, 12(1): 15–27.

Porter, D. (ed.) (1997) *Internet Culture*, London: Routledge.

Portes, P. and Vadeboncoeur, J. (2003) 'Mediation in cognitive socialization: the influence of socioeconomic status', in A. Kozulin, B. Gindis, V. Ageyev and S. Miller (eds), *Vygotsky's Educational Theory in Cultural Context*, New York: Cambridge University Press, pp. 371–92.

Prigogine, I. (1997) *The End of Certainty: Time, Chaos, and the New Laws of Nature*, New York: Free Press.

Prigogine, I. and Stengers, I. (1984) *Order out of Chaos*, London: Heinemann.

Quinn, J. (2003) 'The dynamics of the protected space: spatial concepts and women students', *British Journal of Sociology of Education*, 24: 449–61.

Radford, L., Bardini, C. and Sabena, C. (2007) 'Perceiving the general: the multisemiotic dimension of students' algebraic activity', *Journal for Research in Mathematics Education*, 38: 507–30.

Radford, M. (2006) 'Researching classrooms: complexity and chaos', *British Educational Research Journal*, 32(2): 177–90.

——(2007) 'Action research and the challenge of complexity', *Cambridge Journal of Education*, 37(2): 263–78.

Rattansi, A. (1995) 'Just framing: ethnicities and racisms in a postmodern: framework', in L. Nicholson and S. Seidman (eds), *Social Postmodernism: Beyond Identity Politics*, Cambridge: Cambridge University Press.

Rheingold, H. (1993) *The Virtual Community*, Reading, MA: Addison-Wesley.

Rimpiläinen, S. (2010) 'Knowledge in networks – knowing in transactions?', paper presented at the Practicing Science and Technology, Performing the Social Conference, EASST 2010, Trento, Italy, 2–4 September, http://stir.academia.edu/SannaRimpilainen/Papers (forthcoming in *International Journal of Actor-Network Theory and Technological Innovation*).

Rimpiläinen, S. and Edwards, R. (2009) 'The ANTics of educational research: researching case-based learning through objects and texts', paper presented to Objects – What Matters? Technology, Value and Social Change Conference, University of Manchester, 2 September. www.tlrp.org/tel/ensemble/files/2009/09/cresc_paper_final0109.pdf

Ritchie, S., Tobin, K., Roth, W.-M. and Carambo, C. (2007) 'Transforming an academy through the enactment of collective curriculum leadership', *Journal of Curriculum Studies*, 39: 151–75.

Rizvi, F. (2000) 'International education and the production of global imagination', in N. Burbules and C. Torres (eds), *Globalisation and Education: Critical Perspectives*, New York: Routledge.

Robbins, D. and Stetsenko, A. (eds) (2002) *Voices within Vygotsky's Non-Classical Psychology: Past, Present, Future*, New York: Nova Science.

Robertson, R. (1992) *Globalisation: Social Theory and Global Culture*, London: Sage.

Robertson, S. (2007) 'Public–private partnerships, digital firms, and the production of a neoliberal education space at the European scale', in K. Gulson and C. Symes (eds), *Spatial Theories of Education*, London: Routledge.

Robins, K. (1993) 'Prisoners of the city: whatever could a postmodern city be?', in E. Carter, J. Donald and J. Squires (eds), *Space and Place: Theories of Identity and Location*, London: Lawrence & Wishart.

Rogers, C. (1983) *Freedom to Learn for the '80s*, Columbus, OH: Charles E. Merrill.

Rogoff, B. and Lave, J. (eds) (1984) *Everyday Cognition: Its Development in Social Context*, Cambridge, MA: Harvard University Press.

Roth, W.-M. (1996) 'Knowledge diffusion in a grade 4–5 classroom during a unit on civil engineering: an analysis of a classroom community in terms of its changing resources and practices', *Cognition and Instruction*, 14(2): 179–220.

——(2002) 'Taking science education beyond schooling', *Canadian Journal of Science, Mathematics, and Technology Education*, 2: 37–48.

——(2005) 'Organizational mediation of urban science', in K. Tobin, R. Elmesky and G. Seiler (eds), *Improving Urban Science Education: New Roles for Teachers, Students, and Researchers*, Lanham, MD: Rowman & Littlefield, pp. 91–115.

——(2007) 'Emotion at work: a contribution to third-generation cultural–historical activity theory,' *Mind, Culture, and Activity*, 14(1): 40–63.

Roth, W.-M. and Tobin, K. (2001) 'Learning to teach science as praxis', *Teaching and Teacher Education*, 17: 741–62.

——(2002) 'Redesigning an "urban" teacher education program: an activity theory perspective', *Mind, Culture, and Activity*, 9(2): 108–31.

Roth, W.-M., Lawless, D. and Tobin, K. (2000) 'Co-teaching/co-generative dialoguing as praxis of dialectic method', *Forum Qualitative Sozialforschung/Forum Qualitative Social Research*, 1(3). www.qualitative-research.net/index.php/fqs/article/view/1054/2283

Roth, W.-M., Lee, Y.-J. and Hsu, P.-L. (2009) 'A tool for changing the world: possibilities of cultural–historical activity theory to reinvigorate science education', *Studies in Science Education*, 45(2): 131–67.

Routledge, P. (2006) 'Acting in the network: ANT and the politics of generating associations', *Environment and Planning D: Society and Space*, 26: 199–217.

RRU (2009) 'MA in leadership', Victoria, Canada: Royal Roads University, www.royalroads.ca/program/leadership-ma

Russell, D. (1997) 'Rethinking genre in school and society: an activity theory analysis', *Written Communication*, 14(4): 504–54.

Salomon, G. (1993) *Distributed Cognitions: Psychological and Educational Considerations*, Cambridge: Cambridge University Press.

Sannino, A. (2008). 'From talk to action: experiencing interlocution in developmental interventions', *Mind, Culture, and Activity*, 15: 234–57.

Sannino, A., Daniels, H. and Gutiérrez, K. (eds) (2009) *Learning and Expanding with Activity Theory*, New York: Cambridge University Press.

Sawada, D (1991) 'Deconstructing reflection', *Alberta Journal of Educational Research*, 37(4): 349–66.

Sawchuk, P. (2003) *Adult Learning and Technology in Working-Class Life*, New York: Cambridge University Press.

——(2006) 'Activity and power: everyday life and development of working-class groups', in P. Sawchuk, N. Duarte and M. Elhammoumi (eds), *Critical Perspectives on Activity: Explorations Across Education, Work and the Everyday Life*, New York: Cambridge University Press, pp. 238–67.

Sawchuk, P. and Stetsenko, A. (2008) 'Sociological understandings of conduct for a non-canonical activity theory: exploring intersections and complementarities' *Mind, Culture, and Activity*, 15(4): 339–60.

Sawchuk, P., Duarte, N. and Elhammoumi, M. (2006) *Critical Perspectives on Activity: Explorations Across Education, Work and Everyday Life*, New York: Cambridge University Press.

Schatzki, T.R. (2001) 'Practice theory', in T.R. Schatzki, K. Knorr Cetina and E. von Savigny (eds), *The Practice Turn in Contemporary Theory*, London and New York: Routledge, pp. 1–14.

——(2002) *The Site of the Social: A Philosophical Account of the Constitution of Social Life and Change*, University Park, PA: Pennsylvania University Press.

Scott, D. (2010) *Education, Epistemology and Critical Realism*, London and New York: Routledge.

Sennett, R. (2008) *The Craftsman*, New Haven, CT: Yale University Press.

Serres, M. (1995) *Genesis*, Ann Arbor, MI: Michigan University Press.

Sfard, A. (1998) 'On two metaphors for learning and the dangers of choosing just one', *Educational Researcher*, 27(2): 4–13.

Sheller, M. and Urry, J. (2006) 'The new mobilities paradigm', *Environment and Planning A*, 38: 207–26.

Shields, R. (1997) 'Spatial stress and resistance: social meanings of spatialisation', in G. Benko and U. Strohmayer (eds), *Space and Social Theory: Interpreting Modernity and Postmodernity*, Oxford: Blackwell.

——(1999) *Lefebvre, Love and Struggle: Spatial Dialectics*, London: Routledge.

Singh, M., Kenway, J. and Apple, M. (2005) 'Globalising education: perspectives from above and below', in M. Apple, J. Kenway and M. Singh (eds), *Globalising Education: Policies, Pedagogies and Politics*, New York: Peter Lang.

Singh, M., Rizve, F. and Shrestha, M. (2007) 'Student mobility and the spatial production of cosmopolitan identities', in K. Gulson and C. Symes (eds) *Spatial Theories of Education*, London: Routledge.

Singleton, V. (2005) 'The promise of public health: vulnerable policy and lazy citizens', *Environment and Planning: Society and Space*, 23(5): 771–86.

Singleton, V. and Michael, M. (1993) 'Actor-networks and ambivalence: general practitioners in the UK cervical screening programme', *Social Studies of Science*, 23(2): 227–64.

Slattery, P. (1995) *Curriculum Development in the Postmodern Era*, New York: Routledge.

Smith, J. and Jenks, C. (2005) 'Complexity, ecology and the materiality of information', *Theory, Culture & Society*, 22(5): 141–63.

Snyder, I. (ed.) (2002) *Silicon Literacies: Communication, Innovation and Education in the Electronic Age*, London: Routledge.

Soja, E. (1989) *Postmodern Geographies: The Reassertion of Space in Critical Social Theory*, London: Verso.

Soja, E. and Hooper, B. (1993) 'The spaces that difference makes: some notes on the geographical margins of the new cultural politics', in M. Keith and S. Pile (eds), *Place and the Politics of Identity*, London: Routledge.

Sørensen, E. (2007) 'The time of materiality', *Forum: Qualitative Social Research/ Sozialforschung*, 8(2). www.qualitative-research.net/index.php/fqs/issue/view/6

——(2009) *The Materiality of Learning: Technology and Knowledge in Educational Practice*, Cambridge and New York: Cambridge University Press.

Spillane, J.P., Halverson, R. and Diamond, J.B. (2004) 'Towards a theory of leadership practice: a distributed perspective', *Journal of Curriculum Studies*, 36: 3–34.

Spinuzzi, C. (2007) 'Texts of our institutional lives: accessibility scans and institutional activity: an activity theory analysis', *College English*, 70(2): 189–201.

Spivak, G. (1993) *Outside in the Teaching Machine*, London: Routledge.

Stacey, R.D. (1995) 'The science of complexity; an alternate perspective for strategic change processes', *Strategic Management Journal*, 16: 477–95.

——(2005) *Experiencing Emergence in Organizations: Local Interaction and the Emergence of Global Pattern*, London: Routledge.

Stanley, D. (2006) 'Comparative dynamics: healthy collectivities and the pattern which connects', *Complicity: An International Journal of Complexity and Education*, 3(1): 73–82.

Sterling, B. (2005) *Shaping Things*, Cambridge, MA: MIT Press.

Stetsenko, A. (2005) 'Activity as object-related: resolving the dichotomy of individual and collective planes of activity', *Mind, Culture, and Activity*, 12(1): 70–88.

——(2008) 'From relational ontology to transformative activist stance on development and learning: expanding Vygotsky's (CHAT) project', *Cultural Studies of Science Education*, 3: 471–91.

——(2009) 'Vygotsky and the conceptual revolution in developmental sciences: towards a unified (non-additive) account of human development', in M. Fleer, M. Hedegaard and J. Tudge (eds), *Childhood Studies and the Impact of Globalization: Policies and Practices at Global and Local Levels*, New York: Routledge, pp. 125–41.

——(2010) 'Teaching–learning and development as activist projects of historical becoming: expanding Vygotsky's approach to pedagogy', *Pedagogies: An International Journal*, 5(1): 6–16.

Stetsenko, A. and Arievitch, I. (2004) 'Vygotskian collaborative project of social transformation: History, politics, and practice in knowledge construction', *International Journal of Critical Psychology*, 12(4): 58–80.

Stetsenko, A. and Vianna, E. (2009) 'Bridging developmental theory and education practice: lessons from the Vygotskian project', in O. Barbain and B. Hanna Wasik (eds), *Handbook of Child Development and Early Education*, London: Guilford Press, pp. 38–54.

Stewart, I. and Cohen, J. (1995) *The Collapse of Chaos: Discovering Simplicity in a Complex World*, Harmondsworth: Penguin.

Stith, I. and Roth, W.-M. (2008) *Students in Action: Cogenerative Dialogues from Secondary to Elementary Schools*, Rotterdam: Sense.

Strathern, M. (1996) 'Cutting the network', *Journal of the Royal Anthropological Institute*, 2(3): 517–35.

Suchman, L. (2007) *Human–Machine Reconfigurations: Plans and Situated Actions*, New York: Cambridge University Press.

Sumara, D. and Carson, T. (eds) (1997) *Action Research as a Living Practice*, London and New York: Peter Lang.

Sumara, D. and Davis, B. (1997) 'Enlarging the space of the possible: complexity, complicity, and action research practices', in D. Sumara and T. Carson (eds), *Action Research as a Living Practice*, London and New York: Peter Lang, pp. 299–312.

Sykes, B. and Kuyper, H. (2009) 'Neighbourhood effects on youth educational achievement in the Netherlands: can effects be identified and do they vary by student background characteristics?', *Environment and Planning A*, 41: 2417–36.

Tabbi, J. (1997) 'Reading, writing hypertext: democratic politics in the virtual classroom', in D. Porter (ed.), *Internet Culture*, London: Routledge.

Thamen, K. (1997) 'Considerations of culture in distance education in the Pacific islands', in L. Rowan, L. Bartlett and T. Evans (eds), *Shifting Borders: Globalisation, Localisation and Open and Distance Education*, Geelong, Australia: Deakin University Press.

Thompson, J. (2003) 'The globalisation of communication', in D. Held and A. McGrew (eds), *The Global Transformations Reader*, Cambridge: Polity Press.

Thompson Klein, J. (2004) 'Prospects of transdisciplinarity', *Futures*, 36: 515–26.

Thompson, T.-L. (2010) 'Assembly required: self-employed workers' informal work-learning in online communities', PhD thesis, Edmonton, Canada: University of Alberta.

Thomson, P. (2007) 'Working the in/visible geographies of school exclusion', in K. Gulson and C. Symes (eds), *Spatial Theories of Education*, London: Routledge.

Thrift, N. (1999) 'The place of complexity', *Theory, Culture & Society*, 16: 31–70.

Tobin, K. and Roth, W.-M. (2002) 'Evaluation of science teaching performance through coteaching and cogenerative dialoguing', in J. Altschuld and D. Kumar (eds), *Evaluation in Science Education in the Twenty-First Century*, Dordrecht, the Netherlands: Kluwer Academic Press, pp. 187–217.

Toomela, A. (2000) 'Activity theory is a dead end for cultural-historical psychology', *Culture & Psychology*, 6: 353–64.

——(2008) 'Commentary: activity theory is a dead end for methodological thinking in cultural psychology too', *Culture & Psychology*, 14(3): 289–303.

Trochim, W.M., Cabrera, D.A., Milstein, B., Gallagher, R.S. and Leischow, S.J. (2006) 'Practical challenges of systems thinking and modeling in public health', *American Journal of Public Health*, 96(3): 538–46.

Tsoukas, H. (2004) *Complex Knowledge: Studies in Organizational Epistemology*, Oxford: Oxford University Press.

Turner, B. (1994) *Orientalism, Postmodernism and Globalism*, London: Routledge.

Turner, S. and Manderson, D. (2007) 'Socialization in a space of law: student performativity at "Coffee House" in a university law faculty', *Environment and Planning D: Society and Space*, 25: 761–82.

Urry, J. (2000) *Sociology Beyond Societies: Mobilities for the Twenty-first Century*, London: Routledge.

Urry, J. (2003) *Global Complexity*, Cambridge: Polity Press.
——(2004) 'The "system" of automobility', *Theory, Culture & Society*, 21(4–5): 25–39.
——(2005) 'The complexities of the global', *Theory, Culture & Society*, 22(5): 235–54.
——(2007) *Mobilities*, Cambridge: Polity Press.
Valsiner, J. and van der Veer, R. (2000) *The Social Mind: Construction of the Idea*, Cambridge, UK: Cambridge University Press.
Van Oers, B., Wardekker, W., Elbers, E. and van der Veer, R. (eds) (2008) *The Transformation of Learning: Advances in Cultural–Historical Activity Theory*, New York: Cambridge University Press.
Vanderbeck, R. (2005) 'Anti-nomadism, institutions, and the geographies of childhood', *Environment and Planning D: Society and Space*, 23: 71–94.
Varela, F.J. (1999) *Ethical Know-How: Action, Wisdom and Cognition*, Stanford, CA: Stanford University Press.
Varela, F.J., Thompson, E. and Rosch, E. (1991) *The Embodied Mind: Cognitive Science and Human Experience*, Cambridge, MA: MIT Press.
van der Veer, R. (1996) 'Vygotsky and Piaget: a collective monologue', *Human Development*, 39: 237–42.
van der Veer, R. and Valsiner, J. (1991) *Understanding Vygotsky: A Quest for Synthesis*, Oxford: Blackwell.
Veresov, N. (2005) 'Marxist and non-Marxist aspects of the cultural-historical psychology of L. S. Vygotsky', *Outlines*, 1: 31–49.
Verran, H. (2001) *Science and an African Logic*, Chicago, IL: University of Chicago Press.
——(2007) 'Metaphysics and learning', *Learning Inquiry*, 1(1): 31–39.
Vygotsky, L. (1978) *Mind and Society: The Development of Higher Psychological Processes*, Cambridge, MA: Harvard University Press.
——(1987) *The Collected Works of L.S. Vygotsky (Volume 1). The General Problems of General Psychology. Including the Volume Thinking and Speech*, New York: Plenum Press.
——(1994) 'The socialist alteration of man', in R. van der Veer and J. Valsiner (eds), *The Vygotsky Reader*, Oxford: Blackwell.
——(1997) *The Collected Works of L. S. Vygotsky (Volume 4)*, London: Plenum Press.
Walby, S. (2009) *Globalization and Inequalities: Complexity and Contested Modernities*, London and Beverly Hills: Sage.
Waldrop, M. (1994) *Complexity: The Emerging Science at the Edge of Order and Chaos*, New York: Simon & Schuster.
Waltz, S.B. (2006) 'Nonhumans unbound: actor-network theory and the reconsideration of "things" in educational foundations', *Journal of Educational Foundations*, 20(3/4): 51–68.
Warmington, P. (2008) 'From "activity" to "labour": commodification, labour power and contradiction in Engeström's activity theory', *Critical Social Studies – Outlines*, 10(2): 4–19.
Waters, M. (1995) *Globalisation*, London, Routledge.
Watts, L. and Urry, J. (2008) 'Moving methods, travelling times', *Environment and Planning D: Society and Space*, 26: 860–74.
Wearn, A., Rees, C., Bradley, P. and Vnuk, A. (2008) 'Understanding student concerns about peer physical examination using an activity theory framework', *Medical Education*, 42(12): 1218–26.
Weisbord, M. and Janoff, S. (2000) *Future Search: An Action Guide to Finding Common Ground in Organizations and Communities*, San Francisco, CA: Berrett-Koehler.

Wells, G. (2004) 'Narrating and theorizing activity in educational settings', *Mind, Culture, and Activity*, 11(1): 70–77.

Wenger, E. (1998) *Communities of Practice*, Cambridge: Cambridge University Press.

Wertsch, J. (1991) *Voices of the Mind: A Sociocultural Approach to Mediated Action*, Cambridge, MA: Harvard University Press.

Westheimer, J. and Kahn, J. (2004) 'What kind of citizen? The politics of educating for democracy', *American Educational Research Journal*, 41(2): 237–69.

Wheatley, M. (1992) *Leadership and the New Science: Learning about Organizing from an Orderly Universe*, San Francisco, CA: Berrett-Koehler.

Wheelahan, L. (2010) *Why Knowledge Matters in Curriculum: A Social Realist Argument*, London: Routledge.

Williams, J. (2009) 'Embodied multi-modal communication from the perspective of activity theory', *Educational Studies in Mathematics*, 70(2): 201–10.

Williams, J., Davis, P. and Black, L. (2007) 'Sociocultural and cultural–historical activity theory perspectives on subjectivities and learning in schools and other educational contexts', *International Journal of Educational Research*, 46(1): 1–7.

Wilton, R. and Cranford, C. (2002) 'Toward an understanding of the spatiality of social movements: labor organizing at a private university in Los Angeles', *Social Problems*, 49(3): 374–94.

Wolf-Branigin, M. (2009) 'Applying complexity and emergence in social work education', *Social Work Education*, 28(2): 115–27.

Yamagata-Lynch, L. (2003) 'Using activity theory as an analytic lens for examining technology professional development in schools', *Mind, Culture, and Activity*, 10: 100–19.

Yamagata-Lynch, L. and Haudenschild, M. (2009) 'Using activity systems analysis to identify inner contradictions in teacher professional development', *Teaching and Teacher Education*, 25: 507–17.

Yamagata-Lynch, L. and Smaldino, S. (2007) 'Using activity theory to evaluate and improve K-12 school and university partnerships', *Evaluation and Program Planning*, 30: 364–80.

Yaroshevskij, M.G. (1989) *Lev Vygotsky*, Moscow: Progress.

Yasukawa, K. (2003) 'Towards a social studies of mathematics: numeracy and actor-network theory', in S. Kelly, B. Johnston and K. Yasukawa (eds), *The Adult Numeracy Handbook: Reframing Adult Numeracy in Australia*, Broadway, Australia: NSW Adult Literacy and Numeracy Research Consortium and Language Australia, pp. 28–34.

Young, M. (1998) *The Curriculum of the Future: From the 'New Sociology of Education' to a Critical Theory of Learning*, London: RoutledgeFalmer.

——(2003) 'Durkheim, Vygotsky and the curriculum of the future', *London Review of Education*, 1(2): 99–117.

Zellermayer, M. and Margolin, I. (2005) 'Teacher educators' professional learning described through the lens of complexity theory', *Teachers College Record*, 107(6): 1275–1304.

Zinchenko, V.P. (2002) 'From classical to organic psychology: in commemoration of the centennial of Lev Vygotsky's birth', in S.P. Shohov (ed.), *Advances in Psychology Research: Volume 18*, New York: Nova Science, pp. 3–26.

Index

action/activity 66
activity concept 64, 65, 68
activity systems 69, 83–84, 87, 91
actor-network theory *see* ANT
actor/actant 98
adaptation 62
after-ANT 95, 96, 127
agency 103–104, 112, 168, 171–74, 176
agential realism 33
Alhadeff-Jones, M. 20, 22–23, 51–52, 182
ANT viii, ix, xi, 1, 4, 5, 6, 10, 12, 13, 93; after-ANT 95, 96, 127; ambivalence 111; ANT-diaspora 96; big actor-networks 116; CHAT comparisons 13; circulating reference 97; connection points 98–100; constructionism 126; counter-networks 100; criticisms of 15; delegation 104; early focus 110; early-ANT 96; educational policy research 113–17; in educational research 110–28; effects and interactions 170; equity 111; folding-unfolding networks 104; heuristics 125; human-non-human elements 96–98; immutable mobiles 103, 105; interessement 100; marginalised actors 117; and material assemblages 178; material semiotics 96; materiality 111–13; materializing processes 111–13; messy research 121–22; mobilization 100; multiple (coexisting) ontologies 106–07, 181; multiple worlds 106–09; multiplicity 107, 111; network breakdown 97; network conception 101–02; network definition 101; network effects 13, 103–06; objects as relational effects 103; ordering practices 174; otherness 111; post-ANT 95; problematization 100; reflexivity 102; scale 105; symmetry 96–98, 104, 109; terminology 95–96; theory 94–109; translation 98–100, 102;
anti-Cartesianism 167
anti-reductionism 167
Arievitch, I. 82
artefacts 62, 63, 75
assemblages 3, 13, 112, 169, 178
autopoeisis 20
autopoetic systems 7, 20, 26
Avis, J. 92

backlash pedagogy 90
Bai, Hesoon 28, 53–54
Barab, S.A. 124
Barad, K. 31, 33, 168, 176
Bayne, S. 157–58
being-ontics 119
Bennett, J. 3, 15, 168, 176
Biesta, G.J.J. 8, 26, 32, 33
Bohr, Neils 33
Bosco, F. 101
Brah, A. 146, 147
Bruner, J. 64
bubbles 148
Buckingham, S. 148–49
Bukatman, S. 139
Byrne, David 18–19, 21, 31, 32, 42–43, 55

Callon, M. 4, 94, 100
Carlisle, K. 89
change as emergence 169
Change Laboratory 79

CHAT viii, ix, xi, 1, 5, 6, 8–9; activity core concept 56, 65; ANT comparisons 13; applications 91; artefacts 62, 63, 75; conceptual departures 62–64; contemporary challenges 91–92; context 92; contradictions 8–9, 12–13; development of 70–71; and dialectical thought 67–68; and distance-learning theory 86; diversity 91; early education research 76–78; and ecological psychology 83; and education research 57, 74–93; emotion 82; empirical generalizations 77; equity 21, 89; everyday concepts 76; and ICT 86; influences of traditions 71; instruction types 77; as interdisciplinary 58; internalization-externalization 67, 68; interventionist studies 79; key concepts 65–70; learning technologies 85; learning-development concepts 56–73; LIW 80, 81, 84; object-relatedness 169; origins 58–61; paradigmatic tension 71; and politics 174–77; and power 174–77; production process 67; research on difference 88–91; research on equity 88–91; research methodology 78–81, 178, 179, 180; research orientation 75; research on pedagogy 81–88; research on power 88–91; research on schools 81–88; scientific concepts 77; social class 91; theoretical generalizations 77; three generation model 70–72
circulating reference 97
co-configuration 91
co-operative learning 4
cognition 28
Cole, M. 70, 79, 89
collateral realities 182
Collected Works (Vygotsky) 61
colonization/anti-colonization 156
communication 64
complex adaptive systems 20, 29
complexity metaphors 30–34
complexity science 18
complexity theory viii, ix, xi, 1, 5, 6, 7–8, 12–13, 167; as analytical tool 177; digital tools in 44–45; dynamics of 40; and educational change 40–45; in educational research 35–55, 177;

emergence 12, 21–30; and ethics 51–54; explanations of 18–34; in interdisciplinary education 45–51; origins of 20–21; and power 51–54; in professional education 45–51; and responsibility 51–54
complicity 24–26, 53
Complicity journal 18
computer learning 9
conceptions of learning 5–6
connections/disconnections 3
connectivity 40–41, 84
constructionism 126
context in education 169
context-as-container 167
context-dependent operations 56–73, 91
continuous adaptive change 26
contracting activity 68
contradiction 92
Cooper, H. 47
Coughenour, C.M. 108
coupling 24–26
CRADLE (Center for Research on Activity, Development and Learning) 178
Cranford, C. 151
Crang, M. 138, 140
critical realism ix-x
cultural historical activity theory *see* CHAT
curriculum 36–39
curriculum spaces 152–54
cyberspace 138–40, 156–59, *see also* ICT
cyborg pedagogy 113

Daniels, H. 80, 81, 178
Davis, Brent 7, 12, 19, 24, 26–27, 29, 37–38, 39, 43, 51, 53, 164, 176
Davis, P. 90
Davydov, V. 74, 76, 77, 78, 82
decentred education 164
delegation 104
Deleuze, G. 139, 157
democracy, material theory of 176
democratic citizenship 181
Dewey, J. 1, 29–30, 59, 60, 92
dialectical contradictions 12
dialectical materialism 69
dialectical thought 67–68
digital technology 44–45, 86

dimension of multiple trajectories 5
disability and learning 88, 90
disequilibrium 36
dislocation and politics 144–47
dissipative structures 20
diversity 21, 27–28, 38, 48
Dodge, M. 137, 138
Doll, W. 37
DWR (Development Work Research)
    79–80, 81, 178

e-learning 177
early education research (CHAT)
    76–78
early-ANT 96
economic inequality 141
educational accountability 114
educational assessment 87
educational change 40–45
educational policy research 113–17
educational responsibility 53
educational spaces 154–60
Edwards, A. 80
Edwards, Richard 111, 122, 152, 156,
    161
Elhammoumi, M. 76
embodiment x
emergence 12, 21–30, 54, 169
emotion 82
empirical generalizations 77
enabling constraints 38
enclosure-openness binary 157
Engeström, Y. 68–69, 70, 78, 79, 80,
    85, 92
enrolment 10
entity 98
Eoyang, G. 32, 41
epistemic objects ix
equity ix, 21, 32, 54, 88, 89, 111, 116,
    117
ethnoscapes 136
everyday concepts (CHAT) 76
expansive activity 68, 89

Fazio, X. 38–39
Featherstone, M. 139
feedback 20, 43
feminist theory/writing x, 33, 110–11,
    131, 132, 145, 148, 159–60, see also
    gender
Fenwick, T. 53, 111, 113, 114, 122,
    128

Ferguson, K. 148, 152, 164
Feryok, A. 82
field observations 122–23
field trips 84
5th Dimension research 79, 89
Fletcher, G. 44–45
flows metaphor 139
fluid objects 10
flux 139
force of things 3
Fordism 141
Foucault, M. 162
Fountain, R.M. 108, 113
Fox, S. 117
fractals 27
Freire, P. 54
Fullan, M. 40
fundamentalism 137
Future Search 42

Gallagher, T.L. 38–39
Galperin, P. 66, 76, 77
gendered space 159–60
generational approach (CHAT)
    70–71
geographers on education 148–52
Gherardi, S. 99
Gindis, B. 90
Gladwell, M. 24, 43
globalization 132–37, 138, 141; of
    educational spaces 154–56
goal-directed action 56–73
Gordon, T. 152, 160
Gough, N. 112–13
Greenhill, A. 44–45
Guattari, F. 139, 157
Gutiérrez, K. 89–90
Gyorke, A. 85

Habib, L. 87
Haggis, T. 32
Hall, P. 44
Hannam, K. 143, 144
Harman, G. 99
Harris, Jonathan 44
Harvey, D. 140–41, 155
Hassard, J. 95, 98
Haudenschild, M. 87, 88
Henare, A. 181
Hetherington, K. 102, 105
heuristics 125
hidden geography 174

Holdsworth, C. 149–50
Holzman, L. 58
Hubbard, P. 150
humanist psychology 162
Hunter, S. 117
hybridity 146, 147, 156

ICT 137, 138, 140, 151, 155, 156–58,
    see also cyberspace
Ilyenkov, E.V. 74, 78
immobilities 11–12, 142–44
immutable mobiles 103, 105
interconnected diversity 27–28
interessement 100
interiorization 62
interprofessional practice and education
    36, 46, 47, 48, 49, 80–81
intersubjectivity-interobjectivity in
    research 179
interventionist studies 79, 82
intra-activity 33

Jensen, C.B. 3
Johnson, S. 8, 37
Johnston, M. 161
juxtaposition 182

Kahn, J. 181
Kamvar, Sepp 44
Kang, H. 86
Kaplan, C. 139
Kaptelinin, V. 65
Karpiak, I. 36
Kelly, G. 83
Kinti, I. 80
Kitchen, R. 138
Knorr Cetina, K. ix
Knowledge in Motion 94
Koszalka, T. 79
Koyama, J.P. 115, 116
Kramerae, C. 139
Kwa, C. 123

Lahelma, E. 152, 160
Lakoff, G. 161
Landri, P. 112
Lankshear, C. 156–57, 158
Lather, P. 128
Latour, B. 13–14, 31, 94, 96, 97,
    98, 99, 103, 109, 114, 123, 174,
    183
Lave, J. 92, 162–63

Law, J. 94, 95, 96, 98, 101, 102, 103,
    105, 106, 107, 122, 123, 177, 179,
    181
Leander, K.M. 123–24, 128
learning: conceptions 5–6; 170–171; and
    change 117–121; enactments 181;
    factors 88; technologies 85
Lefebvre, H. 131, 132, 134, 140, 154,
    155
leisurescapes 136
Leontiev, A.N. 58, 63, 65, 66, 67, 71,
    74, 76, 80, 88, 92
liminality 149
literary practice and space-time 123
LIW (Learning in and for Inter-agency
    Working) project 80, 81, 84
location and politics 144–47
looking down 123
Lovvorn, J.F. 123–24, 128
Luria, A.R. 58, 59, 71, 74, 76, 78, 88

McGregor, J. 104, 112, 152, 153, 159
McLean, C. 98
McMurtry, A. 38, 47–48
Manzanares, M.R. 85
marginalised actors 117
margins of intelligibility 128
Margolin, I. 49–50
Martin, D. 58
Marxist theory 12, 68, 72, 90, 131, 132,
    134, 135, 140, 144, 174
Mason, M. 40, 43
Massey, D. 5, 131, 142, 144, 146
material semiotics 96
material theory of democracy 176
materialist (re)turn in framings of space
    131
materiality 111–13, 132; in education
    168–71; and social processes 168
materialization 16
materializing processes 111–13
matter 30, 31, 33
matter-meaning binaries 166
Maturana, H. 20, 25
meaning-sense binaries 166
mediascapes 136
mediation 62–64
memory, semiotic-materialized 63
method in ANT research 121–127;
    in CHAT research 78–81, 178, 179,
    180; in socio-material approaches
    177–182

metaphors of complexity 30–34, 37
metaphors of spatiality 160–163
Michael, M. 126
micro-interactions 5
Miettinen, R. 65, 84, 102, 178
Minick, N. 63–64
mobilities 11–12, 131, 142–44, 145, 149–50, 158
mobilization 10
Mol, A. 106, 107
moments of translation 100
Morin, Edgar 22–23, 28–29, 51
Morley, D. 138
Morrison, K. 36
Mulcahy, D. 94, 116, 123
multi-voicedness 91
multiple ontologies 106–07, 181
Murphy, C. 89
Murphy, E. 85
mutual specification 26

naturalistic observation 124
nature-society binaries 166
NCLB (No Child Left Behind) policy 115–16
Nespor, J. 94, 96, 100, 101, 109, 110, 114, 118, 122, 125, 152, 153
nested systems 48
network effects 153–54
networks see ANT
Nick, J. 44
Nicolini, D. 99
non-linear dynamics 23–24, 31, 34, 35, 39, 43, 45, 54

object relations ix
object-motive 65–67
object-relatedness 169
objects as relational effects 103
observation 124
occasions 38
Open Space 41–42
operation 66
organizational learning 126
organizational development 18, 31–32, 41–42
organized complexity 20
Osberg, D. 8, 24, 26, 32, 33, 34, 52, 176
overlapping activity systems 83–84
Owen, H. 41

Paechter, C. 154, 159, 161
Paley, J. 36
paradigm of complexity 22–23
paradigmatic tension (CHAT) 71
pedagogy 36–39, 47, 48, 54, 75, 76, 90, 113, 156, 157, 161
Peim, N. 58
perspective 2
perturbation 36
Piaget, J. 1, 58, 59, 60
play 63, 89
policy 113–116
political economy framing of space 131
politics and socio-materiality 175–77
poly-contextuality 91
Porter, D. 158–59
positive feedback 24–26
post-ANT 95
post-humanism 14–15
postmodern curriculum 37
power relations and politics 15, 51–54, 174–77
practice theory ix, 14, 64
prepositional approach 124
Prigogine, I. 19, 20, 23–24, 27, 30, 37, 38, 55, 176
problematization 100
professional development 38–39
professional education and learning 18, 45–50

quantum physics 33
quasi-objects 10
Quinn, J. 159–60

Radford, L. 43, 82
Rancière, Jacques 15
recursion 36
redundancy 27–28
reflexivity 102
regional heterogeneity 137
relational agency 80
religious fundamentalism 137

responsibility 51–54
Rewiring the spy 44
Rheingold, H. 138–39
rhizomatic branching networks 139
Rimpiläinen, S. 126–27
Robins, K. 138, 144, 145

Rogers, C. 162
root metaphors 144
Roth, W.M. 68, 79, 82–83, 88, 120–21, 122, 124

Sawchuk, P. 9, 91, 92
Schatzki, T.R. ix
scientific concepts (CHAT) 77
Seddon, T. 148, 152, 164
self-organizing systems 7, 20, 26
self-similarity 20, 26
semiotic-materialized memory 63
Senge, P. 41
Sennett, R. 33
Sheller, M. 142, 143
Shields, R. 133
simplistic complexity 32
Singleton, V. 103, 105, 106, 126
situated learning 14
social class 5, 88, 89, 90, 91, 146, 150, 175
social justice ix, 51, 71, 88, 116, 176, 181
socio-cultural participation 6
sociology of translation 98
Sorensen, E. 1, 4, 31, 111–12
spaces of enclosure 156
spatiality theory viii, ix, xi, 1, 4–5, 6, 11–12; and ANT 132, 143; boundaries 166–67; and capitalism 141; curriculum spaces 152–54; economic inequality 141; in educational research 148–64, 177; feminist framing of space 131; and gender relations 159; and globalization 132–37, 138, 141; homelessness 146; knowing locations 153; materialist (re)turn in framings of space 131; network effects 153–54; political economy framing of space 131; space as dynamic multiplicity 129; space and territory 141; space-time 130, 131, 140–42, 145; spatial metaphors 160–64; spatial ordering 132, 134, 146; spatial relations 130; technologized spaces 137–40; trialectics of spatial practices 131
special education 90
Spencer-Dawe, E. 47
spimes 44
stabilization 10

standards 116–117
Stacey, R.D. 40
Stanley, D. 41
Stengers, I. 37
Stetsenko, A. 59–60, 61, 71, 77, 88, 92, 178
Strausfield, Lisa 44
strong emergence 8, 26
structural coupling 20, 25
student-centred learning 162
studentification 149, 150
subject-object binaries 166
subjectivity 171–174
Suchman, L. 15, 16
Sumara, D. 7, 12, 19, 26–27, 38, 39, 43, 51, 53, 164, 176
Swan, E. 117
symmetry 10, 96–98, 104, 109, 178
systems 22, 38
systems thinking 32

Tabbi, J. 158
teacher agency 104, 112
teacher development 38–39
teacher as knowing location 103
technological invention 121
technologized spaces 137–40
technology learning 9
technoscapes 136
Thamen, K. 155
Thinking and Speech (Vygotsky) 61
third space 149
Thompson Klein, J. 46–47
Thompson, T.L. 125–26
Thrift, N. 35
Tobin, K. 68, 79
topographical approach 152
transactional realism 29–30
transcendent collectivity 26
transformative human agency 172
translation 10, 98–99
trialectics of spatial practices 131
Tsoukas, H. 40

uncertainty 22, 23–24, 36, 115
Urry, J. 11, 21, 25, 35, 131, 139, 142, 143
Usher, R. 152, 156

Varela, F. 20, 25, 26, 55
Verran, H. 94, 119, 181
Vianna, E. 77

Vygotsky, L. S. 1, 57, 58, 59, 60, 61, 62, 63, 64, 65, 67, 70–71, 72, 74, 75, 76, 77, 78, 88, 89, 90, 92

Walby, S. 21, 25
Waldrop, M. 20
Waltz, S.B. 4, 116
Wenger, E. 162–63
Westheimer, J. 181
Wheatley, M. 41
Williams, J. 83
Wilton, R. 151

Wittek, L. 87
Wolf-Branigin, M. 49
women's training spaces 148–49
world culture theory 133
Wu, C. 79

Yamagata-Lynch, L. 87, 88
Yasukawa, K. 120

Zellermayer, M. 49–50
ZPD (zone of proximal development) 75, 78, 84, 89, 91, 92

Taylor & Francis

eBooks

FOR LIBRARIES

ORDER YOUR FREE 30 DAY INSTITUTIONAL TRIAL TODAY!

Over 23,000 eBook titles in the Humanities, Social Sciences, STM and Law from some of the world's leading imprints.

Choose from a range of subject packages or create your own!

Benefits for you
- ▶ Free MARC records
- ▶ COUNTER-compliant usage statistics
- ▶ Flexible purchase and pricing options

Benefits for your user
- ▶ Off-site, anytime access via Athens or referring URL
- ▶ Print or copy pages or chapters
- ▶ Full content search
- ▶ Bookmark, highlight and annotate text
- ▶ Access to thousands of pages of quality research at the click of a button

For more information, pricing enquiries or to order a free trial, contact your local online sales team.

UK and Rest of World: **online.sales@tandf.co.uk**

US, Canada and Latin America:
e-reference@taylorandfrancis.com

www.ebooksubscriptions.com

ALPSP Award for BEST eBOOK PUBLISHER 2009 Finalist

Taylor & Francis eBooks
Taylor & Francis Group

A flexible and dynamic resource for teaching, learning and research.

University Library of Columbus
4555 Central Avenue, LC 1600
Columbus, IN 47203-1892